I0127670

ALTRUISM
NARCISSISM
COMITY

ALTRUISM NARCISSISM COMITY

Research perspectives from *Current Psychology*

Nathaniel J. Pallone

EDITOR

Routledge
Taylor & Francis Group

LONDON AND NEW YORK

Chapters 1, 2, 4, 5, 6, 7, 10, and 11 originally published as a special issue of *Current Psychology* (Summer/Fall 1998).

Published 1999 by Transaction Publishers

Published 2017 by Routledge
2 Park Square, Milton Park, Abingdon, Oxon OX14 4RN
711 Third Avenue, New York, NY 10017, USA

Routledge is an imprint of the Taylor & Francis Group, an informa business

Copyright © 1999 by Taylor & Francis.

All rights reserved. No part of this book may be reprinted or reproduced or utilised in any form or by any electronic, mechanical, or other means, now known or hereafter invented, including photocopying and recording, or in any information storage or retrieval system, without permission in writing from the publishers.

Notice:
Product or corporate names may be trademarks or registered trademarks, and are used only for identification and explanation without intent to infringe.

Library of Congress Catalog Number: 98–33870

Library of Congress Cataloging-in-Publication Data

Altruism, narcissism, comity : research perspectives from Current
    psychology / edited by Nathaniel Pallone.
        p. cm.
    Includes bibliographical references and index.
    ISBN 0–7658–0467–0 (pbk. : alk. paper)
    1. Altruism. 2. Narcissism. 3. Courtesy. 4. Helping
behavior. 5. Helping behavior—Religious aspects.—Christianity
I. Pallone, Nathaniel J. II. Current psychology (New Brunswick, N.J.)
BF637.H4A465   1999
155.2'32—dc21   98–33870
                                                              CIP

ISBN 13: 978-0-7658-0467-9 (pbk)

Contents

Editor's Foreword

*Nature, who for the perfect maintenance of
the laws of her general equilibrium, has sometimes need of vices and sometimes of virtues,
inspires now this impulse, now that one, in
accordance with what she requires . . . Wolves
which batten upon lambs, lambs consumed by
wolves, the strong who immolate the weak, the
weak victims of the strong: there you have Nature, there you have her intentions, there you
have her scheme: a perpetual action and reaction, a host of vices, a host of virtues, in one
word, a perfect equilibrium resulting from the
equality of good and evil on earth . . .*

—Donatien Alphonse François, le
Comte de Sade, 1791

One need not search beyond the day's headlines for evidence of
both the immediacy and the elusiveness of the issues addressed in this
volume. In today's *New York Times,* there appears the report that a
criminal court in Rwanda has imposed the death penalty on two Ro-
man Catholic priests for organizing the execution of 2,000 Tutsi citizens who were "lured to seek shelter in churches . . . only to be crushed
to death by bulldozers." (To his credit, albeit he has made no secret of
his opposition to capital punishment, John Paul II is quoted as commenting that "members of the church hierarchy who played a role in
genocide should face the consequences of their actions.") For its part,
the *Times Sunday Magazine* at length analyzes the shared system of
beliefs and values that gave rise to concentration and death camps in
Tito's former domain but a few months past. And the *Times Book
Review* features a revisionist history of the Spanish Inquisition that
seeks to correct the record of that much maligned institution by revising downward the number of *conversos*, whether originally Jewish or

Moslem, who were tortured, killed, or exiled in the cause of ethnic purity during its period of sway.

What engines generate a sense of basic fairness? of selflessness? of self-aggrandizement? of acquisitive selfishness? Is such a sense exhibited in behavior pervasively, or only in limited arenas? Within the individual actor, does one or the other indeed pervade, or can we discern melds, blends, or even conflicts? How does it happen that one person displays arrogant self-centeredness equally in the family and in the workplace, while another displays an equal level of self-centeredness in the family but the most meticulous attention to the welfare of others in the workplace? Is there sufficient evidence to distinguish either altruism or narcissism as enduring "traits" of personality apart from their manifestation in very specific behavioral "states"? More fundamentally, are altruism and narcissism points on a continuum in any sense save that we have so grouped them conceptually? And, if so, are they related diametrically, orthogonally, or in some other fashion? Or, as de Sade (and perhaps also those who follow the psychoanalytic tradition) would hold, are altruism and narcissism each the flower of radically different, never intertwining, roots?

To paraphrase Sidney Jourard three decades ago in a somewhat variant context, the improvement both of the species and of the relationship between humankind and the environment which sustains us demands that we understand, first, the mechanisms by which self-absorption metamorphoses, is extruded, otherwise transmutes into, or is supplanted or at least "containerized" by, altruism; and, second, the mechanisms by which altruism (however grudgingly, as Wagstaff brilliantly illuminates later in this volume) in its turn yields to a sense of comity that seasons the demands of the self with recognition of the fundamental rights, needs, and aspirations of others. Few topics hold more contemporary significance in "real world" terms or have proved more elusive to specification in scientifically precise terms—one is tempted to say, perhaps the more so under strictures imposed on the scientific community in the United States via the several legislative acts governing research on human subjects that effectively limit scientific inquiry on such issues to perhaps inevitably pale laboratory analogue approximations to real world behavior.

A range of current research perspectives on altruism, narcissism, and comity by accomplished behavioral scientists from around the world were brought together in a special issue of the journal *Current*

Psychology published in Fall 1998. Collectively, these studies not only provide insights into the dynamics of altruistic and narcissistic behavior, but (and perhaps equally importantly) they also illuminate the many inventive ways in which investigators have sought to devise methods of inquiry that operationalize by approximation the multifaceted and complex antecedents, correlates, and concomitants of self-centered, self-absorbed, and/or selfless behavior and thus render such behavior amenable to study at a scientifically acceptable level of precision. They are here offered in a "fastback" for students, researchers, and practitioners in the psychological sciences, sociology, political science, philosophy, law, and other disciplines concerned with the nature of selflessness, heroism, justice, their variants–and their contraries and contradictories.

In the opening chapter in this collection, Graham Wagstaff masterfully reviews the evidence for conceptual models that attribute a sense of equity alternately to selfishness and to "just desert," in the process exploring as well putative relationships between justice, altruism, and the imperatives of evolutionary biology. Sidney Rosen and Shannon Wheatman report a marvelously inventive study in which the misappropriation of intellectual property provides the stimulus for the analysis of interaction between a sense of fairness, self-satisfaction at flattery by imitation, and self-esteem. Gordon Flett, Paul Hewitt, Kirk Blankstein, and Donna Pickering explore the nexus between perfectionism and self-serving or self-excusing explanations for task success and failure in an investigation that yields some understanding of the remote wellsprings for that level of self-absorption and/or self-aggrandizement that may evolve toward narcissism.

In a study that in a micromatic way may reflect today's headlines, Helen Linkey and Sheldon Alexander set out to discern the variables that affect judgments about the level of financial compensation that should be accorded to the formal agents of socialization who carry forward the values of one's own membership (if perhaps not quite reference) group. Robert Hill and Greg Yousey array characteristic levels of narcissism by occupation and distinguish between types of narcissism that prove adaptive or maladaptive, reporting that members of the clergy demonstrate lower levels of maladaptive narcissism than either politicians or university faculty (and not incidentally, thus yielding a shard of evidence that there is still hope for the species).

Complementary studies that explore both the motives that underlie help-giving and how those motives are perceived by others are reported by Mark Barnett, Guy Vitaglione, Jeffrey Bartel, Birgit Valdez, Lee Ann Steadman, and Kimberly Harper. What happens to members of a helping profession when an offer of help is spurned is investigated among nurses in Hong Kong by Wai Hing Cheuk, Bridget Swearse, Kwok Wai Wong, and Sidney Rosen. How formal religion affects belief and behavior is explored in studies by C. Edward Snodgrass and Larry Gates, who investigate anthropocentrism, and Richard Clements, who analyzes attitudes toward death.

Finally, pathological forms of extreme narcissism are investigated in chapters by James J. Hennessy and myself, in an analysis of the "heroic rescue fantasy" in relation to what is known or surmised about genuine heroism, and by Louis Schlesinger, who focuses on serial murder as the ultimate behavioral expression of pathological narcissism–and one that seems but a few conceptual links away from genocide.

Or does the latter formulation reveal more about our tendency to aggregate what may be discrete behaviors into global taxonomic categories (like "trait narcissism," to which we are likely further to link "xenophobia") than about the character of the discrete behaviors we can observe and/or measure?

—Nathaniel J. Pallone

1

Equity, Justice, and Altruism

Graham F. Wagstaff

Is altruism a justice norm? Is justice based on selfishness? And if justice is based on selfishness, can altruism be morally right, yet unjust? I doubt whether many modern psychologists would be prepared to offer an answer to either of these questions with any degree of conviction. A few decades ago, however, things might have seemed rather different.

The Decline of Equity

During the 1960s and early 1970s, the psychological study of justice was dominated by the theory of psychological equity. Indeed, some psychologists saw the equity principle as the basic principle of justice; a principle which governs not only economic relationships between people, but also social relationships (Adams, 1963; 1965; Austin and Walster, 1974; Walster, Berscheid, and Walster, 1973; Walster and Walster, 1975; Walster, Walster, and Berscheid, 1978; Walster, Walster, and Traupman, 1978; Hatfield, Utne, and Traupman, 1979). In its basic form, the equity principle states that a relationship between two people is just or fair when individuals who have made large contributions receive large outcomes, and those who have made small contributions receive small outcomes. The contributions or inputs can be either assets which entitle one to rewards, or liabilities which incur penalties. So, for example, if you work harder than someone else you should receive more than them, and if you commit a crime, the more serious the crime, the more you should be punished.

Importantly, however, when describing equity theory, Hatfield (previously Walster) and her colleagues start from the fundamental assumption that man is selfish (see Walster et al., 1973, p.151; Walster et al., 1978, p.7). The central idea is that individuals will try to maximize their outcomes (outcomes equal rewards minus costs), and they can do this best by evolving accepted systems, or social contracts, for equitably apportioning resources among members. This basis for justice contrasts considerably with the popular notion of altruism which, according to Sabini (1995), "is doing something for someone else. . . . with no benefit to oneself, often with the possibility of risk to oneself" (p. 290). The idea of altruism as self-sacrifice seems to be clearly at odds with an equity principle motivated by self-interest. Moreover, if it is considered morally right to be benevolent or altruistic towards people regardless of their actions, or inputs, then, according to equity theory, one can indeed be altruistic, morally right, yet unjust.

However, during the 1970s an increasing number of critics expressed discontentment with the notion that equity is the most important psychological principle of justice; in particular, there was a growing adherence to multiprinciple perspectives on justice; researchers argued that when individuals are placed in a position of distributing rewards or resources, there are other allocation principles they can, and sometimes do use, particularly those of equality and need (Lerner, 1974, 1975, 1977; Deutsch, 1975, 1983, 1985; Leventhal, Karuza and Fry, 1980; Mikula, 1980; Schwinger, 1980; Sampson, 1975; Schwartz, 1975). Also, although equity as formulated by Walster et al. (1978) also makes promising predictions regarding retributive justice (such as punishment must fit the crime), there was a tendency to ignore or downgrade its predictive explanatory value in this respect (Hogan and Emler, 1981; Miller and Vidmar, 1981).

The multiprinciple perspective has since flourished, and with it the number of different rules of justice posited. For example, Reis (1984) has described seventeen so-called rules of justice, and Desmarais and Lerner (1994) no fewer than eighteen rules, ranging from heroics and self-sacrifice, which would seem to imply altruistic intent, to formal contest and justified self-interest, which would obviously not. However, as a result of these developments, the distinction between rules of justice and any social rule or convention now seems to have been blurred. The problems are compounded by the fact that there are other concepts, such as attributions of responsibility, that are clearly related to justice concerns, but cannot readily be accommodated by any of the other perspectives (Cohen, 1982; Shaver, 1985; Utne and Kidd, 1980).

Justice, Selfishness, Altruism, and Morality

Particularly troublesome for modern perspectives on justice is that there tends to be little consensus as to the nature of the relationship between the concepts of justice, selfishness, altruism, and morality. For example, according to Lerner and his colleagues (Lerner, 1977, 1980; Miller, 1977), the motive for justice (even the norm of justified self-interest) is not based on selfishness; instead people are motivated to restore justice because injustice threatens the whole stability of their social environment (what Lerner terms their "personal contracts" to interact with others in certain defined ways). However, arguably, if the main motive to seek justice for others is to defend oneself against threats against the stability of one's environment, then this does not seem to constitute any altruistic intent. Indeed, Hogan and Emler (1981) have actually categorised Lerner's theory with equity theory and argued that both approaches adopt self-interest as the prime motive for maintaining justice.

There would, however, seem to be more obvious connections between the idea of human altruism and the idea of an ethic of care, or a desire for the welfare of others; that is, something akin the idea of justice as need. Schwartz (1975), for example, suggests that there is a justice of need that is motivated solely by humanitarian norms or the norms of social responsibility. As such, he says, "Need-based norms differ in that they do not prescribe a relative balance of inputs and outcomes between claimants. . . . Further, these norms are unique in that the person called on to forgo resources has performed no act justifying either a reduction in his own claims or an increase in others claims" (p. 112). In other words, when humanitarian need norms are invoked, the acts and attributes of the person in need, and those of the benefactor, are presumed to be irrelevant.

One difficulty with this view, however, is that some theorists and researchers argue that, within the context of justice, the characteristics of the recipient are an important determinant of whether a needy person should be benefitted. Thus, Lerner (1977) argues that "Undeserved suffering elicits compassion and help; but people react with indifference or satisfaction to deserved suffering, depending upon whether the suffering was caused by the victim's blameworthy act or was the 'deserved' fate meted out to a villain by the agents of goodness and truth" (p. 1). Empirical data from numerous studies on both adults and children support this general proposal (see, for example, Brabant and Lerner, 1975; Berkowitz, 1969; Lerner, 1977; Utne and Kidd, 1980; Schmidt and Weiner, 1988; Wagstaff, 1994; Weiner, 1980, 1985; Meyer and Mulherin, 1980).

Perhaps more fundamentally, however, Gilligan (1982) has argued that the ethic of care is a moral principle that is to be differentiated from the concept of justice; thus, justice involves using rules and making judgments of fairness, whereas the ethic of care is not rule bound in this way. However, according to those who argue that need is a rule of justice, if caring is seen as a humanitarian norm, then caring, too, is a part, or a requirement, of justice. Thus, for example, referring to a need orientated justice scheme, Furby (1986) notes, "There is also a certain similarity between Gilligan's 'ethic of care' and the humanitarian standard of justice outlined here" (p. 187).

This all reflects a general difficulty that theorists have in differentiating between rules of justice and other principles of moral conduct. Thus, whilst Gilligan differentiates between rules of justice and other moral principles, often discussions about justice seem indistinguishable from discussions of morality in general (see, for example, Bayley, 1981; Sher, 1981; Furby, 1986; Karniol and Miller, 1981; Montada, 1980). Indeed, according to Furby (1986), "Justice involves an evaluative judgment about the moral rightness of a person's fate" (p. 153), and Kohlberg (1971, 1976) argues that all sets of moral principles used by children and adults are justice structures. Kohlberg says, "The core of the specifically moral component of moral judgment is a sense of justice" (1976, p. 50). Adding to the confusion is the idea proposed by some psychologists that justice also encompasses the famous moral principle of utility (Baron, 1993); a principle that, in theory, prescribes that it is morally right to ignore or even murder those in need of care if, as a result, it would provide greater net benefits for a well-off, selfish majority (Posner, 1981).

Given these considerations, it is perhaps not surprising that many theorists have commented on the rather chaotic state of the psychological literature on justice; thus, Folger, Sheppard, and Buttram (1995) have recently commented that, "New principles of justice seem to spout like weeds in a garden"; they also refer to Greenberg's survey of the justice literature which notes "a burgeoning terminological and conceptual confusion" in the area (p. 261) (see also Deutsch, 1983; Tornblom, 1992; Wagstaff, 1994).

According to Wagstaff (1994), however, it may be possible to unify some of the disparate and fragmented psychological literature on justice by reference to the core principle of Equity as Desert; this is a principle that combines the idea of equal ratio equity with the ancient philosophical tradition of desert. In the rest of this article, it will be argued that this principle can perhaps usefully be extended to clarify some of the relationships between the concepts of justice, altruism, selfishness, and morality.

Equity as Desert (EAD)

The popular view of the equity principle, as promulgated by many modern theorists, is that it is essentially only one of a number of principles of distributive justice that operate in certain defined circumstances. So, for example, it is popularly asserted that equity, or the contributions rule, operates when there is little or no intimacy or affection (these are neutral) and, although the relationship possesses a degree of cooperation, it is impersonal, and there is a sense of conflict and competition; also, the goal of the interaction is to maximize economic productivity. On the other hand, where there is more intimacy, and slightly less potential for conflict; an affective bond and attraction are present; the relationship is cooperative, and the group goal is one of group solidarity, harmony, and enjoyable social relations, then an equality rule will be preferred. And in situations in which there is intimacy, affection, empathy, attraction, an absence of conflict, and welfare is the shared goal, a need rule will be adopted. (See, for example, Deutsch, 1975, 1985; Mikula, 1980; Schwinger, 1980; Leventhal, Karuza and Fry, 1980; Folger, Sheppard, and Buttram, 1995.) Moreover, within this multiprinciple context, psychologists have tended to see psychological equity as ideologically conservative or right wing in nature (Tornblom, 1992) and its influence on modern thought as a feature of "the marketplace economic system of Western capitalism" (Sampson, 1975, p. 51).

However, historically, equity seems to have been more ubiquitous than is often implied. For example, in the ancient cultures of Sumeria, Egypt, and Greece, the terms we now connect with the concept of justice were more associated with a grand state of cosmic order or equilibrium (see Russell, 1979; MacIntyre, 1982). An essential feature of this scheme was that those who contributed services to others through the roles they adopt should be rewarded in proportion to value of their services; and those who harmed the good of others should be punished, again in strict proportion (the term deserve itself derives from the Latin *deservio,* to serve zealously). The Greeks called this the principle of geometrical equality; that is, a principle which, according to Plato (1960), "assigns more to the greater than to the lesser" and "deals proportionately with either party, ever awarding a greater share to those of greater worth." Moreover, Plato asserts that this principle of proportionality is more than simply "true and real equality," it is, he says, "The very award of Zeus; it is 'sheer justice' or 'absolute and perfect justice' " (p. 757). The same principle is described in mathematical form by Aristotle (1984), whose formula for justice, as geometrical proportion, is essentially the same as Adams's (1965) equity formula; that is, one that awards outcomes (rewards) in equal proportion to inputs (contributions or worth). Aristotle further allows this distribution to be "corrected" whenever it is disturbed by some obtaining unjustified gains, such that, essentially "punishment should fit the crime."[1]

Although the best way to formulate equity mathematically has been the source of considerable controversy (Harris, 1983, 1993), recently Wagstaff and Perfect (1992) have proposed that the ancient justice principle of reward for good and punishment for bad is probably best represented by a single formula: $O_i = aI_i$, in which, O represents the value of outcomes, I represents the value of the inputs, and "a" is a constant number greater than zero (that is, a > 0) for all participants, who are denoted by the term "i," in a relationship; this is, in fact, Harris's (1983) linear formula, with an intercept of zero. This formula is essentially a revision of Adams's (1965) equity rule, and Aristotle's principle of geometrical proportion, but with some mathematical constraints. Thus, the main assumptions for perfect equity can be summarized as follows (for mathematical details see Wagstaff and Perfect, 1992):

1. *Outcomes should be distributed in equal proportion to inputs, such that the more one inputs or contributes, the more one should receive.* For example, if A contributes twice as much as B, A should receive twice as much as B.

2. *Positive inputs must always be returned with positive outcomes, and negative inputs with negative outcomes.* So, from a starting point in which equity exists, it is always unjust to reward someone for a harmful act or disservice to others, or punish them for a positive contribution to the good of others. (As the nineteenth-century philosopher J.S. Mill says, "The precept of returning good for evil has never been regarded as a case of the fulfilment of justice, but as one in which the claims of justice are waived, in obedience to other considerations," [1993, p. 46].)

3. *Zero inputs must always be returned with zero outcomes. If one does nothing positive or negative, one should receive nothing positive or negative. It also follows that when all inputs are zero, the most equitable, or least inequitable distribution is one that distributes outcomes equally amongst the participants.* It is unjust to reward or punish people who have done nothing at all to deserve such treatment; however, in cases in which there are rewards or punishments to be distributed amongst people who have done nothing good or bad to others to deserve them, the least unjust or inequitable distribution is an equal distribution (mathematically, this minimizes the deviations from equity). However, to make psychological sense of any equity formula we must add another condition.

4. *When perfect equity exists, the outcomes that individuals receive should be commensurate with their inputs. When the outcomes exceed those commensurate with the inputs the least inequitable solution is one that distributes the commensurate outcomes between participants in equal proportion to their inputs, and the incommensurate excess equally between them.* For example, suppose that a group of workers consensually agree that £20 is an appropriate or commensurate reward for one hour of work; if this is so, then, other factors being equal, equity will normally demand that a person who works for one hour should receive £20, and a person who works for two hours should receive £40. However, if instead there is an excessive incommensurate amount, say a £20 million windfall to distribute, we cannot distribute it with perfect equity (because most of it is undeserved); so, to distribute between the two persons, the least inequitable solution is to first give each person the commensurate outcomes the each has 'earned', £20 to one and £40 to the other, and then divide the rest of the unearned £20 million equally between them (again, mathematically, this minimizes the deviations from equity).

EAD and Input/Outcome Commensurateness

However, whilst there may be an intuitive logic to the idea of commensurateness between outcomes and inputs, we still need some theoretical construction for ideal commensurateness. The most obvious one is that provided by Sadurski (1985) who argues that "social equilibrium means that everyone's work, effort, action, and sacrifice yields a benefit equivalent to the contribution: in other words that a person's 'outcomes' are equal to his 'inputs'" (p. 105). However, this still does not resolve the problem of how one's contribution or input is to be measured; is one's contribution determined by the social benefits one has produced, or by the costs or burdens one has incurred in terms of the amount of effort, skill, responsibility, etc. one has exercised in performing the service? For the moment, therefore, in keeping with the historical scholastic tradition of desert (see Fogarty, 1961), I will simply propose that, within a model of equal ratio equity, commensurateness between inputs and outcomes exists when *all receive outcomes equivalent to the social benefits and harms that they might reasonably expect their inputs or contributions to generate.*

From this perspective, therefore, equity can be construed as a form of sophisticated reciprocity, in which individuals receive favors and punishments in proportion to those favors and harms they have, or could reasonably have expected to have, bestowed on others. It can also be noted that, in keeping with the traditional scholastic idea of desert, outcomes are not awarded according to the extent to which people take responsibility, take risks, put in effort, make themselves look beautiful, incur material costs etc., for their own sakes, but to the extent to which, through these activities, they could reasonably be expefcted to benefit or harm others. Hence, we would not normally reward people for hours of inefficient effort that is of no conceivable use to anyone, or compensate criminals for the costs they have incurred (through loss of earnings, etc.) whilst planning their crimes.

Equity and Responsibility

However, since ancient times, the idea of proportional desert has been inextricably linked with the idea of choice or responsibility. To be truly deserving, one must be able to choose whether or not to perform the inputs. Thus, to Aristotle, the ideal input is that of virtue or excellence and this must be voluntary or chosen; similarly one cannot be held guilty of an offence, unless one could have chosen otherwise. Similar ideas are expressed by Plato, except that some of the most important choices in life, of one's role status or input, are allegedly chosen in a previous existence (Plato, 1987)[2] and are inherent in most modern philosophical conceptions of positive and negative desert (for example, Franklin, 1968; Evans, 1981; Hospers, 1961; Sadurski, 1985).

It will be noted, however, that implicit in this argument is the idea that to be considered more or less deserving than others, one has to be given the same choices. So, for example, if A, as a result of an accidental disability, is unable to perform services to the level of B, then given that A did not choose, or could not help her disability, it could be argued that she cannot be deemed less deserving of a reward for her performance than B. If we link this to the idea of perfect equity identified earlier, the result is a compound principle termed Equity as Desert or EAD (Wagstaff, 1994). If we assume commensurateness between outcomes and inputs, then this principle states that: *A just distribution is one in which the outcomes of participants are equally proportional to their inputs, but under conditions in which each participant has an equal choice or opportunity, either real or hypothetical, to provide the relevant inputs.*

It must be emphasized that, as the principle states, it is not necessary for the participants to be given the same choices in a literal sense; the choices may be equivalent, or may even be hypothetical. In the latter case, we might judge someone's desert to be based on what we might reasonably have expected of them and of others given the same choices (adjusted for outcome costs incurred by others). The idea of equal choice in relation to the performance of inputs for which punishment is deserved may seem unfamiliar, but it is very much implicit in the way that English law assigns blame to offenders. In fact, Hart (1968) has argued that criminal liability can be founded on the simple idea that "unless a man has the capacity and a fair opportunity or chance to adjust his behaviour to the law, its penalties ought not to be applied to him" (p. 181). If a "fair opportunity" is construed as an equal opportunity, and a "chance" is a real choice, then Hart's statement captures the idea well (for other examples of this reasoning in the literature on criminal justice, see Cross, Jones, and Card, 1988).

Equality and Need

Having described the basic proportional desert principle, it is now possible to see how the concepts of equality and need might be accommodated. EAD requires that when inputs are equal, then outcomes should be equal. Thus, all participants should receive equal outcomes under the following conditions:

1. When all inputs are equally positive or negative; that is, all participants have performed either services or disservices to an equal extent;
2. When all inputs are zero or neutral; that is, when no one has any choice at all, and consequently, no one is responsible for his or her behavior (note also, if the outcomes to be distributed exceed those commensurate with the zero inputs, then the least inequitable distribution will always be an equal distribution); and
3. When, under conditions of equal opportunity, all would have provided the same inputs.

Within this model need then operates, not as an input (need is not a chosen contribution to the good of others) but primarily as an outcome adjustment. Thus, for example, a woman who accidentally loses a proportion of outcomes and falls into a state of need, or due to circumstances beyond her control, requires more to maintain the same levels of outcomes compared to others who have similar inputs, is truly deserving of help for her plight, because, relative to others, she is receiving less than is equitable on the basis of her inputs. In contrast, as both Feinberg (1970) and Lerner (1977) argue, if people fall into a state of need through deliberate choice or carelessness, we are less obliged to help them, than if the loss is accidental. Thus, if a man chooses to exchange an outcome for an equivalent outcome that provides temporary pleasure and, thereby, ends up destitute, there is no inequity; he has simply chosen to substitute one outcome with an equivalent outcome that afforded a more temporary outcome satisfaction. And, if the outcome loss or need arises from a negative input (such as voluntary laziness that might be judged detrimental to the community, or a fine for a criminal act), then the need could be construed as an appropriate negative return for a negative action or input. As has been noted, there is considerable empirical evidence that both adults and children make these discriminations (Brabant and Lerner, 1975; Berkowitz, 1969; Lerner, 1977; Utne and Kidd, 1980; Thomas,

Wagstaff, and Brunas-Wagstaff, 1996; Schmidt and Weiner, 1988; Wagstaff, 1994; Weiner, 1980, 1985; Meyer and Mulherin, 1980).

Also, within the Equity as Desert model, the satisfaction of basic needs may be an important requirement for the zero outcomes baseline. According to EAD, if your inputs are zero, your outcomes should be zero, but zero outcomes do not necessarily refer to receiving nothing in a material sense. Even if one had done nothing positive or negative, to be in extreme need relative to others, such that one's life is painful and impoverished (death through starvation, thirst, and exposure to the elements being the obvious extremes) could be construed as a distinctly negative outcome; something that some might want to reserve only for serious criminals, but certainly undeserved by a zero or neutral input. Hence, the zero outcomes position is to be conceptualized as a neutral point within a family of positive and negative values, and provision for basic needs, therefore, can be viewed as fundamental to the maintenance of the zero outcomes baseline.

Also, if Equity as Desert also requires an equal choice or opportunity to perform the inputs within the scheme, then the zero baseline should also include some provision for the maintenance of equal opportunity. In other words, even people whose inputs are zero deserve an opportunity to increase their inputs should they choose. This obviously requires both the financial and material means to be able to choose between inputs, and the physical liberty to do so. Wagstaff et al. (1994) found experimental evidence for this general idea in relation to the award of positive outcomes. In one study, we gave a sample of the general public some scenarios in which one worker's input was ten hours, another's was five hours, and a third worker's input was nothing. We then varied information about the zero input worker's opportunity to work, and her previous work history. Our results showed that when the zero input worker had clearly chosen not to work, she was awarded nothing, as EAD demands (none of the workers was in undeserved need). However, when the zero worker was prevented from working through no fault of her own (she was stuck in a lift), there was a tendency to award her a payment according to her previous work record (that is, what she would have done had she been given the same opportunities as others).

Relative Need and People Who Do Nothing

All this has obvious implications for how we view the appropriate outcomes for a participant who has contributed nothing in a material sense. In a number of empirical studies, we have demonstrated that, unless choice or responsibility are clearly absent or unequal, or differential need is made very salient, or the outcomes are incommensurate with the inputs, then the preferred allocation (followed by the overwhelming majority of participants) is to follow the perfect equity, equal proportionality rule with the available outcomes; that is, award rewards (and punishments) in equal proportion to inputs (positive or negative), and give a zero input worker zero outcomes. When a person does nothing, he or she receives nothing (see, for example, Wagstaff, 1994; Wagstaff and Perfect, 1992; Wagstaff and Worthington, in press; Wagstaff, Chadwick, and Brunas-Wagstaff, 1996; Wagstaff, Huggins and Perfect, 1996; Wagstaff et al., 1994). However, Wagstaff and Worthington (in press) have also shown that allocation to a zero input worker "in need" (that is, a person who does nothing at work, but requires money for basic food and shelter) is very much dependent on the context. Thus, in the absence of comparative information, subjects tend to be unsympathetic towards a needy worker who does nothing, and award him nothing. However, when subjects are surreptitiously reminded that criminal offenders in British prisons (that is, those whose inputs are negative) have their basic needs for food and shelter met, subjects are far more willing to offer the zero input worker money for food and shelter. In other words, the zero outcomes position is to be conceptualized as a relative neutral point within a family of positive and negative values, not an absolute anchor.

As suggested above, this kind of comparative analysis allows an explanation as to why even the most rigid supporter of proportional desert might still consider it perfectly just or equitable to satisfy the basic needs of those who have chosen to be lazy, or have otherwise made themselves destitute.

Justice and Other Reasons

Within the framework of EAD, therefore, people will only apply equality as a principle of justice when they consider inputs to be equal or neutral (as when opportunities to perform inputs are unequal), and they will only make an adjustment for need when they perceive that the need is deserved in some way. This is not to say, however, that people do not use the contribution, equality, and need principles in the ways suggested by the multiprinciple theorists, only that most of the reasons that psychologists have put forward to explain why people operate these principles may have little or nothing to do with people's intuitions about justice (for discussions of this point see, for example, Cohen and Greenberg, 1982; Leventhal, Karuza, and Fry, 1980; Lissak and Sheppard, 1983; Tornblom, 1992; Tyler, 1987). Ironically, it may the case that it is precisely because EAD is a core principle of justice that these allocations can have the effects attributed to them. Indeed, the idea that people attempt to operate a single principle of justice may be able to provide some insight into how people apply and react to different allocation rules, and may help to explain some of the empirical findings that seem to fit uneasily with the multiprinciple view. As researchers such as Adams (1965), Lerner (1980), and Walster et al. (1978) have noted, people appear to have a strong desire to view both their own actions and those of others as just, to the extent that they will not alter inputs and outcomes accordingly, but also make attributions such that inequitable situations look just. Both these reactions may serve to make sense of how individuals react to various allocation rules.

Suppose, for example, we want to maximize productivity. If we distribute proportionally according to raw contribution, then so long as people feel that they have a more or less equal chance to contribute, rewarding those who work hardest will tend to motivate all or most workers, productivity will increase and, in accordance with EAD, the situation should be considered by most people as fair. However, if workers feel that they have not had equal opportunities to contribute, they may find such a system of reward divisive, unjust, and resentment may be created. In the latter instance, productivity may still be maintained, but perhaps at the expense of group cohesion because it will be judged unfair. This would help to explain why, when asked to make a fair allocation, people prefer reward effort or output (inputs over which we can exercise most choice), rather than ability or capability even though the latter might help more to maximize productivity (Stake, 1983).

Suppose now we want to foster a cooperative and enjoyable atmosphere. If we award shares equally, then because people want justice to obtain, and EAD to exist, they will tend to assume that all are "pulling their weight," and inputs are equal. An equal shares allocation gives out the message that people can be trusted to do the best they can; thus fostering an enjoyable cooperative environment in which people trust each other, and do not feel they are in competition for rewards; they all deserve equal. Problems will result, however, if some abuse this trust, clearly do not pull their weight, and a situation of unequal inputs becomes transparent. Under such circumstances productivity may be curtailed as those who have input more attempt to adjust their input/outcome ratios to suit the equal distribution, and resentment may again develop. This would then explain the findings that, even amongst friends, in situations where there were sizeable differences in performance, an equal distribution may generate conflict, hence subjects may consider that harmony is best preserved by applying an unequal distribution that takes contributions into account (Lamm and Kayser, 1978; see also, Leventhal, Karuza, and Fry, 1980).

And, finally, suppose we want to maximize the welfare of the group. We are most likely to be sensitive to the needs of others when we know them and are familiar with them; if they are strangers, we may not know their circumstances. Moreover, if we see others being given shares of some good according to their needs and we want justice, again we will be more likely to assume that those receiving the need are innocent victims, worthy of help, and are legitimate objects of our compassion. Hence, distribution according to need can itself, through our desire for justice, in terms of EAD, evoke feelings of compassion, promote trust that each is inputting as much as anyone else, and sensitize us to the welfare of the group. In line with research findings, however, EAD also predicts that distribution according to need may still operate if the needs of strangers or competitors are made salient, may be moderated by differences in contributions, and it may break down when we feel that the people have placed themselves in a position of need through their own choices; either by lack of, or negative inputs, or through unwise and impulsive outcome substitutions (Brabant and Lerner, 1975; Berkowitz, 1969; Elliott and Meeker, 1986; Lerner, 1977; Utne and Kidd, 1980; Schmidt and Weiner, 1988; Wagstaff, 1994; Wagstaff, Huggins, and Perfect, 1993; Weiner, 1980, 1985; Meyer and Mulherin, 1980).[3]

Justice, Altruism, and Morality Reconsidered

If the preceding analysis has any merit, we are now hopefully in a better position to make more meaningful distinctions between the terms justice, altruism, and morality.

In the philosophical literature, the term morality is problematical. Historically, the term was used to refer simply to one's characteristic ways of behaving, but now it is usually applied to the analysis of those rules of conduct that one characteristically "ought to adopt" because they have intrinsic worth, or they achieve some end that is assumed to be a good (for discussions see Hospers, 1961; MacIntyre, 1982). From the perspective of EAD then, if caring per se, and provision for need per se are seen as altruistic rules that ought to be adopted for some reason, and applied unconditionally to everyone, regardless of unequal desert, or the benefits received by the benefactor, then justice and altruism represent different moral principles. Such an analysis would bring psychological definitions in line with those of many moral and political philosophers. For instance, Lucas (1980) says, "I can be just yet lack many moral virtues." Campbell (1988) also argues that "common humanity, or even generous beneficence, may sometimes be in conflict with, and even more important than, the claims of justice" (p. 35), and in his classic statement Sidgwick (1907) comments, "benevolence begins where justice ends" (p. 242).[4]

On the other hand, if we adopt the position of what we could term deterministic egalitarianism—the view that none of us is responsible for, or chooses the assets and liabilities that might be used as inputs (and, therefore, all inputs are effectively zero or neutral)—and assume desert is always equal, then in as much as they act as outcome adjustments, unconditional caring and provision for need will tend to look just, and morally equivalent, so long as they are distributed in such a way that outcomes are effectively equalized, or provide the closest approximation to this end (for a justification of the tendency towards equality along these lines, see Rawls, 1972; Colby and Kohlberg, 1987).

Empirical research strongly supports these propositions. For example, research from a number of countries has shown that those who support inequality also tend to endorse the idea that behavior is mainly internally or dispositionally caused. Thus, members of right-wing organizations not only have more negative attitudes towards the poor and programs directed towards helping the poor, but also tend to blame those who are poor for their plight, claiming that poverty arises from factors such as indolence and recklessness. On the other hand, supporters of center and left wing political parties, whose views tend more towards egalitarianism, are more likely to argue that the poor are largely if not entirely innocent victims who are made poor by circumstances beyond their control (see, for example, Furnham, 1982; Katz, 1989; Kluegel and Smith, 1986; Pandey et al., 1982; Wagstaff, 1984, 1994; Wagstaff and Quirk, 1983; Williams, 1984).

In other words, within the framework of EAD, whether one considers altruistic concepts such as caring, provision for need, and benevolence, to be acceptable unconditionally as principles of justice, depends very much on one's attitudes towards the philosophical position that none of us can truly be held responsible for his or her actions. If one considers that inputs can be unequal, and that outcome deficits can be chosen or blameworthy, yet common morality requires altruism, or unconditional benevolence to those in need, then morality and justice with regard to these issues can part company. But if one considers inputs always to be equal because ultimately humans have little or no choices over what they do with their outcomes, then the altruistic response to all inequalities created by need becomes a principle component of justice, and in as much as both reflect some popular notions of how we ought to behave, they become equivalently morally acceptable. It can he noted, however, that even from the position of deterministic egalitarianism, unconditional altruism that creates further inequities (such as financial help to those already well off financially compared to others), would still technically be construed as an injustice.

Justice, Altruism, and the Problem of Selfishness

If we view EAD as a core principle of justice, it may also be possible to clarify the relationships between justice, altruism, and selfishness.

If we define altruism, not as simple helping or prosocial behaviour, but as Sabini (1995) says, "doing something for someone else . . . with no benefit to oneself, often with the possibility of risk to oneself" (p. 290), the issue arises as to why people should be motivated to behave in such a way. Indeed, whether true altruism as so defined ever actually occurs has been a contentious issue in the literature. Thus, it has been argued that even though people may sometimes help others when there are no obvious extrinsic rewards to be gained, they may, nevertheless, benefit intrinsically by experiencing from reductions in negative psychological states, which may include the alleviation of feelings of guilt and the pains of empathy (for discussions of this issue see Batson, 1987; Cialdini et al., 1987). The latter position, sometimes termed subtle cynicism, has a parallel in traditional equity theory, in that the alleged selfish motivation for justice includes the idea of the reduction of inequity distress; that is, people may behave equitably because inequity can produce feelings of psychological distress, including guilt feelings, which they are then motivated to reduce (Walster and Walster, 1975; Walster, Walster, and Berscheid, 1978).

One problem, however, with defining the maximization of any intrinsic reward as selfish behavior, is that it seems to deprive the truly unselfish person of any rational motive for behaving altruistically. The true altruist, in as much as such a person exists, is close to becoming a person who helps others as a response to an irrational impulse. In view of this problem, it may make some sense to look elsewhere for the motives that may underlie apparently selfless behavior; an increasingly popular area in this respect is that of evolutionary psychology. But importantly also, evolutionary psychology may be able to provide us with some possible clues as to origins of EAD.

Evolutionary Theory and the Altruist as a Social Liability

According to Hamilton (1964) natural selection works at the level of the genes not the whole organism. It is gene survival, or inclusive fitness, that really counts. Hence, people will tend to take considerable risks helping others to insure that those who share their genes survive; and the closer the relative, the more risks they will be prepared to take. But how can we account for the fact that people often help those who are not genetically related to them? Trivers (1971) has argued that there may be occasions when it is useful to help unrelated others, if it can be assumed that this will increase the probability of them helping you, should the need arise in future. This strategy has been termed reciprocal altruism. However, once again, it is arguable whether this type of helping behavior can be considered truly altruistic; evolutionary theory seems simply to make the selfish motives behind helping behaviour somewhat more clandestine.

Nevertheless, it is perhaps from evolutionary psychology that we find the closest approximation to the idea of a true altruist; the true altruist could be construed as being someone who goes around unconditionally helping others, regardless of intrinsic or extrinsic rewards, oblivious to the fact that he or she might be doing this to increase the probability that those who share his or her genes might be helped reciprocally in future. However, such an analysis also raises the question as to whether an unconditional impulsive to help others could also be dysfunctional.

According to evolutionary psychologists, for reciprocal altruism to work, it is important that the costs incurred and the benefits received be proportional. So, for example, it is not in your interest to take great risks to save another's life, when all that is likely to return is a very small favor. Big favors demand relatively big favors in return. A major problem, therefore, for those engaging in reciprocal altruism, is cheating. If all members of a species possess an altruistic gene, and no one cheats, there is no problem. However, suppose some members of a species possess a genetic mutation that causes them not to return favors in proportion to those received, or, indeed, at all; whose genes would survive? According to Dawkins (1976), this situation represents a clash between "cheats," who attempt to gain whilst incurring fewer or no costs to themselves, or attempt to gain at the expense of others, and "suckers," who indiscriminately incur costs to benefit others, regardless of the benefits received in return. Computer simulations indicate that if cheats are pitted against suckers, then cheats prosper; the suckers will be driven to extinction. To be a sucker amongst suckers works fine; but to be a sucker amongst cheats is not ultimately an evolutionary stable strategy (ESS).

But enter a third strategist—the *grudger*. Grudgers help those who have previously helped them; but they refuse to help cheats. In fact, they bear a grudge. In other words, grudgers play "tit for tat," helping those who help them, but refusing to cooperate with those who defect. According to the simulations conducted by Dawkins, initially grudgers do not do well as a small minority against cheats and suckers because the suckers tend to sustain the cheats. In the short term, therefore, grudging may not always look like the most adaptive strategy. Ultimately, however, over time, as the cheats gradually eliminate the suckers, the grudgers increase, until grudging dominates as the most evolutionary stable strategy (Dawkins, 1976). But what should be the exact strategy of the grudger? A number of studies suggest that a simple "tit for tat" (TFT) strategy of "cooperate with cooperators and do not cooperate with defectors," can be extremely effective in inducing effective cooperation (Axelrod, 1980a, 1980b, 1984); moreover, a person using a TFT strategy in a prisoner's dilemma game situation is seen, not only as strong and intelligent, but *fair* (McClintock and Liebrand, 1988). However, more recent works suggests that this strategy only works effectively with very small numbers of individuals. As group size evolves, however, the strategy of simply withholding cooperation from noncooperators is less effective than a strategy of deliberate retaliation in some form (Boyd and Richerson, 1992). Boyd and Richerson (1992) term this reaction *retribution*. Indeed, according to Boyd and Richerson's analysis, in larger groups, more cooperation is produced when not only are noncooperators punished, but those who fail to punish noncooperation are punished. In other words, when cheats abound, suckers can be a liability for grudgers, so it makes sense to attempt to modify their behavior.

Also, on the basis of both mathematical models and research on animals and humans, Clutton-Brock and Parker (1995) conclude that negative reciprocity may serve a number of adaptive functions, which include not only the maintenance of dominance relationships, but also as a method of persuading reluctant helpers to cooperate, and of discouraging thieves, cheats, parasites, and even predators (p. 215). In larger groups then, one might expect a joint strategy, that combines both positive and negative reciprocity to be the most effective approach for the grudger. The grudger, thus, returns favors with favors, and returns noncooperation and cheating with penalties.

EAD as a Biological Stratagem

The correspondence between this kind of account and EAD is quite striking. Positive and negative reciprocity are the hallmarks of proportional desert; desert requires that favors be returned in proportion to favors done, and penalties in proportion to harms done. Seen from an evolutionary perspective, therefore, a system of proportional desert could be construed as a sophisticated group version of "tit for tat"; a set of biological algorithms designed to facilitate social exchange for the benefit of all, by encouraging cooperation, discouraging noncooperation, and punishing cheating. Indeed, discussing positive and negative reciprocity, Wright (1995) says, "The intuitively obvious idea of just deserts, the very core of the human sense of justice, is, in this view, a by product of evolution, a simple genetic stratagem" (p. 205); de Waal (1989) comes to a similar conclusion about the core nature of justice having closely observed some of our closest relatives in the animal kingdom, chimpanzees; thus, he says, "Chimpanzee group life is like a market in power, sex, affection, support, intolerance and hostility. The two basic rules are 'one good turn deserves another' and 'an eye for an eye, a tooth for a tooth.'" And de Waal adds that, "Reciprocity among chimpanzees is governed by the same sense of moral rightness and justice as it is amongst humans" (p. 207).

However, one can also see how the concept of responsibility might map onto such a scheme. Under conditions of more or less equal opportunity it would make more sense to reward those who are most efficient in proportion to the value of their services to others; on the other hand, when opportunities are clearly unequal, a more equal distribution of resources to compensate individuals who have been denied an opportunity to provide inputs may be a risk worth taking to ensure future cooperation (and even survival). Provision for those who accidentally find themselves in need could also be construed as an insurance policy should similar accidents befall us.

Indeed, game theorists have shown that although TFT works better than consistent cooperation or pacifism (which gets exploited), or consistent noncooperation (which is returned in kind); if both partners play strict TFT, the effects of defecting in response to "accidental" defections rebound on each, resulting in further unnecessary defections that reduce cooperation and are detrimental to both parties. Further research indicates, therefore, that TFT is even more effective if one cooperates on the first move and is then somewhat forgiving, that is, one allows one's partner to make a few mistakes or have some accidents (say 80 percent cooperation over the last series of trials) (Bendor, Kramer and Stout, 1991; Molander, 1985). However, any scheme that makes allowances for accidents must be sensitive to cheating; people who deliberately place themselves in need or claim falsely they have been denied the opportunity to contribute will be continually building up a reproductive advantage by not incurring the costs involved in contributing to the welfare of others.

There is a considerable overlap between these ideas and some observations made by Cosmides and Tooby (1992). As Cosmides and

Tooby point out, the common characterization of primitive peoples leading a hunter-gatherer life is an orgy of indiscriminate, egalitarian cooperation and sharing (p. 216). Archaeological and ethnographic records show, however, that hunter gathers have engaged in a number of different forms of social exchange (see Cashdan, 1989; Roberts, 1979). Particularly interesting are decision rules that govern reciprocity on food sharing. For instance, amongst the Ache tribe of Paraguay, meat is a very high-variance food item. Its availability varies from day to day, and whether a hunter finds any is very much a matter of luck. In contrast, collected plant foods are a very low-variance item. Their availability depends primarily on the effort that is put in to collect them. It is notable, therefore, that meat tends to be distributed equally throughout the band, whereas plant foods are only shared within the nuclear family.

According to Cosmides and Tooby (1992), this makes good economic sense. If success in finding food is highly variable and based on luck, everyone might come across occasions in which he or she would starve. By pooling the risk, however, the variance decreases, and the food supply becomes more stable. Moreover, to punish someone in such a situation for a failure to contribute is a high risk business. As Cosmides and Tooby state, "If the charge is false, then not only will the ostracized man's survival be jeopardized, but each member of the band will have lost a valuable reciprocation partner" (p. 214). Amongst the Ache, therefore, it is significant that little consideration is given to the idea of punishing those who fail to "pull their weight" when hunting for meat. In contrast, acrimonious arguments erupt over whether various individuals are doing their fair share of work in the garden. However, gardening provides a low-variance food source; an equal distribution would simply act to redistribute food from those who put in most work to those who do nothing. Moreover, punishment is less risky in terms of adverse effects on food supply. Cosmides and Tooby (1992) point to a number of other examples from Africa, such as the Kalahari San bands and the !Kung, that illustrate this same relationship between the variability of the food supply and the way it is distributed.

From an evolutionary perspective, therefore, it could also be argued that the introduction of the notion of personal choice or responsibility into the algorithms for both positive and negative reciprocity might have evolved as a method of fine tuning what would otherwise be a fairly primitive and inefficient instrument for encouraging efficient cooperation and discouraging cheating. Thus, rewarding those who deliberately choose to contribute in an efficient and industrious way may serve to reinforce such behavior in members of the group; on the other hand, withholding rewards from or punishing those who deliberately fail to contribute or choose to offend, may serve to discourage both them and others from repeating the same behavior. On the other hand, withholding resources from or punishing those who fail to contribute, or who harm others by accident, can be costly, unnecessary, and have repercussions that prevent future cooperation.

Not surprisingly, Cosmides and Tooby (1992) comment on the obvious correspondence between these observations and political debates over issues such as the homeless. Thus, they say, those opposing help and sharing will stress the chosen or self-caused dimensions of the situation; the homeless are lazy and have brought it on themselves. In contrast, those wishing to motivate sharing will emphasize the random, variance-driven dimensions of the situation. The potential recipient of aid is viewed as worthy because he or she is the unlucky victim of circumstances, such as unemployment, discrimination, or mental illness (p. 219). It also follows that the former may be more reticent in general about punishing than the latter.

If we accept this account, then the implications for our understanding of the origins of EAD may be considerable. EAD could be construed as a basic psychological model, or set of algorithms, common to all humanity, that has evolved to help us adapt to changing local conditions. Thus, by using the *same* model, with the same set of rationalizing principles, we can switch from allocations based on proportionality—culpability to others based on equality—nonculpability, depending on local circumstances, in a coherent and adaptive way.

Of course, the idea that biological evolution may underlie our most basic core conception of justice is controversial and, in any case, it is a well worn cliche that even if we are influenced by such biological predispositions, we do not necessarily have to act on them. But even if we were to reject all of the assumptions of evolutionary psychology, they do draw our attention to an important characteristic of unbridled altruism. In a world in which exploiters or cheats exist, the strategy of the unconditional, selfless altruist, or sucker who helps the rich, idle gangster as much as the destitute child of a war hero, could be considered dysfunctional. It would not be surprising, therefore, if human societies were to evolve social institutions, or grudging strategies, such as those based round EAD, to control such behavior.

Conclusions

If the preceding analysis has any validity we may now be in a better position to answer the questions posed at the beginning of this article.

According to Barry, the assumption underlying many approaches to justice, both ancient and modern, is that "Justice . . . underwrites mutually advantageous cooperative arrangements, whether they arise from explicit agreement or not" (1989, p. 367). In other words, rules of justice are selfish in as much as they have evolved to maximize the advantages to individuals that may accrue from cooperative arrangements; as mentioned previously, the same idea has been used by psychologists to underpin psychological equity theory (Walster et al., 1973, 1978). If we include here the notion of gene survival as one of the advantages of adopting rules of justice, then there seems to be little reason to dissent from the general principle that at some level, justice for most people is motivated by selfishness, even though many people might be totally oblivious to this when they sacrifice their lives in the name of justice. However, in terms of the present analysis, it is important to distinguish between the underlying motives for employing justice, and how justice deals with different types of selfish behavior.

An important difficulty with much of the debate in this area is that it seems to ignore societal standards with regard to the acceptability of different conceptions of selfishness. For example, in everyday experience people perhaps recognize a possible distinction between helping others so that they will leave you money in their will (extrinsic selfishness), and helping them for the joy of seeing them happy, to prevent guilt, or because one is unconsciously compelled by a selfish motive to perpetuate one's genes (intrinsic and biological selfishness); however, all could be termed instances of *non-exploitative selfishness*. Most societies make a clear distinction between helping behaviors, even if motivated by selfishness, and those behaviors that involve *exploitative-selfishness*, such as rape, murder, and robbery. Arguably, there may be good evolutionary reasons for making such differentiations; those who help others because helping characteristically gives them pleasure, or out of some dispositional impulse they find difficult to explain, can perhaps be more relied upon to provide help than those motivated purely by extrinsic rewards. Helping behaviors motivated by intrinsic selfishness may, therefore, be often construed as more socially desirable, and classed as altruistic, than those motivated by extrinsic selfishness. But, of course, those whose selfishness is manifested in the abuse of others might be considered more dangerous to society and socially undesirable than those whose selfishness is manifested in helping others. Nevertheless, one of the features of EAD is that it identifies only certain forms of exploitative selfishness as unjust, and only certain forms of non-exploitative selfishness, and selflessness (in as much as it exists) as just. If we keep these distinctions in mind, and consider justice in terms of EAD, then according to the present analysis, the following conclusions would appear to follow.

1. Although, for most individuals justice may ultimately be driven by selfishness, the selfishness is primarily non-exploitative and could be considered socially desirable for human groups in that its aim is to mutual advantage (even if only at a biological level). However, justice is also to be construed as a piece of rule-utilitarianism, in that it involves following a set of rules that have evolved to be mutually beneficial in the long run; hence, they may not actually be mutually advantageous in every particular instance.

2. Exploitative selfishness is not actually by itself just or unjust; instead justice aims to discourage only those who from a starting point of equal ratio equity seek to gain selfishly at the expense of others; it is not normally considered unjust (or socially undesirable), for example, for victims to selfishly seek compensation from those who have harmed them, so long as they seek redress through socially acceptable channels that do not result in further inequities.

3. But significantly also, altruism, whether construed in terms of non-exploitative selfishness or unbridled pure selflessness, is also neither just nor unjust. In terms of EAD, altruism towards those who, through inequity, are deserving of help is just in as much as contributes to the restoration of equity; whereas altruism towards those who are not in a state of inequity is always technically unjust. Of course, the degree to which inequities caused by indiscriminate altruism will be tolerated will vary considerably (see Gergen, 1969); however, one of the main aims of justice is that of directing and, if necessary, curbing indiscriminate acts of helping no matter what their motivation, so that socially desirable helping behaviors are encouraged, and undesirable helping behaviors discouraged, in an effective and efficient way.

4. And finally, if one accepts Kohlberg's view that justice is the highest moral principle, then perhaps, in line with the historical views of many philosophers and in terms of the development of moral reasoning, pure unbridled, selfless altruism, in as much as it exists, is not to be con-

strued as the highest moral good; indeed, unconstrained, it could be construed as a social liability.

Of course, given the numerous conceptions of justice that now abound, it cannot be claimed that this kind of analysis can provide a full account of the possible relationships between justice and altruism, but arguably, it may help to provide a conceptual and growing empirical basis for many of our commonsense notions in this regard.

Notes

1. Importantly, we find the same ideas in the allegedly socialistic principles of eighteenth century writers such as Rousseau. Thus, whilst he did indeed advocate measures that would reduce inequalities in wealth and privilege, Rousseau was actually no proponent of the doctrine of equal shares. Indeed he showed a marked preference for the ancient principle of geometrical proportion. Thus, of equality, Rousseau says, "Distributive justice would be opposed to this rigorous equality of the state of nature, even if it were practicable in civil society, and since all members of the state owe it services proportionate to their talents and strengths, citizens must in their turn be distinguished and favoured *in proportion to their services.*" He also adds, "History affords . . . no examples of leaders who fared badly merely by being equitable. . . . To be just, one must be severe: tolerating wickedness, when one has the right and the power to repress it, is being wicked oneself" (1988, p. 68). Neither did the early socialists and Marxists adopt a conception of equality that ignored inputs; indeed, the socialist doctrine on this was actually very strict; assuming all have the opportunity to work then, "He who does not work, neither shall he eat" (see Lenin, 1939, p. 150); thus, those who deliberately place themselves in need will not be tolerated. Marx's (1976, 1978, 1986) egalitarianism rests on the premise that in an ideal communist society no one will voluntarily be idle, and all will work equally within the limits of their natural abilities; the Marxist ideal could perhaps most accurately be construed is equal outcomes (adjusted for need), for equal inputs (adjusted for ability and opportunity), not that all should take, according to their needs, regardless of anything they do; indeed, the idleness of the capitalists and gentlefolk was one of Marx's main complaints about capitalism and aristocracy. It can also be noted here that it may be misleading to assume that the religious doctrines, such as the Christian notion goodwill to all men, reflect egalitarian or need oriented considerations of justice; instead they must be set in the context of a belief systems in which, typically, perfect proportional justice is not meted out in this life, but is dispensed by God in the next. Thus, for example, whilst Kant (1963) advocated benevolence as a moral virtue he also emphasized that, "A benevolent judge is unthinkable. . . . *Divine Justice must reward good conduct and punish bad with unerring precision*"(my emphasis). Divine justice, or holy law, therefore, prescribes that happiness be apportioned exactly according to virtue, and that "of necessity . . . punishment should fit the crime" (p. 107). For this, says Kant, is *jus aequitatis,* the law of equity.
2. Historically, this latter idea of extended or implied choice or responsibility can be found in much religious thought. It underlies doctrines such as the Christian idea

of original sin, and the idea in Brahminical and Buddhist thought that "Every sentient being is reaping as it has sown; if not in this life, then in one or other of the infinite series of antecedent existences of which it is the latest term." According to Huxley, such beliefs attempt to justify various situations by claiming that, "The present distribution of good and evil is, therefore, the algebraical sum of accumulated positive and negative deserts" (1911, p. 60).

3. It can be noted that, from the perspective of EAD, what has been termed procedural justice (Tyler, 1987; Lind and Tyler, 1987) is not a species of justice that is separate from desert (for a similar view, see Sadurski, 1985); rather, in many respects, just procedures are those procedures that are most likely to secure deserved outcomes. For example, Wagstaff and Kelhar (1993) found that although subjects judged an adversarial procedure that enabled them the voice their opinions as giving them more control, the fairness of the procedure was determined more by the ability to produce a correct decision or just outcome. However, perhaps most significantly, much of the problem in the just procedures versus just outcomes debate seems to have arisen from a failure to recognize that the many of features of just procedures can be construed as outcomes in their own right. For instance, Tyler argues that the procedures used in making a decision can convey important messages about self-worth and self-esteem, particularly those that relate to neutral treatment, trustworthiness and respect and dignity (Tyler and Dawes, 1993; Tyler and Belliveau, 1995). This makes sense within the context of EAD because any procedure that lowers a person's sense of self-worth or self-esteem could be seen as producing negative outcomes. Within EAD, people who have done nothing wrong (have no negative inputs), or have yet to be found guilty of wrong, are entitled to impartial treatment and a degree of respect, trust, and dignity; and any procedure that is negative in these respects is one that inflicts undeserved harm and is unjust.

4. If justice is conceptualized in terms of EAD, then this also supports the differentiation often made between justice and the moral principle of utility, which would overrule considerations of justice if expedient in obtaining some aggregated conception of the good (see, for example, Raphael, 1981).

References

Adams, J.S. (1963). Toward an understanding of inequity. *Journal of Abnormal and Social Psychology*, 67, 422–436.

Adams, J.S. (1965). Inequity and social exchange. In L. Berkowitz (Ed.), *Advances in Experimental Social Psychology*, Vol. 2. New York: Academic Press.

Aristotle (1984). Nichomachaen Ethics V. In B. J. Barnes (Ed.), *The Complete Works of Aristotle*. Guilford: Princeton University Press.

Austin, W. and Walster, E. (1974). Reactions to confirmations and disconfirmations of expectancies of equity and inequity. *Journal of Personality and Social Psychology*, 30, 208–216.

Axelrod, R. (1980a). Effective choice in the Prisoner's dilemma. *Journal of Conflict Resolution*, 24, 3–25.

Axelrod, R. (1980b). More effective choice in the Prisoner's dilemma. *Journal of Conflict Resolution*, 24, 379–403.

Axelrod, R. (1984). *The evolution of cooperation*. New York: Basic Books.

Baron, J. (1993). Heuristics and biases in equity judgments: A utilitarian approach. In

B.A. Mellers and J. Baron (Eds.), *Psychological perspectives on justice: Theory and applications*. Cambridge: Cambridge University Press.

Barry, B. (1989). *Theories of justice*. Hemel Hempstead, Herts: Harvester-Wheatsheaf.

Batson, C.D. (1987). Prosocial motivation: Is it ever truly altruistic? In L. Berkowitz (Ed.), *Advances in Experimental Social Psychology*, Vol. 20. New York: Academic Press.

Bayley, J.E. (1981). Human nature and justice. In R.L. Braham (Ed.), *Social Justice*. Boston: Martinus Nijhoff.

Bendor, J., Kramer, R.M., and Stout, S. (1991). When in doubt: Cooperation in a noisy prisoner's dilemma. *Journal of Conflict Resolution*, 35, 691–719.

Berkowitz, L. (1969). Resistance to improper dependence relationships. *Journal of Experimental Social Psychology*, 5, 283–294.

Boyd, R. and Richerson, P.J. (1992). Punishment allows the evolution of cooperation (or anything else) in sizeable groups. *Ethology and Sociobiology*, 13, 171–195.

Brabant, J. and Lerner, M.J. (1975). 'A little time and effort'—Who deserves what from whom? *Personality and Social Psychology Bulletin*, 1, 177–181.

Campbell, T. (1988). *Justice: Issues in Political Thoery*. Basingstoke: Macmillan.

Cashdan, E. (1989). Hunters and gatherers: Economic behavior in bands. In S. Plattner (Ed.), *Economic anthropology*, 31–48. Stanford: Stanford University Press.

Cialdini, R.B., Schaller, M., Houlihan, D., Arps, K., Fultz, J. and Beaman, A.L. (1987). Empathy based helping: Is it selflessly or selfishly motivated? *Journal of Personality and Social Psychology*, 52, 749–758.

Clutton-Brock, T.H. and Parker, G.A. (1995). Punishment in animal societies. *Nature*, 373, 209–216.

Cohen, R.L. (1982). Perceiving justice: An attributional perspective. In J. Greenberg and Cohen, R.L. (Eds.), *Equity and justice in social behavior*. New York: Academic Press.

Cohen, R.L. and Greenberg, J. (1982). The justice concept in social psychology. In J. Greenberg, and R.L. Cohen, (Eds.), *Equity and justice in social behavior*. New York: Academic Press.

Colby, A. and Kohlberg, L. (1987). *The measurement of moral judgment—Volume 1—Theoretical foundations and research validation*. London: Cambridge University Press.

Cosmides, L. and Tooby, J. (1992). Cognitive adaptations for social exchange. In J.H. Barlow, L. Cosmides and J. Tooby (Eds.), *The adapted mind: Evolutionary psychology and the generation of culture*. New York: Oxford University Press.

Cross, R., Jones, P. A. and Card, R. (1988). *Introduction to criminal law*. London: Butterworths.

Dawkins, R. (1976). *The selfish gene*. London: Oxford University Press.

de Waal, F. (1989). *Chimpanzee politics: Power and sex among apes*. London: John Hopkins.

Desmarais, S. and Lerner, M.J. (1994). Entitlement in close relationships: A justice-motive analysis. In M.J. Lerner and G. Mikula (Eds.), *Entitlement and the affectional bond: Justice in close relationships*. New York: Plenum Press.

Deutsch, M. (1975). Equity, equality and need: What determines which value will be used as the basis of distributive justice? *Journal of Social Issues*, 31, 137–149.

Deutsch, M. (1983). Current social psychological perspectives on justice. *European Journal of Social Psychology*, 13, 305–319.

Deutsch, M. (1985). *Distributive justice: A social psychological perspective*. New Haven, CT: Yale University Press.

Evans, C. (1981). Justice as desert. In R.L. Braham (Ed.), *Social justice.* Boston: M. Nijhoff.

Elliott, G.C. and Meeker, B.F. (1986). Achieving fairness in the face of competing concerns: The different effects of individual and group characteristics. *Journal of Personality and Social Psychology,* 50, 754–760.

Feinberg, J. (1970). *Doing and deserving,* Princeton, NJ: Princeton University Press.

Fogerty, M. (1961). *The just wage.* London: Geoffrey Chapman.

Folger, R., Sheppard, B.H. and Buttram, R.T. (1995). Equity, equality and need: Three faces of social justice. In B.B. Bunker and J.Z. Rubin (Eds.), *Conflict, cooperation and justice: Essays inspired by the work of Morton Deutsch.* San Francisco: Jossey-Bass.

Franklin, R.L. (1968). *Freewill and Determinism.* London: Routledge and Paul.

Furby, L. (1986). Psychology and justice. In R.L. Cohen (Ed.), *Justice: Views from the social sciences.* New York: Plenum.

Furnham, A. (1982). Why are the poor always with us? Explanations for poverty in Britain. *British Journal of Social Psychology,* 21, 311–322.

Gergen, K.J. (1969). *The psychology of behavior exchange.* Reading, MA: Addison-Wesley.

Gilligan, C. (1982). *In a different voice.* Cambridge, MA: Harvard University Press.

Hamilton, W.D. (1964). The genetical theory of social behaviour (1 and 2). *Journal of Theoretical Biology,* 7, 1–16; 17–32.

Harris, R.J. (1983). Pinning down the equity formula. In D.M. Messick and K.S. Cook (Eds.), *Equity theory: Psychological and sociological perspectives.* New York: Praeger.

Harris, R.J. (1993). Two insights occasioned by attempts to pin down the equity formula. In B.A. Mellers and J. Baron (Eds.), *Psychological perspectives on justice: Theory and applications.* Cambridge: Cambridge University Press.

Hart, H.L.A. (1968). *Punishment and responsibility.* Oxford: Clarendon.

Hatfield, E., Utne, M.K. and Traupman, J. (1979). Equity theory and intimate relationships. In R.L. Burgess and T.L. Huston (Eds.), *Social exchange in developing relationships.* New York: Academic Press.

Hogan, R. and Emler, N.P. (1981). Retributive justice. In M.J. Lerner and S.C. Lerner (Eds.). *The justice motive in social behavior.* New York: Plenum.

Hospers, F. (1961). *Human Conduct: An Introduction to the Problems of Ethics.* New York: Harcourt Brace and World.

Huxley, T.H. (1911). *Evolution and ethics and other essays.* London: MacMillan.

Kant, I. (1963). *Lectures on Ethics.* Translated by L. Infield. New York: Harper (Written 1775–1780).

Karniol, R. and Miller, D.T. (1981). Morality and the development of conceptions of justice. In M.J. Lerner, and S.C. Lerner (Eds.), *The justice motive in social behavior.* New York: Plenum.

Katz, M.B. (1989). *The undeserving poor.* New York: Pantheon.

Kluegel, J.R. and Smith, E.R. (1986). *Beliefs about inequality.* New York: Aldine.

Kohlberg, L. (1971). From is to ought: How to commit the naturalistic fallacy and get away with it in the study of moral development. In T. Mischel (Ed.), *Cognitive development and epistemology.* New York: Academic Press.

Kohlberg, L. (1976). Moral stages and moralization: The cognitive-developmental approach. In T. Lickona (Ed.), *Moral development and behavior: Theory research and social issues.* New York: Holt Rinehart and Winston.

Lamm, H.E. and Kayser, E. (1978). The allocation of monetary gain and loss following dyadic performance. The weight given to effort and ability under conditions of low and high intra-dyadic attraction. *European Journal of Social Psychology,* 8, 275–278.

Lenin, V. (1939). The teachings of Karl Marx, and Class society and the state. In Oakeshott, M. (Ed.), *The social and political doctrines of contemporary Europe.* Cambridge: Cambridge University Press.

Lerner, M.J. (1974). The justice motive: 'Equity' and 'parity' among children. *Journal of Personality and Social Psychology,* 29, 538–550.

Lerner, M.J. (1975). The justice motive in social behavior: Introduction. *Journal of Social Issues,* 31, 1–20.

Lerner, M.J. (1977). The justice motive: Some hypotheses as to its origin and forms. *Journal of Personality,* 45, 1–52.

Lerner, M.J. (1980). *The belief in a just world: A fundamental delusion.* New York: Plenum.

Leventhal, G.S., Karuza, J. and Fry, W.R. (1980). Beyond fairness: A theory of allocation preferences. In G. Mikula (Ed.), *Justice and social interaction.* New York: Springer-Verlag.

Lind, E.A. and Tyler, T.R. (1988). *Social Psychology of procedural justice.* New York: Plenum.

Lissak, R.I. and Sheppard, B.H. (1983). Beyond fairness: The criterion problem in research on dispute intervention. *Journal of Applied Psychology,* 13, 45–65.

Lucas, J.R. (1980). *On justice.* Oxford: Clarendon Press.

MacIntyre, A. (1982). *After virtue: A study in moral theory.* London: Duckworth.

Marx, K.H. (1976). *Capital: A critique of political economy, Vol.1.* Harmondsworth, Middx.:Penguin.

Marx, K.H. (1978). *Capital: A critique of political economy, Vol.2.* Harmondsworth, Middx.:Penguin.

Marx, K.H. (1986). Critique of the Gotha Programme. In J. Elster (Ed.), *Karl Marx: A Reader.* Cambridge: Cambridge University Press (First published 1875).

McClintock, C.G. and Liebrand, W.B.G. (1988). Role of interdependence structure, individual value orientation, and another's strategy in social decision making: A transformational analysis. *Journal of Personality and Social Psychology,* 55, 396–409.

Meyer, J.P. and Mulherin, A. (1980). From attribution to helping: An analysis of the mediating effects of affect and expectancy. *Journal of Personality and Social Psychology,* 39, 201–210.

Mikula, G. (1980). On the role of justice in allocation decisions. In G. Mikula (Ed.), *Justice and social interaction.* 127–165. New York: Springer-Verlag.

Mill, J.S. (1993) Utilitarianism. In G. Williams (Ed.), *Utilitarianism. On Liberty. Considerations on representative government. Remarks on Bentham's philosophy.* London: Everyman (first published 1861; "On Liberty," 1859).

Miller, D.T. (1977). Personal deserving versus justice for others: An exploration of the justice motive. *Journal of Experimental Social Psychology,* 13, 1–13.

Miller, D.T. and Vidmar, N. (1981). The social psychology of punishment reactions. In M.J. Lerner and S.C. Lerner (Eds.). *The justice motive in social behavior.* New York: Plenum.

Molander, P. (1985). The optimal level of generosity in a selfish, uncertain environment. *Journal of Conflict Resolution,* 29, 611–618.

Montada, L. (1980). Developmental changes in concepts of justice. In G. Mikula (Ed.), *Justice and social interaction.* New York: Springer-Verlag.

Pandey, J., Sinha, Y., Prakesh, A., and Tripathi, R. (1982). Right-Left political ideologies and attribution of the causes of poverty. *European Journal of Social Psychology*, 12, 327–331.

Plato (1960). *The laws*. Translated by A. E. Taylor. London: Dent.

Plato (1987). *The republic*. Translated by D. Lee. Harmondsworth: Penguin.

Posner, R.A. (1981). *The economics of justice*. Cambridge, MA: Harvard University Press.

Raphael, D.D. (1981). *Moral philosophy*. Oxford: Oxford University Press.

Rawls, J. (1972). *A theory of justice*. Oxford: Clarendon.

Reis, H.T. (1984). The multidimensionality of justice. In R. Folger (Ed.), *The sense of injustice: Social psychological perspectives*. New York: Plenum.

Roberts, S. (1979). *Order and dispute: An introduction to legal anthropology*. Harmondsworth: Penguin.

Rousseau, J.J. (1988). *Rousseau's political writings: Discourse on inequality: Discourse on political economy: On social contract*. A. Ritter and J. Bondanella (Eds.). New York: Norton (first published 1755).

Russell, B. (1979). *A history of western philosophy*. London: Unwin.

Sabini, J. (1995). *Social psychology* (2nd Edition). New York: W.W. Norton.

Sadurski, W. (1985). *Giving desert its due: Social justice and legal theory*. Dordrecht: Reidel.

Sampson, E.E. (1975). On justice as equality. *Journal of Social Issues*, 31, 45–64.

Schmidt, G. and Weiner, B. (1988). An attribution-affect-action theory of behavior: Replications of judgments of help-giving. *Personality and Social Psychology Bulletin*, 14, 610–621.

Schwartz, S. (1975). The justice of need and the activation of humanitarian norms. *Journal of Social Issues*, 31, 111–136.

Schwinger, T. (1980). Just allocations of goods: Decisions among three principles. In G. Mikula (Ed.), *Justice and social interaction*. New York: Springer-Verlag.

Shaver, K.G. (1985). *The attribution of blame: Causality, responsibility, and blameworthiness*. Cambridge, MA: Springer-Verlag.

Sher, G. (1981). The historical dimension of justice. In R.L. Braham (Ed.), *Social justice*. Boston: M. Nijhoff.

Sidgwick, H. (1907). *The method of ethics*. London: Macmillan (first published 1874).

Stake, J.E. (1983). Factors in reward distribution: Allocator motive, gender and protestant ethic. *Journal of Personality and Social Psychology*, 44, 410–418.

Thomas, S., Wagstaff, G.F., and Brunas-Wagstaff, J. (1996). The influence of responsibility and need on the assignment of penalties for traffic violations. *Proceedings of the British Psychological Society*, 4, 54.

Tornblom, K.Y. (1992). The social psychology of distributive justice. In K.R. Scherer (Ed.), *Justice: Interdisciplinary perspectives*. Cambridge: Cambridge University Press.

Trivers, R. (1971). The evolution of reciprocal altruism. *Quarterly Review of Biology*, 46, 35–57.

Tyler, T.R. (1987). Procedural justice research. *Social Justice Research*, 1, 41–65.

Tyler, T.R. and Belliveau, M.A. (1995). Tradeoffs in justice principles: Definitions of fairness. In B.B. Bunker and J.Z. Rubin (Eds.), *Conflict, cooperation and justice: Essays inspired by the work of Morton Deutsch*. San Francisco: Jossey-Bass.

Tyler, T.R. and Dawes, R.M. (1993). Fairness in groups: Comparing the self-interest and social identity perspectives. In B.A. Mellers and J. Baron (Eds.), *Psychological perspectives on justice: Theory and applications*. Cambridge: Cambridge University Press.

Utne, M.K. and Kidd, R.F. (1980). Equity and attribution. In G. Mikula (Ed.), *Justice and social interaction*. New York: Springer-Verlag.

Wagstaff, G.F. (1984). Political ideology, intelligence, heredity, and social justice: Is there a paradox? *Psychological Reports*, 54, 286.

Wagstaff, G.F. (1994). Equity, equality and need: three principles of justice or one? *Current Psychology: Research and Reviews*, 13, 138–152.

Wagstaff, G.F. (in press). Equity, equality, and allocations to adults and children. *Journal of Social Psychology*.

Wagstaff, G.F. and Kelhar, S. (1993). On the roles of control and outcomes in procedural justice. *Psychological Reports*, 73, 121–122.

Wagstaff, G.F. and Perfect, T.J. (1992). On the definition of perfect equity and the prediction of inequity. *British Journal of Social Psychology*, 31, 69–77.

Wagstaff, G.F. and Quirk, M.A. (1983). Attitudes to sex roles, political conservatism, and belief in a just world. *Psychological Reports*, 2, 813–814.

Wagstaff, G.F. and Worthington, J. (in press). Equity, relative need, and allocations to zero input workers. *Journal of Social Psychology*.

Wagstaff, G.F., Chadwick, D. and Brunas-Wagstaff (1996). Equity and the distribution of undeserved outcomes. Unpublished manuscript, Department of Psychology, University of Liverpool.

Wagstaff, G.F., Huggins, J.P. and Perfect, T.J. (1993). Equity, equality, and need in the adult family. *Journal of Social Psychology*, 133, 439–444.

Wagstaff, G.F., Huggins, J. and Perfect, T.J. (1996). Equal ratio equity, general linear equity, and framing effects in judgments of allocation divisions. *European Journal of Social Psychology*, 26, 29–41.

Wagstaff, G.F., Bowles, R.J., Hughes, D., Rogers, B., Turner, S. and Perfect, T.J. (1994). Judgments concerning zero inputs in equity situations. *Journal of Social Psychology*, 134, 649–654.

Walster, E. and Walster, G.W. (1975). Equity and social justice. *Journal of Social Issues*, 31, 21–43.

Walster, E., Berscheid, E. and Walster, G.W. (1973). New directions in equity research. *Journal of Personality and Social Psychology*, 25, 151–176.

Walster, E., Walster, G.W. and Berscheid, E. (1978). *Equity: Theory and research*. London: Allyn and Bacon.

Walster, E., Walster, G.W. and Traupman, J. (1978). Equity and premarital sex. *Journal of Personality*, 36, 82–92.

Weiner, B. (1980). A cognitive (attribution)-emotion-action model of motivated behavior: An analysis of judgments of help-giving. *Journal of Personality and Social Psychology*, 39, 186–200.

Weiner, B. (1985). An attributional theory of achievement motivation and emotion. *Psychological Review*, 92, 548–573.

Williams, S. (1984). Left-right ideological differences in blaming victims. *Political Psychology*, 5, 573–581.

Wright, R. (1995). *The moral animal: Evolutionary psychology and everyday life*. Boston: Little-Brown.

2

Reactions to the Fate of One's Brain-Child after Its Disclosure

Sidney Rosen and Shannon Wheatman

> ... What a good thing Adam had—when he said
> a thing he knew nobody had said it before.
> —Mark Twain, cited in Paine, 1935

This study has to do with our emotional and evaluative reactions when our self-generated ideas that we believe to be original are slighted, or when our linkage to them is threatened. It is based on two motivational propositions: (a) People desire that the idea receive origination credit; they want consensual validation from knowledgeable others that the idea, per se, is indeed original and useful; (b) People also desire recognition credit. They want public certification from others as having proposed the idea. Each of these propositions will be considered in turn.

We Desire Origination Credit

It would be gratifying if one's idea received origination credit, but not very gratifying if the idea, per se, were certified as unoriginal. Several converging lines of reasoning are suggestive of this proposition. For instance, some writers have proposed that we come to view our ideas as extensions of ourselves, just as we do our more tangible possessions (e.g., Heider, 1958; James, 1890; Rudmin, 1991; Simmel,

1950). The term, brain-child, captures this proprietary attachment one feels to one's originated idea. Effort expended in its generation (James spoke of work saturated with our labor) justifies the desire to have our intellectual offspring certified as original, for certification would affirm our self-investment in its generation. Failure to obtain certification would threaten our self-concept.

Some cross-cultural research indicates that—at least for adults—possessions give one a sense of efficacy, uncertainty reduction, and control over one's environment (e.g., Belk, 1988; Furby, 1978). Although such research is focused largely on material possessions, some of it points to the symbolic function that they may serve (e.g., Csikszentmihalyi & Rochberg-Halton, 1981). It seems plausible, too, that attainment of origination credit would satisfy "intrinsic epistemic curiosity" (Berlyne, 1960), strivings for personal causation (deCharms, 1968), intrinsic motivation (Deci, 1975), and need for cognition (Cacioppo & Petty, 1982). It would justify that feeling of discovery that Merton (1976) dubbed the Eureka Syndrome.

We come to like our ideational products just as we do our tangible possessions. Heider (1958) advanced the notion of a unit relation, an association arising from the perceptual/cognitive process of linking entities or attributes that appear to belong together, such as being associated with a possession. He regarded a unit relation as interchangeable with a sentiment relation to that entity, given that most people like themselves. Beggan (1992) demonstrated that mere possession (vs. nonpossession) of an otherwise hedonically neutral object enhances our attraction to it. He considered this "mere ownership effect" a case of self-serving, positivity bias. Time of possession strengthens such liking through such processes as thought polarization. Time and the frequency with which we think of an idea also increase our tendency to appropriate the idea as our own (Ross & Sicoly, 1979; Wicklund, 1989), either intentionally (as in plagiarization, or in the behavior of the epigone or the "copy-cat" who openly mimics one's expressed thoughts), or unintentionally (as in "cryptomnesia" with regards to others' or even one's own original idea).

Still, uncertainty may linger as to whether our idea is in fact novel: Perhaps our search of the relevant literature was incomplete, or the idea may have appeared under a different name in a seemingly unrelated context. The uncertainty may prompt us to seek reassurance or consensual validation from ostensibly knowledgeable others (e.g., Fazio, 1979; Festinger, 1954; Swann & Read, 1981), especially in science, where the evidential rules or resources needed to determine the viability or usefulness of the idea may require consultation of a jury of competent others (Hagstrom, 1965). But there are risks in seeking such certification from others: Those others might invalidate our claim to the idea's originality; this would reflect unfavorably on our self-concept, such as on our private self-image of creativity. The invalidation might be well founded, or it could represent others' territorial attempts to suppress the idea because it may appear to threaten their own ideational domain. Others might resort to uninvited intentional or unintentional infringement on our own ideational territory. Such violation of one's "intellectual private property" may well produce "a lesion of the ego at its very center," speculated Simmel (1950, p. 322).

We Desire Recognition Credit

It would be gratifying to learn that we have been publicly certified by knowledgeable others as being linked to an idea. Several kinds of observations converge in support of this proposition. For instance, being recognized as the author appears to reflect favorably on one's public self-image, as in the admiration and prestige that comes with being singled out as a Nobelist. Moreover, at least in Western countries, we appear to use various territorial "markers" or infringement-resisting strategies for identifying the idea as our own, such as in seeking to copyright it (see Altman, 1975, on idea or cognitive territoriality), listing ourselves as its author, labelling it in distinctive ways, and so on. Equity considerations also demand it: We authors only think it fair that the outcome (recognition) be proportional to our inputs, namely, to the perceived abilities and skills we have applied during the generation process together with the effort we expended in creating it. Recognition might also affirm our perceptions of uniqueness with respect to *favorable* self-attributes (Ditto & Griffin, 1993).

Yet there are problems associated with seeking recognition credit, similar to those involved in seeking origination credit. For instance, Lemaine (1974) alludes to the threats to one's social identity that comparison with others may pose, and to the struggle for social priority or social originality. The sociological literature (Hagstrom, 1965; Merton, 1949) points to the ambivalence felt by scientists about communicating with one another about their products. On the one hand, they must face such concerns as to whether, when, and whom they ought to reveal their new ideas and findings, fearing that in such revelations they risk being "scooped," having the idea belittled as premature, unoriginal, and so on. On the other hand, they must deal with the scientific ethos of producing and communicating knowledge for the advancement of science rather than of the scientist. That literature also alludes to the ambivalence of the scientific community regarding granting certification on the plausible grounds that the idea would probably not have emerged were it not for the work of intellectual forebears in the scientific community. That ambivalence is also reflected in the temporal limits attached to copyrights and patents.

A Proviso Regarding Recognition Credit

Strictly speaking, it seems reasonable to propose that the issue of recognition credit would be of greater moment to an originator if the idea, per se, has received origination credit than if the idea has been denied origination credit. Given that our idea did receive origination credit, it would be most gratifying if we were also recognized as its originator. It would be least gratifying if the origination credit for that idea went to someone else—as in the case of successful plagiarization. On the other hand, if the idea was denied certification as truly original, it seems plausible that we would be less concerned over who was the recipient of such dubious credit. The empirical literature is silent on this latter case.

Consider, for example, a study by Merton (1976). After examining the biographies or autobiographies of numerous great scientists from Galileo on, he concluded that many of them were involved in disputes over priority of discovery, or at least independence of discovery (in the case of multiple discoveries). The disputes seem to be more about the particular personage who was entitled to recognition credit for first having advanced an original idea than about whether the originality of the idea, per se, was in dispute. In short, the study is not instructive with regard to the question of whether the desire for recognition credit plays an independent role or an interactive role in combination with the desire for origination credit.[1] A similar limitation applies to simulation experiments some of us conducted years ago (Rosen, Johnson, Case, & Flaks, 1978).

The basic scenario concerned a hypothetical originator who revealed to a friend the intention of entering a novel plan in a competition, only to discover later that the friend proceeded to enter that idea, without the originator's knowledge and consent, before the originator could. Origination credit was then awarded—the idea won honors. Recognition credit was reported to have been allocated to the originator (under whose sole name the friend had submitted the plan), or to both parties (it having been submitted by the friend under both names), or to the friend (it having been submitted only under the friend's name)—a case of plagiarization. The more the friend took sole credit, the more respondents expected that the originator would express negative affect and resolve not to confide future ideas to the friend; their relationship would also suffer. However, we are left in the dark as to how strongly they would have responded to the recognition allocation had the plan not received honors.

This limitation was avoided in the present experiment. Respondents were asked to imagine that they were participant P, who had experienced the following episode: P had attended a creativity workshop after which every attendee was invited to submit an entry to a national Creativity Fair. There would be no prize money for winning entries. Accordingly, P drafts a paper on what P considers a novel, useful method for determining the structure of living and nonliving things, but then decides that the odds of winning were too slim to bother submitting it. Fellow-participant, O, inquires about P's progress on the paper. Being told of P's decision not to submit the completed draft, O, using the pretext of seeking good leads on "writing style," asks to borrow the paper. Days later O returns the draft. A change of heart prompts P to revise the paper and mail it off under a new title, together with a separate cover page containing the critical identifying information (author, name of paper, and so on). Months later a letter of apology arrives stating that P's paper had gotten lost after being separated from its cover page, so could not be judged. A second enclosure lists the names of persons who were identified as having contributed entries and the title of each entry. It also indicates whether the entry was judged one of the few winning entries. The original title of P's draft paper (the one P had later changed) is listed in it as having been contributed either by O alone, or jointly by O and P, or by P alone. Furthermore, the entry is, or is not, identified as a winning entry.

Six dependent variables were used to investigate the affective and evaluative impact of these two credit allocation factors. The first three were: (a) negativity of emotional reaction, (b) evaluation of the judges' competence, and (c) evaluation of O's trustworthiness. The remaining three were included for exploratory purposes. They were (d) self-evaluated creativity, (e) self-evaluated sociability, and (f) desire for future collaboration.

It was predicted that P's emotional reaction would be more positive (less negative) if origination credit were awarded than if it were denied. Our rationale was that the receipt of recognition credit would affirm that this ideational extension of P's self-concept, which P regarded as a novel product, was indeed novel, hence would be a pleasurable experience. On the other hand, the denial of such origination credit would threaten this ideational extension of the self, hence would be an unpleasant experience. In this connection, relatively more negative affect in response to bogus negative than positive performance feedback has been reported by other investigators in other contexts (e.g., Kernis, Cornell, Sun, Berry, & Harlow, 1993; Kernis & Sun, 1994; Swann, Griffin, Predmore & Gaines, 1987).

We predicted, too, that P's emotional reaction would be most positive on P's being the sole recipient of recognition, but least positive on O's being the sole recipient. However, we expected this pattern of differences to be stronger where origination credit was awarded than where origination credit was not awarded. Recall that our early study (Rosen et al., 1978) had only tested for the effects of recognition for an idea that had received origination credit.

We expected P to evaluate the judges as more competent in the event that origination credit was awarded than if it were not. Our rationale was that in the latter case the disconfirmation of one's originality would be inconsistent with one's self-concept, hence unacceptable, hence prompt P to rise to its defense through derogation of the certifying agents. Similar evaluative responses to negative performance feedback have been reported by investigators in other contexts (e.g., Kernis et al., 1993; Kernis & Sun, 1994; Swann et al., 1987), although their findings appear to apply especially to participants with high global self-esteem (see also Schlenker, 1986). No hypothesis was entertained concerning the impact, if any, of the recognition factor on evaluation of the judges' competence; we assumed that the judges could not easily be faulted by P for O's behavior.

Little, if any, effect of origination on evaluation of O's trustworthiness was expected. We assumed that P would find it difficult to hold O responsible for the judges' competence, partly on the grounds that

O was not told that P had submitted an improved version that had gone astray. But O could clearly be faulted for the manner in which recognition credit was awarded. We expected P to evaluate O as most trustworthy in the event that P received sole recognition credit, but least trustworthy if O received sole recognition credit instead.

In exploring the possible effects of credit allocation on self-evaluation we were drawn to a line of reasoning suggested by the work of others (e.g., Brown & Smart, 1991; Lemaine, 1974; Steele, 1988), namely, threats to one's perceived own originality or competence may lead to compensatory coping strategies, such as enhanced self-evaluation on unrelated or different dimensions of evaluation. For instance, Brown and Smart (1991) showed that when participants were led to believe they had performed poorly on a test of intellectual ability, those having high global self-esteem exaggerated the positivity of their social attributes, whereas the reverse was true for those with low self-esteem. However, participants' self-evaluations of their intellectual attributes were relatively unaffected. Beggan (1992), also influenced by these investigators, demonstrated that (bogus) failure feedback on an unrelated task produced the "mere ownership" effect, i.e., enhanced evaluation of a neutral possession previously given the participants, in contrast to evaluation of a nonpossession. A reverse tendency was obtained under success feedback.

We assumed that our own respondents, by and large, had high self-esteem and that their creativity rather than their sociability was implicated more in the present context. This rationale led to the predictions that the denial (as opposed to the awarding) of origination credit would have little impact, if any, on self-evaluated creativity, but it would lead to relatively enhanced self-evaluated sociability. No convincing rationale suggested itself for advancing hypotheses regarding the impact of the recognition factor on the self-evaluation variables.

Other results reported by Brown and Smart (1991) are suggestive in connection with desire for future collaboration. They showed that the feedback x self-esteem interaction effects on self-rated social attributes also spilled over into prosocial behavior, with high self-esteem individuals volunteering to help a stranger more after failure than after success, but that the reverse was the case for low self-esteem individuals. Sharing one's resources would, of course, be another form of prosocial behavior, and willingness to collaborate with others implies a willingness to share in the fruits of such collaboration. We expected that P would express *less* interest in collaborating with a partner on a future project requiring much "imagination," if origination credit had been awarded than if it had not. This is suggested too by the results of an early experiment (Rosen & Case, 1979) in which participants received highly positive or negative feedback concerning their own (but no feedback regarding a fellow-participant's) performance on an administered test allegedly on creativity. Asked to indicate whether they preferred noncollaboration to collaboration (in creating television synopses) with the fellow-participant during the "final" phase of the study, the highly "creative" participants were more in favor of working alone, believed they could do a better job working alone, and were relatively less in favor of showing their work to the other participant for comments, than were their less "creative" counterparts. A conceptual replication allegedly on "creative empathy" (Rosen, Case, & Read, 1979) yielded similar results.

No predictions were advanced with regard to the possible impact of the recognition factor on interest in collaborating. Recall that the present scenario alluded to wanting a partner in the future; it made no allusion to co-participant, O, as a potential associate. As matters turned out, however, we failed to anticipate the obvious, namely, that a situation in which recognition credit is allocated jointly to P and O is one that necessarily implies a de facto credit-sharing arrangement with O. As we will see this also influenced self-evaluation.

Method

Overview

Packets of printed material were randomly distributed within small groups of assembled participants. Each packet contained a single one-page vignette, labelled "A Creativity Fair Episode," and a three-page questionnaire that addressed the dependent variables. Participants were asked to imagine a scenario in which they (P) had drafted a paper for submission to a creativity fair. The paper was based on their idea for a novel method of determining underlying structure. Fellow-participant, O, on learning of P's subsequent decision not to submit the draft, asks to borrow it for a few days, under false pretenses. Months later, P learns that O, acting without P's knowledge and consent, had submitted a copy of P's borrowed draft to the

Creativity Fair, listing O's name, both names, or P's name as author(s), and that the idea was or was not judged as original. P also learns that a revised draft, that P had submitted in the meantime under a different title, had gone astray. (More details of the core scenario and its six variants appear in the Introduction.) Participants were then asked to indicate, via rating scales, their affective and evaluative reactions, and their desire for collaboration in the future. After they completed their questionnaires they were asked to read a debriefing statement, thanked, and assured of participation credit.

Design and Participants

A 2 x 3 between-subjects factorial design was employed, involving two levels of origination credit allocation (not awarded/awarded) and three levels of recognition credit allocation (awarded solely to O/to O and P jointly/solely to P). Ninety-six undergraduates from the Psychology Department's Research Participation Pool agreed to serve as participants in a study "On Imagining a Creativity Fair Episode," in exchange for participation credit. Of this number, seventy-eight were females, and eighteen were males. Because so few males signed up during the recruitment period and because the percentage of undergraduate males in psychology at this institution is distinctly smaller than is the percentage of undergraduate females in psychology, the decision was made to use only the data obtained from the female sub-sample.[2]

Measures

All six measures called for one or more ratings on nine-point rating scales. Participants' emotional reaction was ascertained by having them rate the extent to which each of six emotional terms expressed their feelings about the events in the episode. The terms were: angry, deceived, delighted, felt cheated, happy, irritated. The individual scores were summed, after reverse scoring of "delighted" and "happy," to indicate negativity of emotional reaction (Cronbach's α = .96). Participants' evaluation of the judges' competence was determined by having them rate the extent to which each of six attributes applied to the actions of the judges at the fair. The attributes were: far-sighted, close-minded, wise, perceptive, expert, no imagination. The individual scores were summed, after reverse scoring of "close-minded" and "no imagination," to indicate positivity of evaluation of judges' competence (Cronbach's α = .74). Participants' evaluation of O's trustworthiness was obtained via ratings of the extent to which each of six attributes applied to co-participant O in their judgment. The attributes were: sincere, dishonest, trustworthy, reliable, unfair, and helpful. The individual scores were summed, after reverse scoring of "dishonest" and "unfair," to indicate positivity of evaluation of O's trustworthiness (Cronbach's α = .94).

Self-evaluated creativity was measured via participants' ratings of the extent to which each of seven attributes was descriptive "right now" of their own creativity. The attributes were: inventive, skillful, naive, talented, stupid, resourceful, innovative. The individual scores were summed, after reverse scoring of "naive" and "stupid," to indicate positivity of self-evaluated creativity (Cronbach's α = .75). Similarly, self-evaluated sociability was measured via participants' ratings of the extent to which each of six attributes applied to them personally, in which getting along with people was concerned. The attributes were: altruistic, sensitive, sympathetic, cruel, unfriendly, considerate. The individual scores were summed, after reversing "cruel" and "unfriendly," to indicate positivity of self-evaluated sociability (Cronbach's α = .77). Participants' desire for future collaboration was determined via a single item that asked about the extent to which they would be interested in collaborating with a partner on a *new* project that would require a good deal of imagination. The score was considered an index of P's desire for collaboration.

Results

A multivariate analysis of variance (MANOVA) was carried out involving all six dependent variables and the two independent variables of origination and recognition credit allocation. The factor of origination credit was found to be significant, $F(6, 67) = 3.40$, $p <$ .005 (Pillais' trace). So, too, was recognition credit, $F(12, 136) = 6.64$, $p < .001$ (Pillais' trace). The OC x RC interaction was marginally significant, $F(12, 136) = 1.62$, $p < .10$ (Pillais' trace).

Emotional Reaction

The univariate ANOVA on emotional reaction produced a signifi-

TABLE 2.1
**Emotional Reaction as a Function of Allocation of Origination Credit
and Target Allocated Recognition Credit**

Origination credit	Target allocated recognition credit		
	O as author	O and P jointly	P as author
Awarded	50.38$_a$ (3.25)	40.92$_b$ (12.30)	21.00$_c$ (15.26)
Not awarded	47.77$_a$ (7.54)	47.43$_b$ (6.42)	32.25$_b$ (16.53)

Note: Higher means signify more negative emotion. Parenthetical values are standard deviations. Cell means not sharing the same subscripts *within* a given row differ at the .05 level, by Newman-Keuls test.

cant main effect of origination credit, $F(1, 72) = 3.98$, $p < .05$. There was also a significant main effect of recognition credit, $F(2, 72) = 28.42$, $p < .000$. An OC x RC interaction effect of marginal significance was obtained, too, $F(2, 72) = 2.55$, $p < .10$.

As predicted, P's emotional reaction was more positive (less negative) when origination credit was awarded ($M = 37.44$) than when it was not ($M = 42.87$). Also as expected, under conditions where origination credit was awarded, P's emotional reaction was least negative if P alone received the recognition credit ($M = 21.00$), but most negative if O alone received the recognition ($M = 50.38$), $F(1, 72) = 45.08$, $p < .000$. Under conditions of no-origination credit, however, the obtained effect of recognition credit, though somewhat similar, was weaker, $F(1, 72) = 12.08$, $p < .001$, as anticipated. Recall that an OC x RC interaction effect was expected, but no prediction was made concerning the recognition pattern impact under conditions of no origination credit. Mean recognition treatment differences *within* each origination credit condition are also shown in Table 2.1 based on Newman-Keuls tests.

Evaluation of Judges and of Co-Participant O

Evaluation of Judges' Competence

The relevant ANOVA yielded a highly significant main effect of origination credit, $F(1, 72) = 15.82$, $p < .000$. As predicted, the judges

TABLE 2.2
Mean Evaluation of (co-participant) O as a Function of Allocation of Origination Credit and Target Allocated Recognition Credit

	Target allocated recognition credit		
Origination credit	O as author	O and P jointly	P as author
Awarded	9.08_a (3.66)	14.92_a (9.46)	30.00_b (16.55)
Not awarded	10.38_a (5.35)	11.36_a (5.46)	28.33_b (12.84)

Note: Higher means signify more positive evaluation. Parenthetical values are standard deviations. Cell means not sharing the same subscripts *within* a given row differ at the .05 level, by Newman-Keuls test.

were evaluated as more competent if they awarded origination credit ($M = 36.85$) than if they did not ($M = 30.23$). A marginal main effect of recognition credit was also found, $F(2, 72) = 2.60$, $p < .10$, and a nonsignificant OC x RC interaction, $F(2, 72) = 2.04$. Still, it was felt that the evaluation patterns warranted closer examination. This was done through Newman-Keuls tests. They indicated that the differences due to recognition only occurred under conditions of *no*-origination credit. Particularly noteworthy is that under those conditions the mean in the *joint*-recognition treatment ($M = 25.79$) was significantly less positive than the mean in the no origination-O sole recognition treatment ($M = 31.54$) and the mean in the no origination-P sole recognition treatment ($M = 34.00$); both p's $< .05$.

Evaluation of O's Trustworthiness

An ANOVA on evaluation of O's trustworthiness yielded a highly significant main effect of recognition credit, $F(2, 72) = 27.86$, $p < .000$. Support was found for the prediction that O would be evaluated as more trustworthy in the event P alone received recognition credit ($M = 29.20$) than if O received sole credit ($M = 9.73$), $F(1, 72) = 49.22$, $p < .000$. Neither the main effect of origination (none was expected) nor the OC x RC interaction effect were significant (both Fs < 1). Still, fine-grained analyses seemed called for. Mean recognition treatment differences *within* each origination condition are shown in Table 2.2, based on Newman-Keuls tests. The differences appear between the P-alone treatment and the other two treatments.

Self-Evaluations

Self-evaluated Creativity

We had expected relatively little impact of origination on self-evaluated creativity. None was obtained, $F(1.72) = 1.36$, *ns*. Furthermore, the main effect of recognition, $F(2, 72) = 1.82$, and the interaction effect, $F(2, 72) = 2.02$, were both nonsignificant. Still closer examination of the evaluations appeared to be warranted here, too. Newman-Keuls tests revealed mean differences under conditions of *no*-origination credit. More specifically, the mean in the *joint*-recognition treatment ($M = 39.21$) was significantly less positive ($p < .05$) than the mean in the P-sole recognition treatment ($M = 48.00$), but nonsignificantly less than the mean in the O-sole recognition treatment ($M = 43.85$); the latter two means did not differ significantly. The tests revealed no differences among the recognition treatment means under conditions of recognition credit.

Self-evaluated Sociability

Our hypothesis of greater self-evaluated sociability under no-origination than under origination was not supported; no main effect of origination was obtained, $F(1, 72) < 1$. The main effect of recognition was found to be significant, $F(2, 72) = 3.16$, $p < .05$. Apparently, the treatment mean under *joint*-recognition ($M = 41.74$) was significantly less than in the O = alone condition ($M = 45.88$), $F(1, 72) = 6.15$, $p < .02$, and marginally less than in the P-alone condition ($M = 44.56$), $F(1, 72) = 2.80$, $p < .10$. (There was no interaction effect, $F < 1$.)

A Closer Look at Self-evaluation

To shed further light on whether some components of the respective creativity and sociability measures were mainly responsible for the relatively depressed scores in the joint-recognition condition, ANOVAs were carried out on each component of the two measures. In the case of creativity, the only significant effect was an OC x RC interaction effect on the (reverse-scored) self-rating of "naive," $F(2, 72) = 4.93$, $p < .01$. Newman-Keuls tests indicated that the highest self-rating by far of being naive occurred in the *joint*-recognition treatment of the no-origination-credit condition. In the case of sociability, ANOVAs indicated that the only component showing a significant effect was a main effect of recognition credit on sensitivity, $F(2, 72) = 3.71$, p <.03. Newman-Keuls tests revealed that self-rated sensitivity was significantly lower in the *joint*-recognition condition than in the other two recognition conditions.

Desire for Future Collaboration

No support was found for the hypothesis that P would be less desirous of future collaboration if origination credit had been awarded than if it had not, $(F < .01)$. Instead, we obtained a significant main effect of recognition credit, $F(2, 72) = 3.13$, $p < .05$. Further examination indicated a *smaller* desire for collaboration under *joint* recognition ($M = 5.26$) than under O-sole recognition ($M = 6.85$), $F(1, 72) = 6.27$, p <.02. There were no significant differences between either of these two conditions and the P-sole recognition condition ($M = 5.88$). Newman-Keuls analyses *within* origination conditions indicated that the above pattern of recognition differences arose largely in the origination condition; there were no significant mean differences in the no-origination condition.

Discussion

We had reasoned that reactions to events that affect one's claim to a self-generated idea are influenced by two self-relevant motivational factors, a desire that the idea, per se, be credited as original and a desire to receive recognition credit for the idea. By and large, the present results are consistent with this rationale. The MANOVA carried out across the six measures showed highly significant effects of both the origination and recognition allocation factors. Further analysis provided support for the specific predictions concerning the impact of one or both of these allocations factors on emotional reaction, evaluation of the judges' competence, and evaluation of the co-participant O's trustworthiness. The influence of those factors is also reflected in the unexpected effects obtained on self-evaluation and on the desire for collaboration on a similar project in the future.

People's emotional reaction was shown to be less negative if their idea did publicly receive origination credit than if it did not. Furthermore, the results clearly support our prediction that in the event the idea was awarded origination credit, people's emotional reaction would be least negative on learning that they were also awarded sole recognition credit, but would be most negative on learning that fellow participant O had been awarded sole recognition credit—a case of successful plagiarization of their original idea by O. This effect of recognition, given that origination credit was awarded, successfully replicates an earlier finding (Rosen et al., 1978). Note that the reaction, scale-wise, to P's rightly receiving sole recognition credit could hardly be described as one of being overjoyed (see Table 2.1). We had also proposed that the effects of recognition would be weaker if no origination credit had been awarded. The effect of recognition obtained under no origination credit paralleled the effect obtained under origination credit, but was weaker.

We had reasoned that self-serving bias would lead people to protect their ideational extension of the self by evaluating the judges' competence less positively in the event that their idea was not awarded origination credit than if such credit were awarded. The results clearly support this prediction. No prediction was made regarding an effect of recognition on evaluation of the judges. A marginal effect of recognition was obtained. Further examination revealed that this effect was largely due to the unexpectedly low evaluation elicited in the *no-origination–joint-recognition* treatment.

We saw no reason for predicting an effect of the origination factor on evaluation of co-participant O's trustworthiness; none was found. We did, however, obtain clear support for the prediction that O would be evaluated as most trustworthy if P alone had received recognition credit, but least trustworthy if O alone had received it. Given the fact, however, that the highest treatment mean (see Table 2.2) does not exceed the absolute mean of the measure, it seems plausible that people applied the term trustworthiness to O with a grain of salt.

Recall that, in exploring the possible impact of credit allocation on self-evaluation, we were drawn to a line of reasoning suggesting little effect, if any, of denial (as opposed to the awarding) of origination credit on self-evaluated creativity. On the other hand, the line of reasoning we drew on suggested that such denial would prompt a relatively enhanced self-evaluated sociability.

No significant main effects nor interaction effects were obtained in the case of creativity. Further examination revealed, however, relatively *depressed* creativity under *joint*-recognition conditions in comparison with the other two recognition conditions. As for self-evaluated sociability, the hypothesis of relative enhancement under no-origination than under origination was not supported. A significant main effect of recognition, however, was found with relatively *depressed* sociability under *joint*-recognition conditions, too. Analyses of the components of each self-evaluation measure brought to light that the joint-recognition treatment, compared to the other recognition treatments, made the participants feel relatively naive in the no-origination condition, and relatively insensitive.

We had expected that people who had been awarded origination credit would be relatively less desirous of entering a collaborative relationship in the future on a similar project. Our rationale was that their decision would be guided by the supposition that they did not need to be so encumbered. Moreover, to collaborate would mean to share in the fruits of such collaboration, thus, depreciating (or at least detracting from) the significance of their own achievement as originators. To our surprise, regardless of the origination factor, participants in the *joint*-recognition condition were relatively less in favor of collaborating than were the others.[3]

There are several plausible substantive reasons why P's emotional reaction and evaluation of O's trustworthiness were never very positive even under the best of conditions, namely, when P received sole recognition credit as the true originator. One such reason is that P's goals of achieving, *unaided*, both origination credit for the idea and sole recognition for originating it, was frustrated. Not only does the unsolicited help from O reflect unfavorably on O's competence in pursuing those goals alone, but it also makes P indebted to O for this "favor," a state of implied dependence on others that people often find aversive (Brehm & Cole, 1966; Greenberg & Shapiro, 1971; Morris & Rosen, 1973). It may be, too, that O was perceived as having ulterior motives, or was trying to ingratiate herself. To some extent, the mildly positive evaluation of the judges' competence under the most favorable conditions that prevailed may not be very surprising either. After all, they managed to lose P's revised draft, one which, from P's perspective, might have even increased the likelihood of its acceptance as a creative intellectual product. These possibilities deserve exploration in their own right. Of course, it might be useful in future studies to include control conditions, as for example, one in which no intervention by O occurs, and only the paper that P submits is received and evaluated for originality.

It was intriguing to find that the relatively least favorable means in evaluation of the judges' competence, self-evaluated creativity, and self-evaluated sociability occurred in the *no-origination–joint-recognition* treatment. Perhaps this treatment served to focus participants' attention and perhaps to elicit self-doubts most sharply with respect to their own creativity. It clearly led them to portray themselves as relatively naive. Perhaps this should not have been so surprising given what was probably for them an unanticipated, also probably an undesired, partnership that had been foisted on them by O. To have been so taken in may have made them feel not particularly sociable and altruistic. It did make them portray themselves as relatively less sensitive to others and probably contributed to their relative disinterest in future collaborative arrangements.

Some broader issues should be addressed, too. Consider, for example, the issue of being imitated. O's action in copying P's initial paper for further use might be regarded as a form of imitation. But is such imitation the best form of flattery? While the copying provides implicit endorsement of the idea as original or useful, and tacit acknowledgment that the idea is P's, such endorsements come from someone who lacks the official credentials to confer such status formally. It seems probable, therefore, that P would discount O's action as very informative of the likelihood of P's receiving official recognition as the author of an original idea, unless P had prior information indicating that O was indeed competent in the relevant area.

One might also ask whether such imitation simply constitutes a behavioral version of belief or attitudinal agreement, which would then make attraction to the imitator a plausible outcome (e.g., Thelen, Dollinger, & Roberts, 1975). Such an outcome was neither expected nor obtained in the present study. Moreover, belief/attitude agreement-attraction models do not seem particularly applicable here. The idea being proposed by P has much more to do with issues concerning "knowledge" than with those concerning "belief." Although the difference between the two is not absolute, in practice the rules of evidence and reasoning used to determine whether an item of knowledge is objectively correct are ordinarily not encountered in dealing with matters of belief (Abelson, 1979, 1986; Merton, 1949). It is interesting to note that the epithet of "copy-cat," by which a target child may be labelled by other children, is used to convey an impression of contempt for rather than of attraction to that target; the conditions that prompt such an attribution have yet to be investigated.[4]

It is also difficult to see how the consistency theory known as cognitive balance theory might shed light on the findings obtained under joint recognition. Rudmin (1991) discusses Heider's late work on ownership relationships (1987–1989) which he regards as continuing an ancient philosophical debate between proponents of communal property and proponents of private property. Of the scores of triadic ownership relationships that Heider distinguished, only one comes close to representing our joint-recognition situation. It involves a communal ownership in which, at least from P's perspective, P and O both share a given property—the sharing being a unit relation in its own right. Furthermore, both P and O like that property, a sentiment relation. Now, unit relations, said Heider, are conducive to same-valenced sentiment relations. Accordingly, P and O should become attracted to one another, and the triad would then be balanced. Yet, such attraction of P toward O hardly seems forthcoming in the *present* context.

An unresolved issue deserving attention in the future concerns the question of whether the premises, predictions, and findings presented here are culture-specific. Recent evidence (e.g., Kitayama, Markus, Martsumoto, & Norasakkunkit, 1997) suggests that self-enhancement tendencies (such as self-serving bias, self-perceptions of uniqueness in possessing positive attributes, and relative non-acceptance of failure) are more appropriately associated with Western than with non-Western cultures.

If one were to explore the brain-child metaphor, the results in general can be described as reflecting the territorial, concerned reactions of a doting parent in behalf of an intellectual offspring. Judging from recent conceptual and empirical literature on narcissism, some of the results can also be likened to (nonpathologically) narcissistic coping reactions. Note some of the diagnostic aspects of the "narcissistic personality disorder" (DSM-IV; American Psychiatric Association, 1994): grandiosity, lack of empathy, underestimation of others' contributions, belief in one's superiority or uniqueness, unreasonable expectations of entitlement to highly favorable treatment, and a tendency to become furious when such expectations are unmet.

Those of our participants whose intellectual offspring were denied rather than awarded certification as original ideas reacted with negative affect. In addition they evaluated their judges as relatively lacking in competence. And even where their idea was judged to be original, they reacted with greatest discontent if the recognition to which they were entitled was awarded to an undeserving other who apparently was underequipped for generating worthy ideas. Furthermore, where recognition was awarded jointly both to them and to that undeserving other, this may have primed a distaste against entering a future collaborative relationship with some unknown partner whose ideational contributions would most likely have been inferior to their own. It may be, too, that that joint-recognition experience, which elicited admissions of being relatively naive and insensitive, did not represent for them a serious challenge to their self-views of competence and empathy. Instead, its occurrence may have represented for them an aberration of insufficient attention, of allowing themselves to be caught off guard, and so failing to discern in advance that O was not to be trusted.

This superimposition of a relatively narcissistic patina in interpreting some of our results would need to be followed up empirically. Still, it might be noted, briefly, that others have been investigating the possible moderating effects of the level of narcissism on self-enhancing responses to favorable or unfavorable feedback. Kernis and Sun (1994), in particular, demonstrated that relative (nonpathological) narcissism elicited more favorable judgments of an evaluator's competence who provided positive feedback concerning the participants' "social sensitivity," but less favorable judgments of the evaluator's competence who gave negative feedback. (Subsequent self-evaluations of "sensitivity" were not directly measured.) Global self-esteem independently elicited similar moderating effects. Narcissism failed to moderate participants' emotional reaction to feedback. In commenting on this failure, Kernis and Sun noted that narcissists have been conceptualized as able to mask their negative emotions, and that subtler methods of detecting those negative emotions might prove more successful. It may be that our own paradigm, which differed in so many ways from theirs, did not induce a sufficient need in our participants to mask their negative emotional reaction.

In retrospect, the present topic touches on a variety of theoretical and empirical issues that make it merit further exploration. It touches, for example, on questions regarding the relevance of ideational property for the self-concept, on the implications of cognitive territoriality, and on questions of coping style in dealing with threats and challenges to such ideational self-extensions. It also hints at the conflicts between inclinations toward altruism and those of narcissistic self-interest, conflicts that seem inherent in making decisions concerning the advisability and justice of sharing one's intellectual products with others.

Notes

The authors are indebted to Michael H. Kernis for his valuable comments on an earlier version of this manuscript.

1. We urge *other* investigators in our field to replicate their findings, though the replicator receives less valued recognition than does the true originator. On the occasion of being honored for his contributions, Ekman (1993) remarked, jocularly, "He [Silvan Tompkins] did not tell either of us about the other, which helped science because it provided independent replications, but was an unwelcome surprise when we [Carroll Izard and Ekman] learned that we had not been alone in our discoveries" (p. 384).

2. Examination of the data based on the entire sample indicated that inclusion of the males tended to vitiate the findings. Their responses defied interpretation. It should be noted that one treatment contained only two males, another four males, and the remaining four treatments three males each. Still the question of whether gender serves as a moderator in the present context deserves empirical pursuit.

3. We have been assuming that our sample consisted largely of participants having relatively high global self-esteem. Some of the empirical literature we cited (e.g., on self-evaluation) appeared to apply mainly to people of high self-esteem. Yet Beggan (1992) failed in the attempt to show that level of global self-esteem moderated the ownership (nonownership) x feedback success (failure) interaction effect on object evaluation. One interpretation he offered for his failure is that those participants he had assigned to the low-esteem category were still of relatively high self-esteem, scale-wise. It would be useful to bear this caution in mind if, in further research on the present topic, we wish to determine whether global self-esteem does, in fact, serve to moderate the kinds of effects we have been reporting.

4. An unpublished survey, conducted as a science fair project on related issues, was carried out in her high school by Lindsey Rosen (a fifteen-year-old granddaughter of Sidney Rosen). A sample of seventy-two students, representing both sexes and all four grade levels, rated their extent of agreement with a series of pertinent items. They indicated, for example, that they would "feel great" if they came up with an original idea (Merton's Eureka Syndrome revisited). As for recognition credit, they said they would feel robbed if someone imitated them on important matters, or copied their homework, without asking permission. And (apropos of plagiarization) they would feel angry at a person who takes and passes off their own ideas as though they were that person's.

References

Abelson, R. P. (1979). Differences between belief and knowledge systems. *Cognitive Science, 3,* 355–366.

Abelson, R. P. (1986). Beliefs are like possessions. *Journal for the Theory of Social Behaviour, 16,* 223–250.

Altman, I. (1975). *The environment and social behavior: Privacy, personal space, territory, and crowding.* Monterey, CA: Brooks/Cole.

American Psychiatric Association (1994). *Diagnostic and statistical manual of mental disorders* (4th ed.). Washington, D.C.: Author.

Beggan, J. K. (1992). On the social nature of nonsocial perception: The mere ownership effect. *Journal of Personality and Social Psychology, 62,* 229–237.

Belk, R. W. (1988). Possessions and the extended self. *Journal of Consumer Research, 15,* 139–168.

Berlyne, D. E. (1960). *Conflict, arousal, and curiosity.* New York: McGraw-Hill.

Brehm, J. W., & Cole, A. (1966). Effect of a favor which reduces freedom. *Journal of Personality and Social Psychology, 3,* 420–426.

Brown, J. D., & Smart, S. A. (1991). The self and social conduct: Linking self-representations to social behavior. *Journal of Personality and Social Psychology, 60,* 368–375.

Cacioppo, J. T., & Petty, R. E. (1982). The need for cognition. *Journal of Personality and Social Psychology, 42,* 116–131.

Csikszentmihalyi, M., & Rochberg-Halton, E. (1981). *The meaning of things: Domestic symbols and the self.* Cambridge: Cambridge University Press.

deCharms, R. (1968). *Personal causation.* New York: Academic Press.

Deci, E. L. (1975). *Intrinsic motivation.* New York: Plenum.

Ditto, P. H., & Griffin, J. (1993). The value of uniqueness: Self-evaluation and the perceived prevalence of valenced characteristics. *Journal of Social Behavior and Personality, 8,* 221–240.

Ekman, P. (1993). Facial expression and emotion. *American Psychologist, 48,* 384–392.

Fazio, R. H. (1979). Motives for social comparison: The construction-validation hypothesis. *Journal of Personality and Social Psychology, 37,* 1683–1698.

Festinger, L. (1954). A theory of social comparison processes. *Human Relations, 7,* 117–140.

Furby, L. (1978). Possession in humans: An exploratory study of its meaning and motivation. *Social Behavior and Personality, 6,* 49–65.

Greenberg, M. S., & Shapiro, S. P. (1971). Indebtedness: An adverse aspect of asking for and receiving help. *Sociometry, 34,* 290–301.

Hagstrom, W. O. (1965). *The scientific community.* New York: Basic Books.

Heider, F. (1958). *The psychology of interpersonal relations.* New York: Wiley.

Heider, F. (1987–1989). *The notebooks* (M. Benesh-Weiner, Ed.). Munich: Psychologische Verlag Union.

James, W. (1890). *Principles of psychology* (Vol. 1). New York: Holt.

Kernis, M. H., Cornell, D. P., Sun, Chien-Ru, Berry, A., & Harlow, T. (1993). There's more to self-esteem than whether it is high or low: The importance of stability of self-esteem. *Journal of Personality and Social Psychology, 65,* 1190–1204.

Kernis, M. H., & Sun, C-R. (1994). Narcissism and reactions to interpersonal feedback. *Journal of Research in Personality, 28,* 4–13.

Kitayama, S., Markus, H. R., Matsumoto, H., & Norasakkunkit, V. (1997). Individual and collective processes in the construction of the self: Self-enhancement in the United States and self-criticism in Japan. *Journal of Personality and Social Psychology, 72,* 1245–1267.

Lemaine, G. (1974). Social differentiation and social originality. *European Journal of Social Psychology, 4,* 17–52.

Merton, R. K. (1949). *Social theory and social structure: Toward the codification of theory and research.* Glencoe, IL: Free press.

Merton, R. K. (1976). *Sociological ambivalence and other essays.* New York: Free Press.

Morris, S. C., III, & Rosen, S. (1973). Effects of felt adequacy and opportunity to reciprocate on help seeking. *Journal of Experimental Social Psychology, 9,* 265–276.

Paine, A. B. (Ed.) (1935). *Mark Twain's Notebook* (p. 67). New York: Harper.

Rosen, S., & Case, T. L. (1979). *Opposing collaboration to forestall violation of one's ideational territory.* Paper presented at the meeting of the Southeastern Psychological Association, New Orleans, LA.

Rosen, S., Case., T. L., & Read, G. S. (1979). *Protecting one's ideational turf through noncollaboration.* Paper presented at the meeting of the American Psychological Association, New York.

Rosen, S., Johnson, R. R., Case, T. L., & Flaks, A. (1978). *Territorial reactions to infringement upon creative ideas.* Paper presented at the meeting of the Southeastern Psychological Association, Atlanta, GA.

Ross, M., & Sicoly, F. (1979). Egocentric biases in availability and attribution. *Journal of Personality and Social Psychology, 37,* 322–336.

Rudmin, F. W. (1991). "To own is to be perceived to own": A social cognitive look at the ownership of property. In F. W. Rudmin (Ed.), To have possessions: a handbook of ownership and property [Special Issue]. *Journal of Social Behavior and Personality, 6,* (6), 85–104.

Schlenker, B. R. (1986). Self-identification: Toward an integration of the private and public self. In R. F. Baumeister (Ed.), *Public self and private self* (pp. 21–62). New York: Springer-Verlag .

Simmel, G. (1950). *The sociology of Georg Simmel.* Trans. by K. H. Wolff. New York: Free Press.

Steele, C. M. (1988). The psychology of self-affirmation: sustaining the integrity of the self. In L. Berkowitz (Ed.), *Advances in experimental social psychology,* Vol. 21, (pp. 261–302). San Diego, CA: Academic Press.

Swann, W. B., Jr., Griffin, J. J., Predmore, S. C., & Gaines, B. (1987). The cognitive-affective crossfire: When self-consistency confronts self-enhancement. *Journal of Personality and Social Psychology, 52,* 881–889.

Swann, W. B., Jr., & Read, S. J. (1981). Acquiring self-knowledge: The search for feedback that fits. *Journal of Personality and Social Psychology, 41,* 1119–1128.

Thelen, M. H., Dollinger, S. J., & Roberts, M. C. (1975). On being imitated: Its effects on attraction and reciprocal imitation. *Journal of Personality and Social Psychology, 31,* 467–472.

Wicklund, R. A. (1989). The appropriation of ideas. In P. B. Paulus (Ed.), *Psychology of group influence* (2nd ed.) (pp. 393–423). Hillsdale, NJ: Erlbaum.

3

Perfectionism in Relation to Attributions for Success or Failure

*Gordon L. Flett, Paul L. Hewitt, Kirk R. Blankstein,
and Donna Pickering*

Recently, there has been a growing interest in the study of perfectionism and personal adjustment from an empirical perspective. This research has shown that perfectionism is associated with low personal adjustment (Frost, Marten, Lahart, & Rosenblate, 1990; Hewitt & Flett, 1991a, 1993; Hewitt, Flett, & Turnbull-Donovan, 1992) and related forms of self-destruction (see Blatt, 1995). The association between perfectionism and maladjustment reflects, in part, the fact that perfectionists tend to experience a great deal of punishment in the form of failure or stressful experiences. For instance, *self-oriented perfectionists* tend to have high self-standards and motivation to attain perfection (Hewitt and Flett, 1991b). It is believed that these individuals generate failures for themselves because they engage in an all-or-none thinking whereby the only possible outcomes are total successes or total failures (Burns, 1980; Pacht, 1984). The impact of any failure is further magnified by the self-oriented perfectionists tendency to overgeneralize the failure and perceive it as characteristic of the entire self (Hewitt and Flett, 1991b; Hewitt, Mittelstaedt, and Wollert, 1989). In contrast, *other-oriented perfectionism* involves a focus on the imperfections of other people rather than their own imperfections (see Hewitt & Flett, 1991b). Because other-oriented perfectionism is associated with lack of trust and feelings of hostility toward others, this perfectionism dimension may result in difficult interpersonal relationships. Finally, a third form of perfectionism, *socially prescribed perfectionism*, is associated with imposed failure in the form of other people's unrealistic expectations for the self (see Hewitt & Flett, 1991b). Individuals with high levels of socially prescribed perfectionism believe that significant others have unrealistically high expectations for them. Thus, the failures perceived by socially prescribed perfectionists often are in the form of criticism from significant others, such as parents (Frost et al., 1990).

Given that perfectionists are highly attuned to evaluate feedback and react strongly to outcomes, it is important to examine the manner in which perfectionists interpret their failures and successes. The purpose of the present article is to examine the link between dimensions of perfectionism and attributional tendencies for negative and positive outcomes. Since perfectionism is associated with negative affect, and it is well-established that negative affect is associated with a self-critical attributional style (Sweeney, Anderson, and Bailey, 1986; Weiner, Russell, & Lerman, 1979), it is conceivable that perfectionists and nonperfectionists may differ in their causal explanations for negative and positive outcomes.

At present, indirect evidence indicates that perfectionists and nonperfectionists do indeed differ in their attributional explanations for personal events. Research with global attribution measures of self-blame has shown that these measures are associated with perfectionism (Hewitt and Flett, 1991b; Hewitt et al., 1989). For instance, Hewitt et al. (1989) examined the association between the Burns Perfectionism Scale (Burns, 1980) and a five-item measure of self-blame (Wollert, Mittelstaedt, MacIntosh, Erasmus, & Rawlins, 1986). The Burns scale assesses attitudes involving the self-attainment of perfection. The blame measure is comprised of estimates of the likelihood, frequency, persistence, intensity, and comparative significance of self-blaming behavior. Hewitt et al. (1989) found a positive correlation between perfectionism and self-blame. In a subsequent study, Hewitt and Flett (1991b) administered the Multidimensional Perfectionism Scale and a 16-item self-blame measure to a sample of college students. The Multidimensional Perfectionism Scale assesses the three perfectionism dimensions described above—namely, self-oriented perfectionism (i.e., high self-standards and perfectionistic motivation), other-oriented perfectionism (i.e., high standards for significant others), and socially prescribed perfectionism (i.e., the belief that other people expect oneself to be perfect). Hewitt and Flett (1991b) found that self-blame was correlated with self-oriented perfectionism ($r = .21$, $p < .05$) and socially prescribed perfectionism ($r = .44$, $p < .01$), but it was not correlated with other-oriented perfectionism.

Overall, a general association has been demonstrated between certain perfectionism dimensions and a tendency to engage in self-blame. However, existing research is limited in at least three respects. First, there has been no attempt to examine the association between perfectionism and the specific attribution dimensions that are the basis of classic attribution research and theory. In addition to the general distinction between attribution to internal versus external causes (Heider, 1958; Kelley, 1967), theorists in this field (e.g., Weiner, 1985) have also made an important distinction between attribution to stable and controllable causes versus unstable and uncontrollable causes. According to this formulation, subjects may make an internal attribution to a stable cause (i.e., ability) or they may make an internal attribution to an unstable cause (i.e., effort). Negative affective reactions tend to be more extreme when failures are attributed dispositionally to a lack of ability rather than a lack of effort (for a review, see Shepperd, Arkin, Strathman, and Baker, 1994). It is important to examine ability versus effort attributions in perfectionism because the factors that contribute to the self-blame and self-criticism of perfectionists are not well understood; it is not known, for instance, whether the self-blaming tendency of perfectionists is due to a perceived lack of ability, lack of effort, or an inability to overcome uncontrollable causes.

Second, there is need for additional research on perfectionism and attribution because there have been no empirical attempts to distinguish attribution ratings for achievement outcomes versus affiliation outcomes. It has been shown elsewhere that attributions often differ for social versus asocial events (Anderson and Arnoult, 1985; Metalsky, Halberstadt, and Abramson, 1987). Because recent perfectionism research has differentiated the personal and social aspects of the construct (see Frost et al., 1990; Hewitt and Flett, 1990, 1991b), it seems necessary to compare the attributions made by perfectionists for successes and failures in both the achievement and affiliation domains.

Finally, there is need for research on attribution and perfectionism because there has been no investigation of perfectionists' attributions for positive outcomes. Presumably, perfectionists who attain perfection would attribute these successes to some aspects of themselves. However, it is not known whether successes would be attributed to ability or to effort; in addition, no research has examined how the various dimensions of perfectionism relate to perceptions of positive outcomes.

In light of these observations, a cross-sectional study was conducted to obtain some initial data on the association between dimensions of perfectionism and attribution. The participants in this research were administered the Multidimensional Perfectionism Scale (Hewitt and Flett, 1991b) and the Multidimensional-Multiattributional Causality Scale (Lefcourt, von Baeyer, Ware, and Cox, 1979). The MMCS was selected as the attribution measure because it provides separate measures of internal (i.e., effort and ability) and external (i.e., luck and situational context) attributions for positive and negative outcomes in both the achievement and affiliation spheres.

The MMCS was also selected because its format is consistent with recent research on attributional complexity. Research on specific causes has shown that individuals often make complex attributions to two or more causes (Fletcher, Danilovics, Fernandez, Peterson, and Reeder, 1986; Flett, Blankstein, Ochiuto, and Koledin, 1994; Flett, Pliner, & Blankstein, 1989; Howe, 1987). For instance, Flett et al. (1989) found that students with elevated scores on a self-report measure of depressive symptoms experience events that are attributed jointly to internal factors reflecting the self and external factors reflecting the environment. A multidimensional measure such as the one employed in the present research acknowledges the possibility that individuals may make attributions to two or more causal factors and that these complex attributions may involve both internal and external causes.

Summary of Hypotheses

In summary, the present research examined the association between the perfectionism dimensions represented on the Multidimensional Perfectionism Scale and the attribution dimensions represented on the MMCS. Past evidence has indicated that self-oriented perfectionism is associated with internal self-control, while socially prescribed perfectionism is associated with an external locus of control (Flett, Hewitt, Blankstein, & Mosher, 1995; Flett, Hewitt, Blankstein, and O'Brien,

1991; Hewitt & Flett, 1991b). Thus, it was expected that self-oriented perfectionism would be associated with a tendency to attribute events to internal causes reflecting the self whereas socially prescribed perfectionism would be associated primarily with an external attributional style. A link between socially prescribed perfectionism and external attributions would be consistent with a tendency to view other people as responsible for outcomes that involve the self. Unfortunately, more specific predictions involving the various attribution dimensions (i.e., ability, effort, context, and luck) for positive and negative outcomes were precluded by the paucity of investigation in this area.

Finally, it should be noted that we conducted analyses that investigated the association between perfectionism and attribution in the total sample, as well as separate analyses for men and women. The need to examine gender differences is indicated by some gender differences detected in the attribution literature (Sohn, 1982), as well as in the perfectionism literature (Joiner & Schmidt, 1995).

Method

Subjects

The sample consisted of 124 subjects (84 women, 40 men) from York University. Subjects were approached randomly in various locations throughout the university and were asked to participate in a brief "personal perceptions" study. The mean age of the subjects was 22.46 years ($SD = 6.54$).

Materials and Procedure

As noted above, subjects completed the following measures:

Multidimensional Perfectionism Scale (MPS). The MPS (Hewitt and Flett, 1991b) is a 45-item measure designed to measure self-oriented, other-oriented, and socially prescribed perfectionism. Subjects make seven-point ratings of such statements as "When I am working on something, I cannot relax until it is perfect" (self-oriented perfectionism), "I have high expectations for the people who are important to me" (other-oriented perfectionism), and "I feel that people are too demanding of me" (socially prescribed perfectionism). Hewitt and Flett (1991b) presented extensive data supporting the reliability, dimensionality, and validity of the MPS in both clinical and nonclinical samples. Coefficient alphas have ranged between .74 and .88 for the three subscales (Hewitt & Flett, 1991b), and test-retest reliabilities over three months were .75, .65, and .78 for the self-oriented, other-oriented, and socially prescribed perfectionism subscales, respectively. Several studies have demonstrated that the subscales correlate highly with theoretically similar constructs (Hewitt and Flett, 1991b). For instance, self-oriented perfectionism is associated positively with other measures of high self-standards and the self-importance of high performance, while socially prescribed perfectionism is associated with the fear of negative social evaluation (Hewitt and Flett, 1991b). Finally, there is evidence that the MPS subscales are not influenced significantly by response biases (Hewitt and Flett, 1991b; Hewitt, Flett, Turnbull-Donovan, & Mikail, 1991).

Multidimensional-Multiattributional Causality Scale (MMCS). The MMCS is comprised of two 24-item Likert scales representing achievement and affiliation outcomes (Lefcourt et al., 1979). One-half of the items refer to success outcomes and the remaining items refer to failure outcomes. As noted above, each scale is subdivided into specific internal attributions and external attributions. The internal attribution dimensions are ability (i.e., The most important ingredient in getting good grades is my academic ability. It seems to me that failure to have people like me would show my ignorance in interpersonal relationships) and effort (i.e., Whenever I receive good grades, it is always because I have studied hard for that course. If I did not get along with others it would tell me that I hadn't put much effort into the pursuit of social goals). The external attribution dimensions are contextual factors (i.e., My enjoyment of a social occasion is almost entirely dependent on the personalities of the other people who are there. Some low grades I've received seem to me to reflect the fact that some teachers are just stingy with marks), and luck (i.e., In my experience, making friends is largely a matter of having the right breaks. Some of my bad grades may have been a function of bad luck, being in the wrong course at the wrong time). The MMCS is a well-known scale that has been used in numerous studies (Ashkanasy and Gallois, 1987; Lefcourt, Martin, Fick, and Saleh, 1985; Lewinsohn, Steinmetz, Larson, and Franklin, 1981). Psychometric investigations have confirmed the MMCS's factor structure, as well as the reliability and validity of the subscales (Chandler, Shama, Wolf, and Planchard, 1987; Lefcourt,

1981; Lefcourt et al., 1979; Powers, Douglas, and Choroszy, 1983; Powers, Douglas, Lopez, & Rossman, 1985).

Results

Correlations for Total Sample

The correlations between the MPS and MMCS dimensions for the total sample are shown in Table 3.1. It can be seen that self-oriented and other-oriented perfectionism were not correlated significantly with any MMCS dimension in the total sample. In contrast, socially prescribed perfectionism was correlated significantly with numerous MMCS measures. In terms of achievement outcomes, socially prescribed perfectionism was associated with attributions to external factors (i.e., context and luck) for both positive and negative achievement outcomes. The pattern of correlations was somewhat more complex for affiliation outcomes. In terms of positive outcomes, socially prescribed perfectionism was associated with greater attributions to ability, $r = .31$, $p < .001$, and to luck, $r = .41$, $p < .001$. In terms of negative affiliation outcomes, socially prescribed perfectionism was associated with greater attributions to ability, $r = .23$, $p < .05$, luck, $r = .24$, $p < .05$, and contextual factors, $r = .19$, $p < .05$.

Correlations Involving Achievement Outcomes for Males versus Females

Separate correlation analyses by gender illustrated the need to consider possible gender differences in this area. Whereas analyses with the total sample found no significant correlations involving self-oriented and other-oriented perfectionism, several correlations involving these perfectionism dimensions attained or approached statistical significance when the data were examined separately for men and women. Analyses of the data from the males showed that male self-oriented perfectionists were relatively less likely to attribute positive achievement outcomes to luck, $r = -.30$, $p < .10$. Males with high levels of self-oriented perfectionism were less likely to attribute negative achievement outcomes to luck, $r = -.40$, $p < .05$, contextual factors, $r = -.40$, $p < .05$, and ability, $r = -.31$, $p < .10$. Instead, there was a marginally significant tendency for male self-oriented perfectionists to attribute negative achievement outcomes to effort, $r = .31$, $p < .10$. The only significant

TABLE 3.1

Correlations between Perfectionism and Attribution Measures for Males (M), Females (F), and the Total Sample (T)

Attribution Measures	Self			Other			Social		
	M	F	T	M	F	T	M	F	T
Achievement Outcomes									
Positive									
Ability	.14	.13	.13	−.08	.20*	.13	.17	.16	.16
Effort	.16	−.01	.03	.19	.03	.06	−.06	.13	.10
Context	−.06	.02	.00	−.24	.01	−.03	.34**	.11	.19**
Luck	−.30*	.17	.03	−.14	.08	.04	.26	.27**	.28**
Negative									
Ability	−.31*	.15	.00	−.04	.01	−.01	.16	.24**	.16
Effort	.31*	.02	.09	−.05	.14	.10	.24	.00	.08
Context	−.40**	.15	−.03	−.05	.07	.04	.21	.25**	.27**
Luck	−.40**	.24**	.03	−.28*	−.01	−.07	.09	.35**	.29**
Affiliation Outcomes									
Positive									
Ability	−.27*	.25**	.12	.10	.01	.03	.25	.33**	.31**
Effort	−.06	.04	.01	.24	.07	.11	.00	.05	.01
Context	.07	.12	.10	−.29*	.03	−.03	.20	.12	.16
Luck	−.21	.12	.02	.03	.09	.08	.36**	.40**	.41**
Negative									
Ability	.05	.03	.03	.02	−.23**	−.17	.42**	.15	.23**
Effort	−.03	−.05	−.04	.07	−.14	−.09	.17	.09	.11
Context	−.20	.11	.01	−.05	−.04	−.04	.34**	.13	.19**
Luck	−.26	.13	.01	−.32**	.08	−.02	.04	.31**	.24**

Note: * $p < .10$; ** $p < .05$ or greater. Based on the responses of 124 students (40 men, 84 women).

correlation for females involving self-oriented perfectionism was a tendency for female self-oriented perfectionists to attribute negative achievement outcomes to luck, $r = .24$, $p < .05$.

No correlations involving other-oriented perfectionism and attributions for achievement outcomes attained conventional levels of statistical significance. As for socially prescribed perfectionism, it was found that males with high levels of socially prescribed perfectionism were more likely to attribute positive achievement outcomes to contextual factors, $r = .34$, $p < .05$. There were no significant correlations for males between socially prescribed perfectionism and the attributions for negative achievement outcomes. Females with high levels of socially prescribed perfectionism attributed positive achievement outcomes to luck, $r = .27$, $p < .05$, while negative achievement outcomes were attributed to ability, $r = .24$, $p < .05$, contextual factors, $r = .25$, $p < .05$, and luck, $r = .35$, $p < .05$.

Correlations Involving Affiliation Outcomes for Males versus Females

Examination of the ratings given for the causes of the affiliation outcomes also demonstrated the need to examine gender differences. For instance, it was found that male self-oriented perfectionists were less likely to attribute positive social outcomes to ability, $r = -.27$, $p < .10$, while female self-oriented perfectionists were more likely to attribute positive social outcomes to ability, $r = .25$, $p < .05$. No other correlations involving self-oriented perfectionism and attributions for affiliation outcomes were significant.

As for other-oriented perfectionists, male other-oriented perfectionists were less likely to attribute positive affiliation outcomes to contextual factors, $r = -.29$, $p < .10$, and they were less likely to attribute negative affiliation outcomes to luck, $r = -.32$, $p < .05$. The only significant effect for females involved a reduced tendency for other-oriented perfectionists to attribute negative affiliation outcomes to ability, $r = -.23$, $p < .05$.

Finally, males with high levels of socially prescribed perfectionism were more likely to attribute positive social outcomes to luck, $r = .36$, $p < .05$. These same males were more likely to attribute negative social outcomes to ability, $r = .42$, $p < .05$, and to contextual factors, $r = .34$, $p < .05$. Females with high levels of socially prescribed perfectionism attributed positive social outcomes to luck, $r = .40$, $p < .05$, and to ability, $r = .33$, $p < .05$. These same females attributed negative social outcomes to luck, $r = .31$, $p < .05$.

Gender Differences in Mean Scores

Given these differences in the pattern of correlations, possible gender differences in mean scores were also investigated. A multivariate analysis of variance (MANOVA) was conducted on mean MPS subscale scores. The multivariate effect of gender was not significant. Four separate MANOVAs were conducted with the four sets of attribution scales as dependent measures. The multivariate effect of gender was significant for the four attribution dimensions for achievement successes, $F (4, 120) = 2.45$, $p < .05$. The subsequent univariate ANOVAs

TABLE 3.2
Mean Perfectionism and Attribution Scores for Males, Females, and the Total
Sample

Measures	Males		Females		Total	
	M	SD	M	SD	M	SD
Perfectionism Scores						
Self-Oriented	71.60	15.00	71.70	15.40	71.70	15.21
Other-Oriented	60.05	8.43	59.31	11.65	59.55	10.68
Socially Prescribed	58.65	11.10	54.63	13.49	55.93	12.86
Attribution Scores						
Positive Outcomes						
Achievement						
Ability	8.25	2.24	8.13	2.20	8.17	2.20
Effort	9.08	1.56	8.86	2.08	8.93	1.93
Context	7.10	2.01	5.87	2.64	6.27	2.52
Luck	6.98	2.20	5.98	2.53	6.30	2.46
Affiliation						
Ability	7.03	1.92	6.76	2.54	6.85	2.34
Effort	8.03	2.09	8.67	2.22	8.46	2.19
Context	8.33	1.66	7.91	2.02	8.04	1.91
Luck	5.85	2.66	4.61	2.68	5.01	2.73
Negative Outcomes						
Achievement						
Ability	5.50	2.76	7.26	2.53	6.69	2.72
Effort	8.98	1.94	8.19	2.39	8.44	2.23
Context	7.60	2.45	5.95	2.31	6.48	2.47
Luck	5.60	2.46	4.37	2.31	4.77	2.42
Affiliation						
Ability	6.60	2.19	5.99	2.63	6.19	2.51
Effort	6.23	2.11	6.13	2.53	6.16	2.39
Context	5.68	2.49	5.45	2.59	5.52	2.55
Luck	6.18	2.35	5.73	2.47	5.87	2.43

indicated that males were less likely to attribute positive achievement outcomes to external factors involving the context, $F (1, 123) = 6.80$, $p <.05$, and luck, $F (1, 123) = 4.59$, $p <.05$. The means associated with these effects are shown in Table 3.2.

Several differences emerged in the analysis of attributions for achievement failures. In addition to the overall multivariate effect, $F (4, 119) = 11.22$, $p <.001$, the ANOVAs revealed significant gender differences in attributions of ability, $F (1, 122) = 12.39$, $p <.01$, context, $F (1, 122) = 13.25$, $p <.001$, and luck, $F (1, 122) = 7.40$, $p <.01$. There was also a marginally significant difference with effort, $F (1, 122) = 3.27$, $p <.08$. Examination of the means provided in Table 3.2 indicates that males were characterized by a tendency to make more self-serving attributions. That is, males were more likely than females to attribute negative achievement outcomes to external factors and a lack of effort rather than a lack of ability.

The multivariate effect was also marginally significant for the MANOVA conducted on the four causes of positive affiliation outcomes, F (4, 119) = 2.20, p <.08. The only significant univariate effect was obtained with the luck measure, F (1, 122) = 5.85, p < .05. Males felt that luck would play a greater role in positive social outcomes. Finally, the MANOVA conducted on attributions for negative social events found no evidence of significant gender differences.

Discussion

The purpose of the present study was to examine the association between perfectionism dimensions and the attributions made for successes and failures in the academic and social domains. The main finding was the expected positive association between socially prescribed perfectionism and external attribution to such factors as luck and the situational context. The correlation between socially prescribed perfectionism and luck is consistent with past indications that socially prescribed perfectionism is associated with a perceived lack of control (Flett, Hewitt, Blankstein, & O'Brien, 1991; Hewitt and Flett, 1991b). Meanwhile, the obtained link between socially prescribed perfectionism and attribution to contextual factors probably reflects the fact that the presence of other people is a key component of many situations and the role of other people is reflected in the attributions tapped by the MMCS context scales. Consistent with the definition of socially prescribed perfectionism, individuals with high socially prescribed perfectionism scores tended to blame other people for much of their misfortune. These individuals endorsed such MMCS context statements as "In my experience, once a professor gets the idea you're a poor student your work is much more likely to receive poor grades than if someone else handed it in," and "Some people just seem predisposed to dislike me." It appears then that the link between socially prescribed perfectionism and context attributions may reflect a generalized tendency to blame other people for one's problems. This tendency to blame others for misfortune is regarded as a robust predictor of emotional problems (Tennen & Affleck, 1990). The tendency to attribute outcomes to external causes is associated with high levels of anxiety (Bandalos, Yates, &Thorndike-Christ, 1995), and this attributional style is believed to reflect negative self-conceptualizations about the availability of personal resources (Leppin, Schwarzer, Belz, Jerusalem, and Quast, 1987).

In the introduction, it was noted that past studies have shown that socially prescribed perfectionism is associated with self-blame (e.g., Hewitt and Flett, 1991b) and self-criticism (Frost et al., 1990; Hewitt and Flett, 1991b, 1993). Why would socially prescribed perfectionists persist in blaming themselves and being self-critical even though they clearly acknowledge the role of external factors in negative outcomes? The overall pattern of findings is similar to the seemingly paradoxical tendency of depressed individuals to engage in self-blame even though they acknowledge the presence of uncontrollable circumstances (Abramson & Sackeim, 1977). One explanation for this paradox was advanced by Covington (1986). On the basis of his data, Covington (1986) concluded that self-blame and uncontrollability may be related because certain individuals are disappointed by their own inability to change an aversive, uncontrollable situation. In the present instance, it is possible that socially prescribed perfectionists maintain a high level of self-criticism because of a belief that they should be able to overcome external influences, such as other people's high expectations.

Other findings in the current study indicated that socially prescribed perfectionism is also associated with a tendency to make external attributions for positive outcomes, in both the achievement and affiliation domains. This finding has important implications for the link between socially prescribed perfectionism and negative affective states such as depression and anxiety. Socially prescribed perfectionists are exposed to a great deal of punishment due to their inability to meet the perceived perfectionistic demands imposed on themselves by others. This punishment may be mitigated somewhat by a tendency to attribute these failures to external factors. Unfortunately, however, these individuals also suffer from a relative absence of positive self-reinforcement because successes will also be attributed to external factors. A low rate of positive self-reinforcement may contribute to the association between socially prescribed perfectionism and depression.

Overall, the results obtained with socially prescribed perfectionism are in keeping with the view that a sense of personal helplessness is a core feature of this perfectionism dimension. In the present study, helplessness is indicated by the fact that a high level of socially prescribed perfectionism appears to be associated with a pervasive tendency to attribute positive and negative outcomes to external factors. According to Mikulincer (1994), an important aspect of the helpless-prone personality is the adequacy of personal resources when personal commitments are threatened. Mikulincer maintains that people are especially likely to experience depression and related forms of maladjustment when they lack personal resources and respond to learned helplessness deficits by engaging in avoidance coping. Previous research accords with the view that the link between socially prescribed perfectionism and depression is rooted in maladaptive reactions to helplessness; it has been established that socially prescribed perfectionism is associated with avoidant coping and a deleterious problem-solving orientation (see Hewitt and Flett, 1996). Moreover, it has been shown that perceptions of low resourcefulness and low self-efficacy are moderators of the link between between socially prescribed perfectionism and depressive symptoms (Flett, Hewitt, Blankstein, and O'Brien, 1991; Martin, Flett, Hewitt, Krames, & Szantos, 1996). Collectively, these findings suggest that further investigation of perfectionism and helplessness is warranted.

Self-Oriented Perfectionism and Attributions

Returning to the current study, our analyses found little support for the prediction that self-oriented perfectionism would be associated with an internal attributional style. In fact, analyses of data from the total sample revealed no significant correlations between attributional indices and the dimensions of self-oriented and other-oriented perfectionism and attributional indices for the total sample. One interpretation of our results is that they underscore the importance of examining the perfectionism construct as a multidimensional entity; different findings emerged depending on the MPS dimension in question.

Although self-oriented perfectionism and attribution were not linked in the overall sample, separate analyses for males and females suggested that the link between self-oriented perfectionism and attribution may be complex and may depend on characteristics of the individual (i.e., male or female) as well as the valence and type of event being attributed. For instance, analyses of males' responses indicated that self-oriented perfectionism was associated with a tendency to attribute negative *achievement* outcomes to a lack of *personal effort* rather than a lack of ability or the presence of external factors. This pattern of findings was not obtained for females nor was it obtained for the perceived causes of social failures. Analyses of mean scores revealed that males were also distinguished by a tendency to attribute achievement failures to a lack of effort. The latter finding is consistent with numerous other studies that have reported similar gender differences in ability-related attributions for achievement outcomes whereby males attribute failure to effort and females attribute failure to lack of ability (Feather, 1969; Sohn, 1982; Zuckerman, 1979). Clearly, the current findings need to be replicated and must be interpreted cautiously, especially given the relatively low number of males in the present study. However, they may have important implications for self-oriented perfectionism. First, they highlight the importance of examining separately the results for males and females. Second, the findings for males are consistent with some research which suggests that individuals with high levels of achievement motivation tend to attribute negative outcomes to a lack of persistence rather than a lack of skill. Janoff-Bulman and Brickman (1982) have proposed that people with overly high expectations are likely to perceive a lack of personal effort when they fail. They observed that these individuals will persist at tasks even when they should no longer do so. This dogged persistence may result in a wide variety of negative personal consequences (see Feather, 1989). One particularly important consequence for perfectionists is the growing realization that one has failed despite expending maximum effort. These individuals must either engage in some form of self-handicapping behavior that provides an excuse for the failures or they must confront the possibility that they are solely responsible for the failures. Although the above sequence is admittedly speculative, it would appear that an examination of persistence, failure, and reactions to failure over an extended time period represents an important direction for future research in the perfectionism field.

Another important direction for future investigation will be to examine whether attributions serve as mediators or moderators of the association between perfectionism and adjustment. The present research has focused directly on the association between perfectionism and attribution, but future research must expand by addressing the possibility that negative affect is most likely to result from particular combinations of perfectionism and attribution. Self-regulation theorists (Kanfer and Hagerman, 1981; Rehm, 1977) predict that pathology such as depression is most likely to be experienced by individuals with high personal standards and a self-critical attributional style. High personal standards lead to consistent failure. The impact of failure should be significantly greater for individuals who blame themselves for these failures.

Although the current findings have provided substantial insight into the association between perfectionism and attribution, the limitations of the current findings must be noted. First, the generalizability of our results needs to be examined, both in terms of other types of subjects (e.g., psychiatric patients) and other types of events. It is possible, for instance, that different findings would have emerged if subjects had made attributions for actual events rather than the hypothetical outcomes described on the MMCS. Second, the causality issue needs to be examined. Our findings enable us to conclude that dimensions of perfectionism and attribution are related but there is presently no basis to assume that perfectionism causes certain attributional tendencies.

Conclusion

In summary, the results of the present study indicated that socially prescribed perfectionism was associated with a tendency to make external attributions. Moreover, this tendency to make attributions to such factors as luck and the situational context was present for both positive outcomes and negative outcomes. Whereas past research has demonstrated that exposure to controlling feedback (i.e., high social expectations) may undermine motivation (Deci & Ryan, 1985), the present results suggest that controlling feedback in the form of socially prescribed perfectionism may also have a negative influence on the attributions that are made by individuals who experience success. Unfortunately, one consequence is that these individuals with high levels of socially prescribed perfectionism may have little opportunity to experience the feelings of pride and happiness that usually accompany attributions of success to the self.

Note

This research was supported by grant #410–93–1256 from the Social Sciences and Humanities Research Council of Canada awarded to the authors. The authors wish to thank Shawn Mosher for his assistance with the data collection.

References

Abramson, L. Y., & Sackeim, H. A. (1977). A paradox in depression: Uncontrollability and self-blame. *Psychological Bulletin, 84*, 838–851.

Anderson, C. A., & Arnoult, L. H. (1985). Attributional style and everyday problems in living: Depression, loneliness, and shyness. *Social Cognition, 3*, 16–35.

Ashkanasy, N. M., & Gallois, C. (1987). Locus of control and attributions for academic performance of self and others. *Australian Journal of Psychology, 39*, 293–305.

Bandalos, D. L., Yates, K., & Thorndike-Christ, T. (1995). Effects of math self-concept, perceived self-efficacy, and attributions for failure and success on test anxiety. *Journal of Educational Psychology, 87*, 611–623.

Blatt, S. J. (1995). The destructiveness of perfectionism: Implications for the treatment of perfectionism. *American Psychologist, 50*, 1003–1020.

Burns, D. D. (1980). *Feeling good: The new mood therapy.* New York: The New American Library.

Chandler, T. A., Shama, D. D., Wolf, F. M., & Planchard, S. K. (1987). Multiattributional causality: A five cross-cultural sample study. *Journal of Cross-Cultural Psychology, 12*, 207–221.

Covington, M. V. (1986). Anatomy of failure-induced anxiety: The role of cognitive mediators. In R. Schwarzer (Ed.), *Self-related cognitions in anxiety and motivation* (pp. 247–263). Hillsdale, NJ: Erlbaum.

Deci, E., & Ryan, R. M. (1985). *Intrinsic motivation and self determination in human behavior.* New York: Plenum.

Feather, N. T. (1969). Attribution of responsibility and valence of success and failure in relation to initial confidence and perceived locus of control. *Journal of Personality and Social Psychology, 13*, 129–144.

Feather, N. T. (1989). Trying and giving up: Persistence and lack of persistence in failure situations. In R. C. Curtis (Ed.), *Self-defeating behaviors: Experimental research, clinical impressions, and practical implications* (pp. 67–95). New York: Plenum.

Fletcher, G. J. O., Danilovics, P., Fernandez, G., Peterson, D., & Reeder, G. D. (1986). Attributional complexity: An individual differences measure. *Journal of Personality and Social Psychology, 51*, 875–884.

Flett, G. L., Blankstein, K. R., Occhiuto, M., & Koledin, S. (1994). Depression, self-esteem, and complex attributions for life problems. *Current Psychology, 13*, 263–281.

Flett, G. L., Hewitt, P. L., Blankstein, K. R., & Mosher, S. W. (1995). Perfectionism, life events, and depressive symptoms: A test of a diathesis-stress model. *Current Psychology, 14*, 112–137.

Flett, G. L., Hewitt, P. L., Blankstein, K. R., & O'Brien, S. (1991). Perfectionism and learned resourcefulness in depression and self-esteem. *Personality and Individual Differences, 12*, 61–68.

Flett, G. L., Pliner, P., & Blankstein, K. R. (1989). Depression and components of attributional complexity. *Journal of Personality and Social Psychology, 56*, 757–764.

Frost, R. O., Marten, P. A., Lahart, C., & Rosenblate, R. (1990). The dimensions of perfectionism. *Cognitive Therapy and Research, 14*, 449–468.

Heider, F. (1958). *The psychology of interpersonal relations.* New York: Wiley.

Hewitt, P. L., & Flett, G. L. (1991a). Dimensions of perfectionism in unipolar depression. *Journal of Abnormal Psychology, 100*, 98–101.

Hewitt, P. L., & Flett, G. L. (1991b). Perfectionism in the self and social contexts: Conceptualization, assessment, and association with psychopathology. *Journal of Personality and Social Psychology, 60*, 456–470.

Hewitt, P. L., & Flett, G. L. (1993). Dimensions of perfectionism, daily stress, and depression: A test of the specific vulnerability hypothesis. *Journal of Abnormal Psychology, 102*, 58–65.

Hewitt, P. L., & Flett, G. L. (1996). Personality traits and the coping process. In M. Zeidner & N. S. Endler (Eds.), *Handbook of coping* (pp. 410–433). London: Wiley.

Hewitt, P. L., Flett, G. L., & Turnbull-Donovan, W. (1992). Perfectionism and suicidal potential. *British Journal of Clinical Psychology, 31*, 181–190.

Hewitt, P. L., Flett, G. L., Turnbull-Donovan, W., & Mikail, S. (1991). The Multidimensional Perfectionism Scale: Reliability, validity, and psychometric properties in psychiatric samples. *Psychological Assessment, 3*, 464–468.

Hewitt, P. L., Mittelstaedt, W., & Wollert, R. (1989). Validation of a measure of perfectionism. *Journal of Personality Assessment, 53*, 133–144.

Howe, G. W. (1987). Attributions of complex cause and the perception of marital conflict. *Journal of Personality and Social Psychology, 53*, 1119–1128.

Janoff-Bulman, R., & Brickman, P. (1982). Expectations and what people learn from failure. In N. T. Feather (Ed.), *Expectancies and actions: Expectancy value models in psychology* (pp. 207–237). Hillsdale, NJ: Erlbaum.

Joiner, T. F., & Schmidt, N. B. (1995). Dimensions of perfectionism, life stress, and depressed and anxious symptoms: Prospective support for diathesis-stress but not specific vulnerability among male undergraduates. *Journal of Social and Clinical Psychology, 14*, 165–183.

Kanfer, F. H., & Hagerman, S. (1981). The role of self-regulation. In L. Rehm (Ed.), *Behavior therapy for depression: Present status and future directions* (pp. 143–179). New York: Academic Press.

Kelley, H. H. (1967). Attribution theory in social psychology. In D. Levine (Ed.), *Nebraska Symposium on Motivation*, Vol. 15 (pp. 192–238). Lincoln, NE: University of Nebraska.

Lefcourt, H. M. (1981). The construction and development of the Multidimensional-Multiattributional Causality Scales. In H. M. Lefcourt (Ed.), *Research with the locus of control construct, Vol. 1: Assessment methods* (pp. 245–277). New York: Academic Press.

Lefcourt, H. M., Martin, R. A., Fick, C. M., & Saleh, W.E. (1985). Locus of control for affiliation and behavior in social interactions. *Journal of Personality and Social Psychology, 48*, 755–759.

Lefcourt, H. M., von Baeyer, C. L., Ware, E. E., & Cox, D. J. (1979). The Multidimensional-Multiattributional Causality Scale: The development of a goal-specific locus of control scale. *Canadian Journal of Behavioural Science, 11*, 286–304.

Leppin, A., Schwarzer, R., Belz, D., Jerusalem, M., & Quast, H. H. (1987). Causal attribution patterns of high and low test-anxious students. In R. Schwarzer, H. van der Ploeg, & C. Spielberger (Eds.), *Advances in test anxiety research*, Vol. 5. (pp. 97–106). Hillsdale, NJ: Erlbaum.

Lewinsohn, P. M., Steinmetz, J. L., Larson, D. W., & Franklin, J. (1981). Depression-related cognitions: Antecedent or consequence? *Journal of Abnormal Psychology, 90*, 213–219.

Martin, T. R., Flett, G. L., Hewitt, P. L., Krames, L., & Szantos, G. (1996). Personality in depressive symptoms and health problems: A test of a self-regulation model. *Journal of Research in Personality, 30,* 264–277.

Metalsky, G. I., Halberstadt, L. J., & Abramson, L. Y. (1987). Vulnerability to depressive mood reactions: Toward a more powerful test of the diathesis-stress and causal mediation components of the reformulated theory of depression. *Journal of Personality and Social Psychology, 52,* 386–393.

Mikulincer, M. (1994). *Human learned helplessness: A coping perspective.* New York: Plenum.

Pacht, A. R. (1984). Reflections on perfection. *American Psychologist, 39,* 386–390.

Powers, S., Douglas, P., & Choroszy, M. (1983). The factorial validity of the Multidimensional-Multiattributional Causality Scale. *Educational and Psychological Measurement, 43,* 611–615.

Powers, S., Douglas, P., Lopez, R. L., Jr., & Rossman, M. H. (1985). Convergent validity of the Multidimensional-Multiattributional Causality Scale with the Mathematics Attribution Scale. *Educational and Psychological Measurement, 45,* 689–692.

Rehm, L. (1977). A self-control model of depression. *Behaviour Therapy, 8,* 787–804.

Shepperd, J. A., Arkin, R. M., Strathman, A., & Baker, S. M. (1994). Dysphoria as a moderator of the relationship between perceived effort and perceived ability. *Journal of Personality and Social Psychology, 66,* 559–569.

Sohn, D. (1982). Sex differences in achievement self-attributions: An effect-size analysis. *Sex Roles, 8,* 345–357.

Sweeney, P. D., Anderson, K., & Bailey, S. (1986). Attributional style in depression: A meta-analytic review. *Journal of Personality and Social Psychology, 50,* 974–991.

Tennen, H., & Affleck, G. (1990). Blaming others for threatening events. *Psychological Bulletin, 108,* 209–232.

Weiner, B. (1985). An attributional theory of achievement motivation and emotion. *Psychological Review, 92,* 548–573.

Weiner, B., Russell, D., & Lerman, D. (1979). The cognition-emotion process in achievement-related contexts. *Journal of Personality and Social Psychology, 37,* 1211–1220.

Wollert, R., Mittelstaedt, W., MacIntosh, C., Erasmus, M., & Rawlins, L. (1986). *Sanctions, attributions, and scores on the Beck Depression Inventory.* Paper presented at the Western Canada Clinical Psychology Conference, Saskatoon, Canada.

Zuckerman, M. (1979). Attribution of success and failure revisited or: The motivational bias is alive and well in attribution theory. *Journal of Personality, 47,* 245–287.

4

Need Norm, Demographic Influence, Social Role, and Justice Judgment

Helen E. Linkey and Sheldon Alexander

Most studies of distributive justice have focused on the equity norm of justice (Greenberg, 1982; Walster, Walster, and Berscheid, 1978). This justice norm indicates that persons' outcomes should be proportional to their contributions. Under the influence of equity theory, much attention has been focused on pay equity in employment situations (Greenberg, 1982; Lane and Messe, 1971; Mowday, 1983; Prentice and Crosby, 1987) where contributions such as performance level, length of service or seniority, special training, or level of skills have been important. Other fairness norms, such as equality and need, have received much less attention than equity (Deutsch, 1975, 1985).

While the equality norm—which states that outcomes should be equal for all—has not been studied as extensively as equity, research exists showing that the equality principle is indeed used in certain distribution situations (Brickman and Bryan, 1975; Morgan and Sawyer, 1967; Kahn, O'Leary, Krulewitz, and Lamm, 1980; Leventhal and Lane, 1970; Shapiro, 1975). Least studied has been the need norm, which states that resources should be allocated on the basis of need. Nonetheless, there is some research that has demonstrated that the need norm may be used in distribution situations (Batson, Klein, Highberger, and Shaw, 1995; Grover, 1991; Lamm and Schwinger,

1980, 1983). However, previous research—which examined allocations that included the issue of need—did not investigate third-party salary allocations, the most common pay situation. The present study does so. In third-party allocations neither the allocator nor the other employees are impacted directly by the recipient's salary allocation.

Some authors (Deutsch, 1975; 1985; McClintock, 1972; Schwinger, 1980) believe that the social orientation of group members, the type of group task, the characteristics of the situation, and the individual goals of the allocator(s) determine which of the three major justice norms will be used. Deutsch (1975) has described the conditions that he believes determine which norm will apply in a given situation. If a competitive orientation exists in the group, or if the resource distribution is to be used to increase productivity, then the equity norm will be used. If the task is cooperative, or if the group social climate is very friendly, or if the goal is group cohesion, then the equality norm will be used. If the social climate is one of caring for group members, or if the allocators are held responsible for the welfare of the recipients, then the need principle will be used.

It has been assumed that if one is dealing with a work setting in which a pay allocation is being made, then the equity norm would be the primary allocation rule used (e.g., Mowday, 1983). We believe such an assumption may not always be correct. Even when a salary distribution is involved, the context of the allocation situation, the goals of the allocation, or the social values of the participants involved may determine which justice rule is used. If the situational context makes a recipient's needs most salient, then the need norm may become the most important rule used to judge the fairness of the distribution, even in a work setting.

Social role also may influence fairness and satisfaction judgments. Social roles are social structures imposed on role occupants by others and the self through norms and expectations for behavior attached to the occupant's role position. Normative standards about role behaviors serve as guides to one's own behavior and to expectations about appropriate behavior from others (McGrath, 1984; Shaw and Costanzo, 1982). Occupants of different social roles may find different information salient and useful; occupants of similar social roles are likely to be regarded as a group (e.g., nurses in a hospital). So social roles will define people who are expected to be similar in terms of values, goals, and judgments related to their social function. This has indeed been the case. For example, it has been found that occupation of a social role produces a bias in attributions (Nisbett and Ross, 1980; Ross, 1977).

Thus, the different social role groups in an organization, such as administrators and subordinates, may have different expectations for behavior in response to an employee's need. Employees should find information about the need for an increased salary more salient, available, and influential than would administrators or observers, producing differences between such groups in judgments of fairness, satisfaction, organizational obligation, or employee entitlement. The present study uses members of three different naturally occurring social roles in an organization: employees (lay teachers in a religious school), allocators (members of the Church council), and less directly involved observers (Church members).

Criterion judgments of fairness, satisfaction, employee entitlement, and organizational responsibility were obtained in this field study involving a salary allocation. We expected that judgments about the need norm would be the most influential of the three justice norms for predicting these four criterion judgments in relation to a salary allocation where an employee's need was made salient. In such a context it was expected that the need norm would predict more unique variance than the other two norms, equity and equality.

We expected that the social roles of the respondents, whose real-life social roles were similar to the social role perspective taken in the material they were responding to, would generate differential responses to the four criterion measures. We predicted that the allocators, who are responsible for the macrojustice of the organization, would be more aware of the organizational dimensions of the allocation and would judge a salary increase given to an employee on the basis of need to be less fair and less satisfying than would employees whose roles were similar to that of the recipient of the allocation. Further, we expected that the allocators would rate the recipient employee as being less entitled to the salary increase and the organization as less obligated to help than would the other social role groups.

Method

To increase external validity, subjects were solicited from five Catholic Church parishes with elementary and secondary schools in a large metropolitan area. There were several reasons for using Catholic parishes for this study of need. Catholic parishes and schools have greater flexibility in salary allocation than public schools because there are often no unions and only advisory salary schedules. Each administrator negotiates with each employee individually concerning salary. Some degree of inequity can occur. Because parish schools are usually smaller than public schools the administrators and faculty are more likely to know one another personally. This would incline administrators to respond positively to a need of an employee. Employees of religious schools are usually paid significantly less than public school employees. Thus, meeting an unusual need may appear reasonable. Finally, there is an emphasis on "helping the needy" in the Catholic religion that could incline participants of this setting to respond favorably to a request for help.

Among a total of 223 subjects, 68 were teachers in the parish schools, 76 were parish council members, and 79 were other parish members who were neither teachers nor members of the parish council; 91 were men, 129 were women, and 3 did not indicate gender. Ages ranged from 16 to 85 years with a mean of 45.6 years.

Subjects were tested at their local parishes when they were functioning in their respective roles. Teachers were tested during a regular teaching day. Parish council members were tested during a parish council meeting. Parish members were tested either during a meeting of their parish organization or whenever they could be met to answer the questions of the study. All respondents were asked to imagine themselves as a person who is part of the situation described by a story involving a female teacher in a Catholic school who has a need for increased salary because of a serious family medical situation. Each subject responded to a description involving a parish teacher whose child was seriously injured, leading to major increased family expenses. The teacher whose child was injured requested a $1,500 salary increase. Respondents were directed to put themselves personally in the role in the story that matched their real-life role (i.e., a teacher or Church council member or Church member). For example, teacher respondents were asked to imagine themselves as a teacher at that school whose co-worker requested the increased salary. Church council members were asked to put themselves in the allocator's role of a member of the Church council that had to decide about the salary increase request.

After reading the story, respondents made judgments of fairness, satisfaction, employee entitlement, and organizational obligation using 6-point Likert scales. Then general attitudes toward each of the norms of equity, equality, and need were obtained. The equity (contributions) norm was measured using 4 items based on performance level, skills level, and seniority. The 3 need norm items were based on family need. One equality item was used. Personal demographic information about age, gender, yearly family income level, and education level was obtained from each respondent. Yearly family income was measured on a 6-level scale ranging from very low income ($0 to $10,000) to higher income (over $50,000). Education level was indicated using 7 categories ranging from some high school (1) to graduate or professional degree (7).

Results

Relative importance of the justice norms. Hierarchical 2-step and 3-step multiple regressions were carried out to determine the unique variance in the dependent variables predicted by each of the three justice norm preferences for equity, equality, and need (Tabachnick and Fidell, 1983). That is, we looked at the remaining variance after all the variance shared with the other predictors had been accounted for. When the predictor variable is entered into the regression equation last, the unique variance which only it can account for is obtained.

Inspection of Table 4.1 shows that the need norm predicts the most unique (last step) variance for each one of the dependent variables. The need norm predicted significant amounts of unique variance for all 11 measures. Equity and equality norms yielded little. The equity norm was significant in only 2 judgments, and the equality norm never predicted significant unique variance. On the distributive and procedural fairness dependent measures, the unique variance predicted by the need norm ranged from 4 to 10 percent. Need also predicted 7 to 9 percent of the unique variance for the satisfaction measures. On the organizational obligation measures, the need norm predicted 10 to 13 percent of the unique variance. Finally, on the employee entitlement measures, 8 to 10 percent of the variance was uniquely accounted for by need. It is clear from these results that the need norm was more useful for uniquely predicting responses to the allocation in this situation than were the norms of equity and equality, confirming our prediction.

TABLE 4.1
Unique Variance Explained by the Justice Norms*

Dependent Variables	Unique variance (R^2)			F value
	Equity	Need	Equality	
Fairness to organization	.01	.10**	.00	9.87**
Fairness to other employees	.00	.04**	.01	4.30**
Fairness to recipient	.00	.04**	.00	3.37**
Procedural fairness	.01	.04**	.00	3.62**
Satisfaction of respondent	.02**	.07**	.00	7.14**
Satisfaction with allocators	.01	.09**	.00	7.72**
Organizational responsibility	.01	.11**	.00	10.03**
Obligation to employee	.01	.10**	.01	9.54**
Obligation to help	.00	.13**	.01	11.58**
Employee deservingness	.02**	.10**	.01	9.93**
Employee entitlement	.01	.08**	.00	7.88**

Note: *$N = 223$; **$p < .05$.

Social role analysis. ANOVA analyses showed significant main effects for social role conditions only for judgments of fairness (see Table 4.2). Those in the recipient's co-workers' role indicated the highest agreement (M = 4.4) that the allocation was fair to the organization, while those who took the allocators' role (M = 3.5) and those who took the role of observers (M = 3.8) indicated less agreement. Teachers in the recipient's co-workers' role indicated more agreement (M = 3.4) that the allocation was fair to the other employees than did those in the allocators' role (M = 2.8). Respondents in the social roles of the recipient's co-workers and observers agreed that the procedure by which the decision was made was fair (M = 3.8 and M = 3.9,

TABLE 4.2
Means for Fairness Variables, Demographics, and Norms for Social Role Groups*

| | Social Role Conditions | | | |
	Recipient's Co-workers (N=68)	Observers (N=79)	Allocators (N=76)	F value
Fairness items				
Fair to organization	4.4***	3.8†	3.5†	6.51**
Fair to other employees	3.4***	2.9***,†	2.8†	3.41**
Fair to recipient	4.5	4.2	4.0	2.27
Procedural fairness	3.8***	3.9***	3.2†	3.47**
Demographics				
Age	39.8***	49.8†	46.5†	8.65**
Gender	1.7	1.5	1.6	1.15
Income level	3.9***	4.0***	4.6†	4.71**
Education	6.3***	4.1†	5.2††	39.63**
Justice norms				
Equity	19.7***	18.7†	18.7†	3.38**
Need	10.9***	8.9†	9.4†	9.02**
Equality	3.6	3.2	3.2	2.02

Note: $*N$ = 223; $**p < .05$; ***, †, †† Different symbols on means indicate significant differ ence at $p < .05$.

respectively), while those in the allocators' role indicated less agreement (M = 3.2).

Significant main effects for social role were found for the demographic variables. Those in the recipient's co-workers' role (teachers) were younger (M = 39.8 years) than those in the allocators' or observers' roles (M = 46.5 and 49.8 years, respectively). The allocators (Church council members) had the highest family income level (M = 4.6 or $36,000) compared to the teachers (M = 3.9 or $29,000) and the observers (M = 4.0 or $30,000). Those similar to the recipient—who were all professional teachers—had the highest education level (M = 6.3 or some graduate education), the observers had the lowest level (M

TABLE 4.3
Unique Variance Predicted by Justice Norms, Demographics, and Social Role*

| Dependent variables | Unique Variance (R^2) | | | F value*** | Total R^2 |
	Norms	Demographics	Social role		
Fairness to organization	.11**	.10**	.03**	8.07**	.25
Fairness to other employees	.05**	.07**	.02	4.15**	.15
Fairness to recipient	.04**	.04	.01	2.49**	.10
Procedural fairness	.04**	.05**	.03**	3.66**	.13
Respondent satisfaction	.08**	.07**	.01	4.73**	.17
Satisfaction with allocators	.08**	.10**	.01	6.13**	.21
Organizational responsibility	.10**	.08**	.01	6.44**	.21
Organization owes recipient	.10**	.09**	.01	6.36**	.21
Organizational obligation	.10**	.07**	.00	6.11**	.21
Employee deservingness	.10**	.05**	.01	5.17**	.18
Employee entitlement	.08**	.08**	.01	5.57**	.19

Note: $N = 223$; **$p < .05$; ***Indicates the last step of a hierarchical analysis.

= 4.1 or two years of undergraduate college education), and the allocators were between those two groups (M = 5.2 or a bachelor's degree).

Exploratory multiple regressions. Since main effects of social role on three of the four demographic variables were found and significant correlations exist between several of the demographics and the fairness judgments (see Table 4.3), hierarchical multiple regression was used to examine the unique variance in the criterion measures accounted for by the set of demographic variables (age, gender, family income level, and education level), the norms (equity, equality, and need), and social roles (recipient's co-workers, allocator, and observer).

TABLE 4.4
Correlations Between Demographic and Dependent Variables*

Dependent Variables	Demographic variables			
	Age	Gender	Income	Education
Fairness to organization	–.24**	–.14**	–.17**	.11
Fairness to other employees	–.14**	–.22**	–.13	.03
Fairness to recipient	–.13**	–.09	–.15**	–.02
Procedural fairness	–.16**	–.10	–.15**	.04
Respondent satisfaction	–.12	–.18**	–.20**	.03
Satisfaction with allocators	–.21**	–.16**	–.22**	.09
Organizational responsibility	–.28**	–.06	–.14**	.07
Organizational obligation to employee	–.20**	–.17**	–.21**	.07
Organizational obligation to help	–.29**	–.01	–.10	.11
Employee deservingness	–.14**	–.08	–.22**	.01
Employee entitlement	–.19**	–.14**	–.21**	.04

Note: $*N = 223$; $**p < .05$.

The relative usefulness of the demographics and the justice norms was investigated by comparing the unique variance predicted by the demographics and the justice norms when they were each entered last into regression equations. The justice norms and the demographics each predicted approximately the same amount of unique variance in the dependent variables (Table 4.4). The justice norms uniquely accounted for 4 to 11 percent of fairness variance. Justice norms predicted 8 percent of both satisfaction items and 10 percent of each organizational obligation item. From 8 to 10 percent of the employee entitlement judgments were uniquely predicted by the justice norms.

TABLE 4.5
Standardized Canonical Coefficients for Social Roles

Predictor variables	Function 1	Function 2
Fairness	.3195	−.6418
Just	−.3312	.2042
Needs norm	.3150	.1502
Equity norm	.0906	−.3813
Equality norm	.2169	.0014
Age	−.4158	.0037
Education level	.8168	.2187
Income level	−.0017	.7826

The demographics uniquely predicted 4 to 10 percent of the fairness item variances. Prediction of unique variance for the two satisfaction items was 7 percent (respondent satisfaction) and 10 percent (satisfaction with allocators). The variance predicted by the demographics for organizational obligation judgments ranged from 7 to 9 percent, while 5 to 8 percent of the employee entitlement variance was predicted uniquely by the demographics.

Social role predicted small amounts of unique variance only for the fairness to organization (3 percent) and procedural fairness (3 percent) items. The total R^2 predicted by these three sets of variables ranged from 10 to 25 percent.

Correlations of demographics and dependent variables. Inspection of the correlations of the demographic variables of gender, age, family income level, and education level with the fairness, satisfaction, employer obligation, and employee entitlement judgments allows us to characterize the linear relation between them (see Table 4.4). Females were less favorable toward the salary allocation in response to the female employee's need than were males. Age was significantly negatively correlated to judgments of fairness, satisfaction, organizational obligation, and employee entitlement. The older the respondent, the less favorable were the responses. Correlations between family income level and the dependent variables showed that subjects with higher incomes gave less favorable responses to the increased salary allocation. Education level was unrelated to any of the dependent variables. Thus, subjects who were younger, less wealthy, or male responded more positively than older, more wealthy, or female subjects.

An exploratory discriminant function analysis for the social role groups was obtained on the basis of judgments of fairness, justice, the justice norms, education level, and family income. Two independent functions were revealed, which are presented in Table 4.5. The first function had an eigenvalue of .56, accounted for 88.71 percent of the variance, and had a canonical correlation of .60, Wilks's lambda = .60, $F(16, 426) = 7.80, p, .0001$. This first function is defined by a positive loading from age and a negative loading from education level. The second function had an eigenvalue of .07, accounted for 11.3 percent of the variance, and had canonical correlation of .26, Wilks's lambda = .93, $F(7, 214) = 2.18, p < .04$. The second function is defined by a positive loading from income level and negative loadings from fairness judgments and contribution norm judgments.

Discussion

This study obtained judgments about a need-based salary allocation from a sample of adults actually participating in a setting similar to that in a described allocation situation. The need norm was found to be the most important justice norm related to judgments of fairness, satisfaction, employee entitlement, and organizational obligation in this need-related situation. This demonstrates that the equity (contributions) norm is not always the most important basis for justice judgments of salary allocations in employment situations. This result is consistent with the view that characteristics of the specific situation make one or another justice norm more salient in forming fairness judgments about resource distributions (Deutsch, 1975). If the characteristics of the situation focus attention on some dimension other than contributions, then a norm other than the equity norm may be used to assess the justice of an allocation. This does not argue that equity theory is incorrect but rather suggests that a broader theory is needed to explain which norm will dominate in judging the justice of an allocation. Such a conclusion is consistent with that proposed in Leventhal, Karuza, and Fry (1980); it is also consistent with recent research that found the participants responded to need rather than to equity in a non-work situation (Batson, Klein, Highberger, and Shaw, 1995).

In the situation presented to our respondents, a salary increase was requested due to a need of the allocation recipient. This made the need norm more salient as a basis for a pay decision and led to the need norm being more important than the equity norm in predicting responses to the allocation. It should be noted that justice norm attitudes were measured after the subjects read the stories and made their other judgments. This order of presentation would encourage the judgments of the norms in the context of a need situation.

Although the social role groups (co-workers, allocators, and observers) did not give significantly different judgments about satisfaction, organizational obligation, and employee entitlement, it is noteworthy that the role groups did judge the fairness of the allocation differently. The recipient's co-workers viewed the allocation of higher salary as more fair to the organization and to the other employees than did the allocators and observers. This result is consistent with the idea that people in various social role positions find different information salient, leading to differing judgments of fairness about a situation. In addition, allocators' procedural fairness judgments were lower than those of the recipient's co-workers and observers. We have found then that in spite of agreement about satisfaction with the allocation and agreement about organizational obligation to help and employee entitlement to get help, the different social roles led to different justice judgments.

The variance predicted by demographic characteristics contributes independently of the justice norms. We have seen that individual characteristics of the respondents—such as age, gender, and family income—account for significant amounts of unique variance. It should be noted that the respondents in this study were members of a religious organization that encourages responding to the need of others. While our study did not directly examine the impact of the respondent group's broader social and religious values on our results, such factors could have influenced the findings.

The demographic variables of age, gender, and family income level made significant contributions to the prediction of the dependent variables, ranging up to a maximum unique R^2 of 10 percent. The respondents' justice norm preferences were also useful predictors, accounting for an additional unique 4 to 11 percent of the variance. These results emphasize the importance of measuring such personal characteristics of respondents in relation to justice judgments. The findings for the demographic variables indicate that researchers who use samples of restricted age or income ranges must not overgeneralize to different age or income level groups.

We have seen here that in groups of naturally occurring allocators and recipients, significant differences in demographic characteristics exist, which are in turn associated with social roles that explain significant variance in justice judgments. Not surprisingly, those in the role of recipient's co-workers were younger and had lower incomes than the allocators. Social roles, generally, are associated with different demographic characteristics. Age, income, gender, and social role influence justice judgments and research must take account of such differences. The more limited these are in a subject sample, the less generalizable are the conclusions reached.

The situation used in this study was deliberately selected as one where need was likely to be salient. However, work settings may differ in the amount of openness to the use of non-equity distribution norms. Future research should gather information on other characteristics of the situation as they relate to fairness judgments. Such context variables could include information about the cohesion and friendship level of employees, the degree of organizational paternalism or participation levels by management and labor, and the endorsement of the various justice norms in that setting.

In conclusion, this study indicates that the need norm of justice can be the basis for judgments of fairness, satisfaction, organizational obligation, and employee entitlement in a work situation. It also indicates that such characteristics as age, income level, gender, and social role can uniquely influence such responses.

References

Batson, C. D., Klein, T. R., Highberger, L. & Shaw, L. L. (1995). Immorality from empathy-induced altruism: When compassion and justice conflict. *Journal of Personality and Social Psychology, 68,* 1042–1054.

Brickman, P. & Bryan, J. H. (1975). Moral judgment of theft, charity, and third-party transfers that increase or decrease equality. *Journal of Personality and Social Psychology, 31,* 156–161.

Deutsch, M. (1975). Equity, equality, and need: What determines which value will be used as the basis of distributive justice? *Journal of Social Issues, 31,* 137–149.

Deutsch, M. (1985). *Distributive justice: A social-psychological perspective.* New Haven: Yale University Press.

Greenberg, J. (1982). Approaching equity and avoiding inequity in groups and organizations. In J. Greenberg & R. L. Cohen (Eds.), *Equity and justice in social behavior* (pp. 389–436). San Diego, CA: Academic Press.

Grover, S. L. (1991). Predicting the perceived fairness of parental leave policies. *Journal of Applied Psychology, 76,* 247–255.

Kahn, A., O'Leary, V. E., Krulewitz, J. E., & Lamm, H. (1980). Equity and equality: Male and female means to a just end. *Basic and Applied Social Psychology, 1,* 173–197.

Lamm, H. & Schwinger, T. (1980). Norms concerning distributive justice: Are needs taken into consideration in allocation decisions? *Social Psychology Quarterly, 43,* 425–429.

Lamm, H. & Schwinger, T. (1983). Need consideration in allocation decisions: Is it just? *Journal of Social Psychology, 119,* 205–209.

Lane, I. M. & Messe, L. A. (1971). Equity and the distribution of rewards. *Journal of Personality and Social Psychology, 20,* 1–17.

Leventhal, G. S., Karuza, J., & Fry, W. R. (1980). Beyond fairness: A theory of allocation preferences. In G. Mikula (Ed.), *Justice and social interaction* (pp. 167–218). New York: Springer-Verlag.

Leventhal, G. S. & Lane, D. W. (1970). Sex, age, and equity behavior. *Journal of Personality, 15,* 312–316.

McClintock, C. G. (1972). Social motivation: A set of propositions. *Behavioral Science, 17,* 438–454.

McGrath, J. E. (1984). *Groups: Interaction and performance* (pp. 200–213). Englewood Cliffs, NJ: Prentice-Hall.

Morgan, W. R. & Sawyer, J. (1967). Bargaining, expectations, and the preference for equality over equity. *Journal of Personality and Social Psychology, 6,* 139–149.

Mowday, R. T. (1983). Equity theory predictions of behavior in organizations. In R. M. Steers & L. W. Porter (Eds.), *Motivation and work behavior* (3rd ed., pp. 91–113). New York: McGraw-Hill.

Nisbett, R. E. & Ross, L. (1980). *Human inference: Strategies and shortcomings of social judgment.* Englewood Cliffs, NJ: Prentice-Hall.

Prentice, D. A. & Crosby, F. (1987). The importance of context for assessing deservingness. In J. C. Masters & W. P. Smith (Eds.), *Social comparison, social justice, and relative deprivation* (pp. 165–182). Hillsdale, NJ: Erlbaum.

Ross, L. (1977). The intuitive psychologist and his shortcomings: Distortions in the attribution process. In L. Berkowitz (Ed.), *Advances in Experimental Social Psychology* (Vol. 13, pp. 279–301). New York: Academic Press.

Schwinger, T. (1980). Just allocation of goods: Decisions among three principles. In G. Mikula (Ed.), *Justice and social interaction* (pp. 95–125). New York: Springer-Verlag.

Shapiro, G. (1975). Effects of expectations of future interaction on reward allocations in dyads: Equity or equality. *Journal of Personality and Social Psychology, 31,* 873–880.

Shaw, M. E. & Costanzo, P. R. (1982). *Theories of social psychology* (pp. 295–313). New York: McGraw-Hill.

Tabachnick, B. G. & Fidell, L. S. (1983). *Using multivariate statistics* (pp. 107–109). New York: Harper and Row.

Walster, E., Walster, G. W., & Berscheid, E. (1978). *Equity: Theory and research.* Boston, MA: Allyn and Bacon.

5

Adaptive and Maladaptive Narcissism among University Faculty, Clergy, Politicians, and Librarians

Robert W. Hill and Gregory P. Yousey

While narcissism has received considerable attention in the psycho-analytic literature for many decades, the inclusion of Narcissistic Personality Disorder in the third edition of the *Diagnostic and Statistical Manual of Mental Disorders* (DSM; American Psychiatric Association [APA]) in 1980 spurred increased research into the nature of narcissism. The most recent edition of the DSM (4th ed.; APA, 1994) characterizes narcissism as involving: grandiosity, a need for admiration and attention from others, exaggerated self-importance, a preoccupation with fantasies of unlimited success, power or brilliance, envy, entitlement, exploitiveness, limited empathy, and arrogance. When these characteristics are predominant and pervasive they are maladaptive primarily due to consequent impaired interpersonal relationships.

Empirical studies of narcissism were bolstered by the development of the Narcissistic Personality Inventory (NPI; Raskin and Hall, 1979), a questionnaire designed to measure individual differences in narcissism based on DSM criteria. Multivariate analyses of the NPI indicate that narcissism is a multidimensional construct that can be conceptualized with either seven components (Raskin and Hall, 1979; Raskin and Terry, 1988) or four components (Emmons, 1984, 1987). Emmons's (1984) four NPI dimensions provide a parsimonious set of scales with good validity evidence indicating that several dimensions of narcissism are adaptive (i.e., Leadership/Authority, Superiority/Arrogance, and Self-absorption/Self-admiration) while one dimension appears more clearly maladaptive (Exploitativeness/Entitlement). Emmons (1984) found that the three adaptive NPI scales were positively associated with self-esteem, extroversion, dominance, and independence; and negatively with self-abasement, self-ideal discrepancy, neuroticism, and social anxiety. The Exploitativeness/Entitlement NPI scale was associated with competitiveness, suspiciousness, tenseness, extroversion, anxiety, neuroticism, public self-consciousness, but not with self-esteem. Emmons (1987) also reported that only the Exploitativeness/Entitlement scale was significantly associated with two measures of pathological narcissism as well as affective intensity. Adaptive narcissism was also found to be associated with positive personal adjustment and optimism while the reverse was found for maladaptive narcissism (Hickman, Watson, and Morris, 1996). Individuals with high levels of narcissistic characteristics have also been described as exhibiting a need for attention and admiration from others, and NPI total scores were found to be associated with self-reported concerns for self-presentation, status, power, dominance, and physical beauty (Hill and McFerren, 1995). Narcissism has also been associated with a need for power (Carroll, 1987).

Adaptive narcissistic characteristics may prove advantageous to individuals in social or occupational situations that require leadership, authority, and a confident social presentation. Also, high levels of narcissism may lead some individuals to select occupations that better gratify needs for social attention, prestige, and status. Vocational interests have been observed as an important indicator of personality, and vocational stereotypes have been suggested to have reliable and important psychological and sociological meaning (Holland, 1985). Holland (1985) proposed that individuals both select and perform best with occupations that fit their personality. Holland (1985) describes occupations using three of six personality styles (realistic, investigative, artistic, social, enterprising, and conventional) in rank order of importance. Adaptive narcissism appears to overlap with features of Holland's (1985) "social" personality, which was described as ascendent, friendly, persuasive, sociable, and warm and the "enterprising" personality, which was described as agreeable, possessing leadership and speaking ability, talkative, optimistic, and self-confident. Maladaptive narcissism might also be associated with Holland's (1985) "enterprising" personality which was also described as acquisitive, domineering, exhibitionistic, ambitious, excitement seeking, and aggressive.

The present study pursued the expectation that narcissistic characteristics would be more prevalent in individuals engaged in occupations involving frequent opportunities for attention and admiration from others, social prestige, and power, and that narcissism would be less prevalent in occupations that provide less of these characteristics. The occupations selected for analysis included university faculty, politicians, clergy, and librarians.

University faculty, politicians, and clergy were selected for sampling because these occupations involve frequent appearances before audiences and thus frequent social attention, as well as authority over others, relatively high levels of prestige and status, responsibility, and power. Librarians were selected as an occupation that might be of less interest to individuals with high needs for prestige, social attention, power, and admiration from others. These expectations regarding occupational differences were based on stereotypes of the roles involved rather than an empirical assessment. A literature review revealed no empirical studies of narcissism related to occupational choice with the exception of one study, which found no significant pathological narcissism characteristics in sixty-four ministerial candidates, but above-average dominance scores (Patrick, 1990). Faculty, politicians, and clergy were all expected to exhibit higher levels of adaptive narcissism than librarians, who were expected to manifest lower levels of adaptive narcissism. We did not expect any occupation to manifest high levels of maladaptive narcissism because the interpersonal impairment associated with high Exploitativeness/Entitlement would likely interfere with successful occupational functioning.

Method

Procedure

Participants were randomly selected from occupation-related mailing lists in each of the following four occupational groups: 1) all full-time university faculty at one southeastern United States (U.S.) university with a field-appropriate terminal degree were sampled without regard to department affiliation (except those from Library Services; N = 567); 2) state legislators, from both the state senate and house of representatives, from four southeastern U.S. states were all solicited to participate using mailing lists provided by each state's respective legislative information service ($N = 575$); 3) clergy—including 200 Methodist ministers, 200 Baptist ministers, and 192 Catholic priests located within North Carolina—were solicited from mailing lists provided by the central offices of the respective denominations ($N = 592$); and 4) librarians were solicited from a list of North Carolina Librarian Association members ($N = 600$). All participants were mailed identical questionnaire packets containing: a cover letter requesting participation and explaining voluntary consent, a copy of the NPI, a set of demographic questions, and an addressed, postage-paid return envelope.

Measure

The NPI is a forty-item self-report questionnaire that uses a forced choice format (Raskin and Hall, 1979). In addition to a total narcissism score, four subscales were derived (Leadership/Authority, Superiority/Arrogance, Self-Absorption/Self-Admiration, and Exploitativeness/Entitlement) with alpha coefficients ranging from .69 to .86 (Emmons, 1984). Considerable evidence supporting the stability, internal consistency, and validity of the NPI has been reported (Emmons, 1984, 1987; Raskin and Hall, 1979; Raskin and Terry, 1988).

Results

Of the 2,334 questionnaires mailed out, 459 were returned, resulting in an overall response rate of 19.7 percent. The response rate varied significantly [X^2 (9, $N = 459$) = 1377.0, $p < .001$] between occupation sampled: faculty 21.7 percent ($N=123$), politicians 7.3 percent ($N=42$), clergy 16.7 percent ($N= 99$), and librarians 32.5 percent ($N=195$). The means and standard deviations of the scores for the total NPI and each of the four subscales for each occupation sample are reported in Table 5.1.

An analysis of variance indicated that total narcissism scores were significantly different by occupational group [$F(3,455) = 5.91, p<.001$]. *Post hoc* examination of mean difference scores indicated that politi-

TABLE 5.1
NPI Mean Scores and Standard Deviations by Occupation

Subscale	Professors		Clergy		Politicians		Librarians	
	Mean	SD	Mean	SD	Mean	SD	Mean	SD
Full NPI	12.40	5.87	11.98	5.38	15.19	6.22	11.09	6.00
LA	3.76	2.21	4.47	1.94	5.43	1.84	3.45	2.38
SS	2.90	1.91	2.74	1.78	2.74	1.99	2.47	1.77
SA	1.56	1.43	1.62	1.53	2.02	1.79	1.47	1.43
EE	1.07	1.08	0.69	0.83	1.12	1.17	1.09	1.23

Note: NPI, Narcissistic Personality Inventory; LA, Leadership/Authority; SS, Self-Absorption/Self-Admiration; SA, Superiority/Arrogance; EE, Exploitativeness/Entitlement.

cians were significantly higher in total narcissism (Tukey HSD $p<.05$), with faculty, clergy, and librarians not significantly different from each other in total narcissism. Further analyses of variance were conducted for each of the four NPI subscales in order to determine which subscales contributed to differences in narcissism between occupational samples. Of the four subscales, Leadership/Authority [$F(3,455) = 11.73$, $p < .001$] and Exploitativeness/Entitlement [$F(3,455) = 3.38$, $p = .02$) were significantly different for the occupations sampled. *Post hoc* analyses indicated that politicians scored significantly higher than the other occupations on the Leadership/Authority subscale (Tukey HSD $p <.001$). Clergy scored significantly lower than all other occupation samples on the Exploitativeness/Entitlement subscale (Tukey HSD $p < .05$). The differences in scores on the NPI subscales, which were standardized for the graphical comparison, are represented for each of the four occupations in Figure 1.

Discussion

Differences in the manifestation of narcissistic characteristics were expected among occupational groups which involve differing opportunities for leadership, authority, social attention, prestige, and admiration from others. We found that politicians as a group responded less frequently to the survey packet than the other occupations sampled. Faculty and librarians may be more familiar with academic research surveys, and thus more inclined to participate, and politicians may

FIGURE 5.1
Narcissism Scales by Occupation

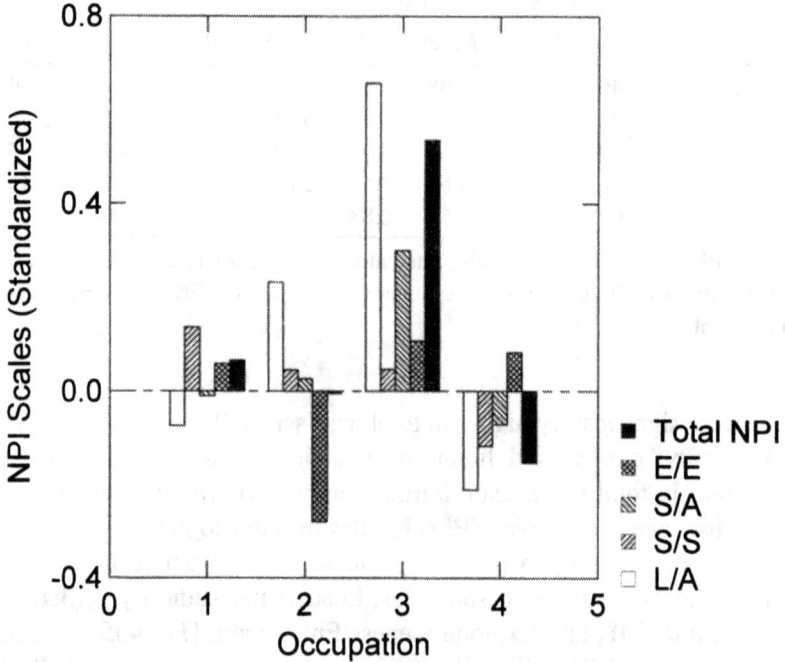

Notes: Mean Narcissistic Personality Inventory Scale Scores (standardized) by Occupational Group. Occupation 1 = faculty, 2 = clergy, 3 = politicians, 4 = librarians. Legend: L/A = Leadership/Authority Narcissism scale; S/S = Selfabsorption/ Self-admiration; S/A = Superiority/Arrogance; E/E = Exploitativeness/Entitlement.

experience a higher volume of mail with less time and inclination to respond to unnecessary correspondence. We could not determine any relationship between response rate and narcissism scores from our data.

Among the different occupations sampled, politicians scored highest in total narcissism as well as the Leadership/Authority dimension. The Leadership/Authority subscale is associated with warmth, dominance, extroversion, and social boldness, and has been described as an adaptive aspect of narcissism (Emmons, 1984). The politicians appeared to manifest strong leadership traits relative to the other occupations sampled, consistent with the demands of political activity. State legislators likely achieve elected office with successful adaptive leadership and authority characteristics.

Holland (1985) suggested that the most important vocational personality types associated with politicians were: (1) enterprising, entailing the manipulation of others to attain organizational goals or economic gain and an acquisition of leadership and persuasive competencies (and less developed scientific skills); (2) social, with a preference for activities that entail informing, training, or developing others, well-developed relationship skills, and an aversion to explicit vocational activities involving materials, tools, or machines; and (3) artistic, with a preference for ambiguous, unsystematized activities entailing the manipulation of materials to create products or art, with an aversion to ordered activities. Holland's enterprising and social vocational personality descriptions appear consistent with the adaptive NPI scales (Emmons, 1984) in describing politicians. In fact, state legislators are modestly compensated part-time politicians with some other occupation during much of the year. We nonetheless correctly anticipated that politicians manifest high levels of adaptive narcissism.

University faculty did not score particularly high or low on any of the narcissism subscales relative to the other occupations. While the role of university faculty might often involve social prestige, authority, and frequent opportunity for attention and perhaps admiration from others, narcissism scores for this group were average among the occupations sampled. The average narcissism scores for these four occupations may be high relative to other groups, but no normative data for the four Emmons (1984) NPI scales has been described. In Holland's (1985) classification of vocational personality, university faculty were characterized as: (1) social (described above); (2) investigative, with a tendency to observe and synthesize physical, biological, or cultural phenomena to better understand and control it with a disposition to acquire scientific and mathematic competencies; and (3) artistic (described above). The descriptors that characterize Holland's (1985) "social" personality appear particularly consistent with adaptive narcissism characteristics.

Of the occupations sampled, clergy were lowest in Exploitativeness/ Entitlement, which represents the more maladaptive aspects of narcissism. Exploitativeness/Entitlement is related to suspiciousness, tenseness, anxiety, and neuroticism, and is manifested by an expectation of special or exceptional importance and a willingness to use others to achieve desired ends. Clergy endorsed less of these characteristics than the other occupations sampled. This low level of maladaptive narcissism is consistent with a more altruistic characterization of clergy with fewer mistrustful, self-serving, and manipulative tendencies than the other occupations sampled. Of the dimensions of narcissism reflected by the NPI, clergy scored highest on the Leadership/Authority subscale indicating an endorsement of social dominance, social boldness, warmth, and extroversion. The NPI scales endorsed by clergy are consistent with Holland's vocational personality descriptions of clergy as social, artistic, and investigative, emphasizing the same characteristics as university faculty in a different order of priority.

While librarians scored lowest in total narcissism, they were not significantly less narcissistic than faculty and clergy, in spite of the relatively lower level of prestige, social attention, and admiration from others that might be stereotypically associated with this occupational role. Sampling librarians as an attempt to identify an occupation low in narcissistic characteristics was not as successful as anticipated perhaps because of our underestimate of the degree of social interaction library work involves. Of the dimensions of narcissism sampled by the NPI, librarians were lowest on the Leadership/Authority scale, especially relative to politicians and clergy, indicating less social dominance and extroversion, which is consistent with a description of librarians as typically more introverted than extraverted (Meyers and McCaulley, 1985). Holland (1985) classified librarians as social, artistic, and investigative (like clergy), emphasizing the preference for interpersonal interactions and responsibility that also characterized faculty and clergy.

This investigation demonstrated some support for differing levels of narcissistic characteristics associated with occupational role. Politicians were found to exhibit markedly high levels of adaptive narcissistic characteristics, and clergy manifest notably low levels of maladaptive narcissism relative to the other occupations sampled. Future research might sample other occupations and include other indices of leadership, experience of attention from others, and beliefs about one's occupational role. Future researchers may also wish to investigate the additional issues of job performance and both occupational and personal satisfaction as a function of the fit between occupation and personality. Among the vocational personality types described by Holland (1985), the "enterprising" personality might better target occupations high in narcissistic characteristics, and the "realistic" and "conventional" vocational types might be investigated for lower levels of narcissism. The results of this investigation support the hypothesis that narcissistically inclined individuals may select occupations that complement their personality by providing social attention, prestige, power, and opportunities for social influence.

Acknowledgment

Support for this investigation was provided by Graduate Studies and Research, Appalachian State University.

References

American Psychiatric Association (1987). *Diagnostic and statistical manual of mental disorders* (3rd ed.). Washington, D.C.: Author.

American Psychiatric Association (1994). *Diagnostic and statistical manual of mental disorders* (4th ed.). Washington, D.C.: Author.

Carroll, L. (1987). A study of narcissism, affiliation, intimacy, and power motives among students in business administration. *Psychological Reports, 61*, 355–358.

Emmons, R. A. (1984). Factor analysis and construct validity of the Narcissistic Personality Inventory. *Journal of Personality Assessment, 48*, 291–300.

Emmons, R. A. (1987). Narcissism: Theory and measurement. *Journal of Personality and Social Psychology, 52*, 11–17.

Hickman, S., Watson, P. J., and Morris, R. J. (1996). Optimism, pessimism, and the complexity of narcissism. *Personality and Individual Differences, 20*, 521–528.

Hill, R. W. and McFerren, B. P. (1995). *Narcissism and a need for approval and admiration.* Presented at the annual meeting of the Southeastern Psychological Association, Savannah, GA.

Holland, J. L. (1985). *Making vocational choices: A theory of vocational personalities and work environments* (2nd ed.). Englewood Cliffs, NJ: Prentice Hall.

Meyers, I. B. and McCaully, M. H. (1985). *Manual: A guide to the development and use of the Meyers-Briggs Type Indicator.* CA: Consulting Psychologists Press.

Patrick, J. (1990). Assessment of narcissistic psychopathology in the clergy. *Pastoral Psychology, 38,(3)*, 173–180.

Raskin, R. and Hall, C. S. (1979). A narcissistic personality inventory. *Psychological Reports, 45*, 590.

Raskin, R. and Terry, H. (1988). A principal-components analysis of the Narcissistic Personality Inventory and further evidence of its construct validity. *Journal of Personality and Social Psychology, 54*, 890–902.

6

Perceptions of Self-Oriented and Other-Oriented Help-Providers

Mark A. Barnett, Guy D. Vitaglione, Jeffrey S. Bartel,
Birgit S. Valdez, Lee Ann Steadman,
and Kimberly K.G. Harper

Altruism has been conceptualized as a helpful act that is motivated by a desire to provide a positive outcome for another without regard for oneself; in contrast, egoistic helping is defined as prosocial behavior motivated by the expectation of rewards for the self or by the desire to avoid aversive consequences to the self (Batson, 1991, 1995; Carlo et al., 1991; Eisenberg, 1986; Shaffer, 1994). Despite psychology's emphasis on "human nature" as primarily egoistically motivated (Batson, 1990; Campbell, 1975; Wallach and Wallach, 1983), altruistic, or other-oriented, helping has consistently been regarded more favorably than egoistic, or self-oriented, helping.

Western philosophers have argued that helping behaviors stemming from "altruistic feelings" are not only present in humanity but reflect the more positive aspects of humanity. For example, David Hume (1963) praised sympathetic (i.e., selfless) helping as a remarkable quality of human nature, and Adam Smith (1966) extolled the virtues of sympathetic acts (i.e., other-oriented helping) as a demonstration of humanity's benevolence. Similarly, contemporary psychologists (Batson, 1991, 1995; Eisenberg, 1982, 1986; Hoffman, 1982, 1989;

Krebs and Van Hesteren, 1994) have viewed other-oriented helping as the more compassionate and morally advanced form of prosocial behavior. For example, Batson (1991) suggests that when individuals act altruistically, they are "more interconnected, more closely tied to one another" and their behavior reflects a higher "moral horizon" than when their help is egoistically motivated (pp. 3–4). In one developmental model consistent with this view, Eisenberg (1982, 1986; Eisenberg, Lennon, and Roth, 1983; Eisenberg et al. 1991) described five levels of prosocial moral reasoning. At the lowest level, young children are reported to display a hedonistic form of helping that is characterized by a focus on personal gain and a concern for oneself. In contrast, the highest level of helping behavior attainable by older individuals reflects a desire to assist others that is based on internal values and the acceptance of helping for the good of others. More recently, Krebs and Van Hesteren (1994) incorporated the developmental stages proposed by ten theorists into an altruistic behavior model, with "egocentric accommodation" at stage 1 and "integrated altruism" and "universal self-sacrificial love" at stages 6 and 7 (the highest stage), respectively. Krebs and Van Hesteren claim that the other-oriented helping associated with the higher stages is more advanced, principled, and humanitarian than the self-oriented helping associated with the lower stages. In sum, theorists and researchers have consistently portrayed altruistically motivated helping as more socially desirable and developmentally mature than egoistically motivated helping.

The notion inferred from the helping literature that other-oriented assistance should be consistently favored over self-oriented assistance appears to contrast sharply with the observation that our culture emphasizes individualism, personal ambition, and the value of endeavors stemming from self-interest (Baumeister, 1995; Markus and Kitayama, 1991). Thus, despite the apparent consensus among authors within the helping literature, an individual whose self-interested behavior also serves to assist and benefit another may well be valued in some situations. For example, media attention on the skills and successes of publicity-seeking, highly paid lawyers (Bart, 1994; Gleick, 1996; Kaplan, 1994) suggests that, under some circumstances and on certain dimensions, a self-oriented help-provider may indeed be perceived in a highly favorable manner.

Study 1: Perceptions of Self-Oriented
and Other-Oriented Lawyers

As the preceding discussion suggests, there is a need to more closely examine the relationship between an individual's motivation to provide assistance and others' evaluations of that individual. Study 1 was designed to assess the relationship between an individual's self-described motivation for being a lawyer (i.e., self-oriented or other-oriented) and college undergraduates' perceptions of that lawyer. Of particular interest in this study was the determination of whether a lawyer's motivation for providing legal assistance influences an individual's desire to seek help from that lawyer. Although some research has been conducted on the influence of the potential helper's characteristics on individuals' desire to receive assistance from that potential helper (e.g., Barnett, 1988; Clark, 1983; Nadler, 1991), little attention has been given to the role of the helper's motivation on individuals' helpseeking. Despite the helping literature's indication that an other-oriented helper would be clearly favored, it was anticipated that a self-oriented lawyer would be rated as desirable as (and, perhaps, even more desirable than) an other-oriented lawyer. Moreover, because individuals tend to seek aid from a help-provider who is perceived as similar to themselves (for a review, see Nadler, 1991), pairs of personality characteristics associated with a concern for self (i.e., selfism, masculinity) and a concern for others (i.e., empathy, femininity) were included as potential correlates in this investigation.

Method

Participants and Experimenters. A total of 171 undergraduates (84 males, 87 females) enrolled in General Psychology classes at Kansas State University participated in Study 1 in groups of 8 to 20. A male served as the experimenter for Session 1 and a female served as the experimenter for Session 2.

Session 1: Materials and Procedure. Lawyer information sheet. Participants were led to believe that they were taking part in two separate studies in consecutive sessions. In the first session, students were provided personal information about a lawyer via a Lawyer Information Sheet (LIS), ostensibly completed by the lawyer as part of a prior study in which lawyers were the "subjects" (all of the lawyer's "responses" were typed on the LIS). The participants were told that the lawyers had granted us permission to use their completed LISs and accompanying photographs in the present study. They were informed that the particular LIS they would review was randomly selected for their group and that other groups of participants would be examining one of the many other LISs available from the prior study. The participants were instructed that after they had reviewed the information provided by the lawyer, they would be asked to complete a brief questionnaire examining their attitudes about the lawyer as well as their willingness to hire him or her for a particular hypothetical case.

With the exception of the lawyers' gender, all of the demographic information provided to participants on the LISs was identical (e.g., the lawyers were presented as thirty-four years old, white, married, with an undergraduate degree in Political Science from the University of Illinois and a law degree from the University of Michigan) and equated the lawyers on objective indices of competence and experience (e.g., they were presented as having had a 3.6 undergraduate GPA, as having passed the bar exam on their first attempt, and as having nine years of experience in an active legal practice). Although the participants were told that there were numerous lawyers being considered in this study, in fact, the lawyers' orientation and gender were the only portions of the LIS that were manipulated in this study.

The lawyer's orientation was "revealed" as either egoistic or altruistic in response to the last request for information on the LIS ("... please describe *why* you chose to be a lawyer and what your aspirations are for the future."). The self-oriented and other-oriented responses read as follows:

- *Self-oriented.* As far back as I can remember, I have always wanted to be a lawyer. Even as a child, it was very important to me to compete against others and to be successful. As a lawyer, I derive a strong sense of personal accomplishment and satisfaction from providing individuals with competent legal representation. In addition, I believe there are few professions besides the law in which hard work and success are so richly rewarded, both in terms of monetary gain and public recognition. In the future, in addition to maintaining my regular law practice, I would like to lecture and write books about the law and my experiences as a lawyer.
- *Other-oriented.* As far back as I can remember, I have always wanted to be a lawyer. Even as a child, it was very important to me to try to help friends of mine who had gotten in some kind of trouble at home or

at school. As a lawyer, I am able to provide assistance to individuals who are in need of competent legal representation. I believe that everyone involved in our legal system should be treated in a fair and just manner, regardless of their status or ability to pay. In the future, in addition to maintaining my regular law practice, I would like to assist in law reform in order to make the legal system more responsive to the needs of all individuals.

The gender of the lawyer was made salient by attaching a photograph of a male or a female to the top of the LIS. These photographs were selected from magazines, and the faces were rated as equally and moderately attractive in pretesting.

Assessment of lawyer's characteristics. After reviewing one of the four LISs used in this study (male/self-oriented, male/other-oriented, female/self-oriented, and female/other-oriented), participants were given a questionnaire that assessed their perceptions of the lawyer's characteristics. The participants were asked to rate on a scale from 1 (*Not at All Descriptive*) to 9 (*Very Descriptive*) the extent to which numerous words and phrases (e.g., trustworthy, intelligent, motivated to succeed) are descriptive of the lawyer who completed the LIS. A manipulation check of lawyer orientation (self- versus other-oriented) was embedded in this questionnaire. Factor analyses of participants' responses to this questionnaire yielded seven multi-item factors (Self-Oriented, Other-Oriented, Likable, Ambitious, Devious, Honest, and Competent). Table 6.1 presents the internal reliability (alpha) for each factor, the items associated with each factor, and their respective item loadings.

Auto accident scenario and associated questions. After evaluating the lawyer's characteristics, participants were presented with a scenario in which they were to imagine that they had been involved in a serious car accident that was the result of their car's brake failure. The participants were instructed to pretend that they had suffered severe and painful injuries as a result of the accident and that they required extensive hospitalization. They were also asked to imagine that they (a) later discovered that the brake failure was a result of manufacturer negligence, which was being covered up by the automobile company, and (b) had decided to sue the manufacturer for physical and emotional damages associated with the accident.

Participants were instructed to rate on a 9-point scale from 1 (*Not at All*) to 9 (*Very Much*) the extent to which they would experience

TABLE 6.1
**Factors Associated with Characteristics of Lawyers and Affective Reponses to
Scenario: Internal Reliabilities, Associated Items, and Item Loadings**

Characteristics of Lawyers Factor (alpha)	Item (loading)
Self-Oriented (.91)	focused on his/her own welfare (.87) self-oriented (.83) egoistic (.83) self-centered (.82) concerned about self (.79)
Other-Oriented (.88)	sensitive to others' needs (.88) caring (.84) compassionate (.84) concerned about others (.78) focused on clients' welfare* (.65) other-oriented (.57) empathic (.50)
Likable (.86)	friendly (.84) a nice person (.80) likable (.78)
Ambitious (.71)	motivated to succeed (.56) determined (.55) hard-working (.54)
Devious (.77)	sly (.83) manipulative (.74)
Honest (.80)	honest (.85) trustworthy (.79) sincere (.61)
Competent (.73)	skillful (.75) successful (.63) intelligent (.63) thorough (.58)
Affective Responses to Scenario Sad (.69)	sad (.77) depressed (.59)
Angry (.48)	angry (.62) resentful (.56) vengeful (.50)
Powerless (.70)	intimidated (.61) confused (.56) scared (.55) helpless (.48)

Note: *In Study 2, the wording was changed to "focused on patients' welfare."

several possible emotional reactions to the auto accident scenario. Factor analysis of participants' affective responses to the scenario yielded three multi-item factors (Sad, Angry, and Powerless). Table 1 presents the internal reliability (alpha) for each factor, the items associated with each factor, and their respective item loadings.

After making their affect ratings, the participants were asked to rate on a 9-point scale from 1 (*Definitely No*) to 9 (*Definitely Yes*) the extent to which they would want to hire the lawyer presented on the LIS, given that other lawyers were available to represent them on the case. The participants were informed that in "personal injury" cases such as this, a lawyer would receive payment only if the lawsuit were successful. Nonetheless, participants were asked to estimate the hourly wage the lawyer on the LIS typically charges for his or her legal services; participants answered this question by circling one number on a 12-point scale ranging from 1 (*$50*) to 12 (*more than $150*).

Session 2: Materials and Procedure. Participants were led to believe that the purpose of the "second study" was to gather data for some attitude scales that were in the process of being developed. In reality, the undergraduates completed three established personality measures: (1) the Empathic Concern subscale of Davis's (1983) Interpersonal Reactivity Index (IRI), (2) Phares and Erskine's (1984) Selfism scale, and (3) Bem's (1974) Sex-Role Inventory (BSRI).

Empathic Concern. This subscale of Davis's (1983) IRI assesses individuals' tendencies to experience feelings that reflect an emotional responsiveness to the needs of others. In completing this subscale, respondents are asked to indicate on a 5-point scale from 1 (*Strongly Disagree*) to 5 (*Strongly Agree*) the extent to which they agree or disagree with seven statements (e.g., "I often have tender, concerned feelings for people less fortunate than me."). The internal reliability (alpha) for this subscale with the present sample was .67.

Selfism. This scale measures the extent to which an individual is self-oriented with regard to a broad range of situations dealing with the satisfaction of needs. In completing this scale, respondents are again asked to indicate on a 5-point scale from 1 (*Strongly Disagree*) to 5 (*Strongly Agree*) the extent to which they agree or disagree with twenty-eight statements (e.g., "Getting ahead in life depends mainly on thinking of yourself first."). The internal reliability (alpha) for this scale with the present sample was .79.

Sex-role orientation. The BSRI assesses the degree to which individuals perceive themselves as having traditionally masculine and feminine characteristics. In completing this scale, respondents are asked to rate on a 7-point scale from 1 (*Never or Almost Never True*) to 7 (*Always or Almost Always True*) the extent to which 20 masculine, 20 feminine, and 20 gender-neutral traits are descriptive of themselves. The internal reliabilities (alphas) for the masculinity and femininity subscales with the present sample were .83 and .76, respectively.

After completing these three measures, the participants were asked to fill out a brief "Post-Experiment Survey" that probed their suspicions about their involvement in the research; no suspicions were expressed. Finally, all participants were fully debriefed and thanked for their assistance.

Results

Effects of lawyer orientation. Participants' responses concerning the characteristics of the lawyer presented on the LIS, their desire to hire the lawyer, and the estimated hourly wage of the lawyer were analyzed in a series of 2 x 2 x 2 (Gender of Participant x Gender of Lawyer x Lawyer Orientation) ANOVAs.[1] Because findings involving Lawyer Orientation were of primary interest, only main and interaction effects involving this variable will be presented in this report.

Responses to the manipulation check items indicated that the manipulation of lawyer orientation on the LISs was successful. As presented on Table 6.2, the self-oriented lawyer was rated higher on the self-oriented factor than was the other-oriented lawyer; similarly, the other-oriented lawyer was rated higher on the other-oriented factor than was the self-oriented lawyer. Although the other-oriented lawyer was rated as more likable, more honest, and less devious than the self-oriented lawyer, the self-oriented lawyer was rated as more ambitious, more competent, and as earning more money per hour than the other-oriented lawyer. The participants displayed no clear preference in ratings of their desire to hire the self-oriented and other-oriented lawyers. Furthermore, none of the significant main effects of Lawyer Orientation were qualified by interactions with Gender of Participant or Gender of Lawyer.

Correlates of the desire to hire the self- and other-oriented lawyer. Although an ANOVA had revealed no clear preference in the partici-

TABLE 6.2
Mean Ratings of Self-Oriented and Other-Oriented Lawyers

| Variable | Lawyer Orientation | | $F(1,163) =$ |
	Self-Oriented	Other-Oriented	
Self-oriented	5.61	3.04	101.78***
Other-oriented	5.23	7.06	88.94***
Likable	5.69	6.54	10.58**
Ambitious	8.13	7.30	28.29***
Devious	3.91	2.52	24.14***
Honest	5.62	6.25	6.11*
Competent	7.36	6.63	17.17***
Hourly wage	7.67	6.26	12.32**
Desire to hire	6.73	6.67	.03

Note: $*p < .05$, $**p < .01$, $***p < .001$.

pants' desire to hire the self- or other-oriented lawyer, bivariate correlations were computed to determine whether the participants' "desire to hire" was associated with their ratings of: (1) the characteristics of the self- and other-oriented lawyer presented on the LIS, (2) their anticipated affective response to the auto accident scenario, and (3) their own personality characteristics (i.e., empathy, selfism, masculinity, and femininity).[2] For participants in both the self- and other-oriented lawyer conditions, three lawyer characteristics were found to be associated ($p < .05$) with their "desire to hire": competent ($r = .25$ and .31 for self- and other-oriented lawyers, respectively), ambitious ($r = .19$ and .34, respectively), and devious ($r = -.22$ and $-.28$, respectively). For the self-oriented lawyer condition only, the "desire to hire" was associated with participants' masculinity ($r = .18$) and the extent to which they anticipated feeling angry in response to the automobile accident scenario ($r = .24$). For the other-oriented lawyer condition only, the "desire to hire" was associated with ratings of the lawyer's honesty ($r = .20$) as well as the participants' femininity ($r = .24$) and empathy ($r = .29$).

Discussion

While theorists and researchers have consistently emphasized the "superiority" of altruistic over egoistic helping (Batson, 1991, 1995;

Eisenberg, 1982, 1986; Eisenberg et al., 1983, 1991; Hoffman, 1982, 1989; Krebs and Van Hesteren, 1994), the main findings of Study 1 suggest that an other-oriented help-provider may not be evaluated more favorably than a self-oriented help-provider on all dimensions. Indeed, the participants in this study appeared to display ambivalent feelings toward the self-oriented and other-oriented lawyers. Although they liked the other-oriented lawyer more and rated him or her as having more integrity (i.e., more honest and less devious), the self-oriented lawyer was perceived as having more drive and ability. This ambivalence may have contributed to the failure to find a significant main effect of lawyer orientation with regard to the participants' "desire to hire." That is, the self-oriented and other-oriented lawyers may have been perceived as having contrasting and offsetting patterns of relative strengths and weaknesses which resulted in participants demonstrating no clear preference in their desire to hire one or the other. Alternatively, information concerning the lawyers' motivations for providing legal assistance may not have been particularly salient in participants' hiring decisions in the context of other information presumably provided by the lawyers.

Interestingly, the self-oriented lawyer was assumed to earn more money per hour than the other-oriented lawyer. This finding may reflect the belief that self-oriented individuals would tend to "demand" higher pay for their services than individuals who are relatively less concerned about their own personal welfare. Similarly, this finding may reflect participants' belief that financial success is related to the characteristics perceived to be more highly associated with a self-oriented than an other-oriented lawyer. Consistent with the latter interpretation, participants' estimates of the lawyer's hourly wage were found to be related ($p < .05$) to their ratings of the extent to which the lawyer was competent ($r = .15$), ambitious ($r = .17$), devious ($r = .21$), and "unlikable" ($r = .15$).

Although the participants' willingness to hire the lawyer presented on the LIS was not influenced by the lawyer's orientation, certain responses and characteristics of the participants were found to be associated with their desire to hire the self-oriented and/or other-oriented lawyers. Regardless of the lawyer's orientation, participants expressed a heightened interest in hiring a lawyer who was perceived as relatively high in competence and ambition, but relatively low in deviousness. In addition, the participants' desire to hire the self-oriented lawyer was associated with the extent to which they anticipated feeling angry in response to the auto accident scenario and their level of masculinity. Perhaps those individuals who expected to be especially angry in response to the scenario, and those with traditionally masculine characteristics (e.g., "forceful," "willing to take a stand," "aggressive"), may have anticipated wanting to seek revenge against the auto manufacturer for intentionally neglecting to correct the flaw in the brake system that resulted in their pain and distress. The self-oriented lawyer, rated as relatively competent, ambitious, *and* devious, may have been perceived as especially able and willing to exact this revenge. In contrast, those participants scoring relatively high on empathy and femininity (e.g., "sensitive to the needs of others," "understanding," "eager to soothe hurt feelings") may have been interested in hiring the other-oriented lawyer because of the perceived similarity between themselves and the other-oriented lawyer, as well as the belief that this lawyer may be particularly sensitive and responsive to their emotional needs.

Study 2: Perceptions of Self-Oriented and Other-Oriented Physicians

The main results of Study 1 appear incongruent with prior literature concerned with individuals' motives for helping (Batson, 1991, 1995; Eisenberg, 1982, 1986; Eisenberg et al., 1983, 1991; Hoffman, 1982, 1989; Krebs and Van Hesteren, 1994) in demonstrating that an other-oriented help-provider may not be evaluated more favorably on all dimensions, nor more sought out for assistance, than a self-oriented help-provider. However, it might be argued that lawyers' stereotypic public image (Caplan, 1995; Fotheringham, 1994; Samuelson, 1992) may result in egoistic motivation being perceived as more common, and perhaps more acceptable, among them than among individuals in other occupations that involve providing assistance to others. In response to this concern, Study 2 was designed as a replication of Study 1 with one major difference—the help-provider that participants were asked to evaluate and to consider for assistance in Study 2 was not a lawyer, but a physician.

Method

Participants and Experimenters. A total of 129 undergraduates (65 males, 64 females) enrolled in General Psychology classes at Kansas State University participated in Study 2 in groups of 8 to 20. The experimenters in Study 2 were the same as those in Study 1.

Overview of Materials and Procedure. The materials and procedures in Study 2 were similar to those in Study 1. Participants were again led to believe that they were taking part in two separate studies in consecutive sessions. In the first session, students were presented with personal information "from an orthopedic surgeon" via a completed Physician Information Sheet (PIS). Again, all of the demographic information ostensibly provided by the male or female physician pictured on the form was identical (the photographs at the top of the PIS were the same as those used in Study 1) and equated the physicians on objective indices of competence and experience. The orthopedic surgeon's orientation was again "revealed" as egoistic or altruistic in response to the last request for information on the form (" . . . please describe *why* you chose to be a physician and what your aspirations are for the future."). The self-oriented and other-oriented responses read as follows:

- *Self-oriented.* As far back as I can remember, I have always wanted to be a doctor. Even as a child, it was very important to me to excel above my peers and to be admired for my accomplishments. As a physician, I derive a strong sense of personal satisfaction from providing individuals with competent medical care. In addition, I believe there are few professions besides medicine in which hard work and success are so richly rewarded, both in terms of monetary gain and public recognition. In the future, in addition to maintaining my regular practice as an orthopedic surgeon, I would like to lecture and write books about medicine and my experiences as a physician.
- *Other-oriented.* As far back as I can remember, I have always wanted to be a doctor. Even as a child, it was very important to me to try to help friends of mine who had injured themselves while playing. As a physician, I am able to provide assistance to a broad range of individuals who are in need of competent medical care. I believe that everyone should have access to good medical personnel and facilities, regardless of their status or ability to pay. In the future, in addition to maintaining my regular practice as an orthopedic surgeon, I would like to assist in medical insurance reform in order to make the health care system more responsive to the needs of all individuals.

After reviewing one of the four versions of the PIS used in this study (male/self-oriented, male/other-oriented, female/self-oriented, and female/other-oriented), participants were given a questionnaire that assessed their perceptions of the orthopedic surgeon's characteristics. This questionnaire contained the same descriptors and 9-point rating scale as in Study 1; the internal reliabilities (alphas) for the seven factors (Self-Oriented, Other-Oriented, Likable, Ambitious, Devious, Honest, and Competent) ranged from .74 to .91 for participants in Study 2.

After evaluating the physician's characteristics, participants were again presented with an "auto accident scenario" in which they were to imagine that they had suffered severe and painful injuries that required hospitalization. Unlike the scenario in Study 1 (which focused on the manufacturer's negligence and "cover-up" associated with the auto's brake failure), the scenario in Study 2 emphasized the recommendation by the medical staff for an orthopedic surgeon "to perform 3 or 4 surgical procedures spread over several months to optimize your chances of a full recovery."

Using the same questionnaire as in Study 1, participants were asked to rate the extent to which they would experience several possible emotional reactions to the auto accident scenario. The internal reliabilities (alphas) for the three affective response factors (Sad, Angry, and Powerless) ranged from .70 to .79 for participants in Study 2.

After making their affect ratings, the participants were asked to rate (on the same 9-point scale used in Study 1) the extent to which they would want to hire the orthopedic surgeon presented on the PIS, given that other orthopedic surgeons were available to perform the necessary operations. Although the participants were instructed to assume that their insurance company would cover most of the costs associated with these procedures, they were asked to "estimate the total amount of money the individual on the 'Physician Information Sheet' earns in a typical year as an orthopedic surgeon"; participants answered this question by checking one alternative on a 10-point scale ranging from 1 (*$50,000–$100,000*) to 10 (*more than $500,000*).

The materials and procedure for the second session of Study 2 were identical to those in the second session of Study 1. The internal reliabilities (alphas) for Davis's (1983) Empathic Concern subscale, Phares and Erskine's (1984) Selfism scale, and the masculinity and femininity subscales of Bem's (1974) Sex-Role Inventory ranged from .81 to .86 for participants in Study 2. The "Post-Experiment Survey" administered at the end of the second session again revealed no suspicions from participants concerning their involvement in the research. All participants were fully debriefed and thanked for their assistance.

Results

Participants' responses concerning the characteristics of the orthopedic surgeon presented on the PIS, their desire to hire the surgeon, and the estimated annual income of the surgeon were analyzed in a series of 2 x 2 x 2 (Gender of Participant x Gender of Physician x Physician Orientation) ANOVAs.[3] As in Study 1, only effects involving Physician Orientation are presented in this report.

Effects of physician orientation. Responses to the manipulation check items indicate that the manipulation of physician orientation on the different versions of the PIS was successful. As presented on Table 6.3, the self-oriented physician was rated higher on the self-oriented factor than was the other-oriented physician; similarly, the other-oriented physician was rated higher on the other-oriented factor than was the self-oriented physician. Although the other-oriented surgeon was rated as more likable, more honest, and less devious than the self-oriented surgeon, the self-oriented surgeon was rated as more ambitious, more competent, and as having a higher annual income than the other-oriented surgeon.[4] The participants displayed no clear preference in ratings of their desire to hire the self-oriented and other-oriented physicians.

Correlates of the desire to hire the self- and other-oriented physician. Although an ANOVA had revealed no clear preference in the participants' desire to hire the self- or other-oriented physician, bivariate correlations were computed to determine whether the participants' "desire to hire" was associated with their ratings of: (1) the characteristics of the self- and other-oriented physician presented on the PIS, (2) their anticipated affective response to the auto accident scenario, and (3) their own personality characteristics (i.e., empathy, selfism, masculinity, and femininity).[5] For participants in both the self-oriented and other-oriented physician conditions, three physician characteristics were found to be associated ($p < .05$) with the "desire to hire": competent ($r = .32$ and .34 for self- and other-oriented physicians, respectively), likable ($r = .35$ and .44, respectively), and honest ($r = .38$ and .50, respectively). For the other-oriented physician condition only, the "desire to hire" was associated with ratings of the physician's

TABLE 6.3
Mean Ratings of Self-Oriented and Other-Oriented Physicians

Variable	Physician Orientation		$F(1,121) =$
	Self-Oriented	Other-Oriented	
Self-oriented	5.60	3.00	72.14***
Other-oriented	5.52	7.29	52.11***
Likable	5.60	6.74	12.59**
Ambitious	8.13	7.23	16.03***
Devious	2.72	1.91	5.37*
Honest	5.95	6.68	4.70*
Competent	7.47	6.95	6.89*
Annual income	4.68	4.06	4.22*
Desire to hire	6.11	6.53	2.26

Note: *$p < .05$, **$p < .01$, ***$p < .001$.

ambitiousness ($r = .38$), deviousness ($r = -.38$), and the extent to which the participants anticipated feeling powerless in response to the automobile accident scenario ($r = .21$). There were no significant correlates of "desire to hire" that were unique to the self-oriented physician condition.

Discussion

The results of Study 2 were highly similar to those of Study 1. Most notably, the pattern of main effects associated with the participants' ratings of the characteristics of the self- and other-oriented orthopedic surgeons (see table 5.3) was identical to the pattern of main effects in the prior study (see table 5.2). Although the participants in Study 2 liked the other-oriented physician more and rated him or her as less devious and more honest (especially the female participants, see note 4), the self-oriented physician was perceived as having more drive and ability. Again, it cannot be determined from the present data whether the failure to find a relation between the physicians' orientation and the participants' "desire to hire" was due to: (1) the self-oriented and other-oriented physicians being viewed as having contrasting and offsetting patterns of relative strengths and weaknesses, or (2) information about the physicians' motives for providing medical assistance to others not being viewed as particularly salient in the participants' hiring decision.

Paralleling the findings of Study 1, the self-oriented orthopedic surgeon was assumed to have a larger annual income than the other-oriented surgeon. This finding may reflect the belief that self-oriented individuals would tend to be especially self-serving in the payment they require for their services. As in Study 1, there is also evidence that the participants viewed a physician's financial success to be associated with some of the characteristics perceived as more descriptive of a self-oriented than an other-oriented help-provider in these studies. Specifically, participants' estimates of an orthopedic surgeon's annual income were found to correlate positively ($p < .05$) with their ratings of the surgeon's competence ($r = .17$) and ambitiousness ($r = .19$).

Although the participants' willingness to hire the physician presented on the PIS was not influenced by the physician's orientation, some of their other responses were again found to be associated with their "desire to hire" ratings. Regardless of the physician's orientation, participants expressed a heightened interest in hiring an individual who was perceived as relatively competent, likable, and honest. The participants' desire to hire the other-oriented physician was associated with rating the physician relatively high on ambition and relatively low on deviousness, as well as the extent to which the participants anticipated feeling powerless in response to the auto accident scenario. It is unclear why the first two correlates emerged for the "desire to hire" the other-oriented physician only, especially given the finding in Study 1 that participants expressed a heightened interest in hiring a lawyer who was rated relatively high on ambition and relatively low on deviousness, regardless of the lawyer's orientation. Concerning the third correlate, perhaps the more participants anticipated feeling powerless and vulnerable in facing the prospect of a series of difficult surgical procedures, the more they desired to be under the care of an other-oriented orthopedic surgeon who might be expected to be particularly sensitive and responsive to their emotional needs.

In sum, the main findings of Studies 1 and 2 suggest that the participants were ambivalent in their attitudes toward the other-oriented and self-oriented help-providers. First, whereas the participants in both studies tended to associate an individual's other-oriented motive for providing assistance with desirable "personal" qualities (e.g., heightened likability and honesty), they tended to associate an individual's self-oriented motive for providing assistance with desirable "professional" qualities (e.g., heightened competence, ambition, and income).

Second, no clear relation was found in either study between the help-provider's orientation and the participants' desire to seek assistance from that help-provider. This pattern of findings may reflect the specific conditions presented in Studies 1 and 2, wherein: (1) the help to be provided would be primarily instrumental in nature (e.g., preparing a lawsuit or performing a series of surgical procedures), and (2) the relationship between the professional help-provider and potential recipient would be, to a considerable extent, formal and impersonal. In a situation in which sensitive, expressive help is needed (e.g., an individual is called upon to comfort someone who is sad or distressed), a help-provider whose motivation for assisting emanates from an empathic concern for the other may be perceived as more effective (i.e., competent) in providing aid than a help-provider whose assistance is motivated by a blatant desire to benefit the self. In a similar vein, the acceptance of help within a close personal relationship is typically predicated on the belief that the other's motive for offering or providing assistance is genuinely other-oriented—any hint that a particular act of help is being offered for a self-serving reason may be viewed as violating a sense of trust and actively rejected.

Perceptions of self-oriented and other-oriented help-providers in "everyday" helping situations: A preliminary study. To explore these notions more systematically, we have begun to examine individuals' perceptions of altruistically and egoistically motivated help-providers in "everyday" helping situations. In a preliminary investigation, sixty-five undergraduates were asked to complete several Helping Incident Evaluation Forms in which a help-provider described: (1) a situation in which he or she had acted alone to offer assistance to another individual, and (2) the reason why he or she had offered the assistance in this situation (participants were led to believe that this information had been gathered in prior research on individuals' self-reported helping behaviors).[6] The forms reviewed by the participants systematically varied the helper's motive (i.e., self- versus other-oriented), the relationship between the helper and recipient (i.e., close versus distant), the type of help provided (i.e., instrumental versus expressive), and the gender of the helper-recipient dyad (i.e., male-male versus female-female). After reading about each instance of helping behavior, participants were asked to rate the degree to which numerous phrases and adjectives were descriptive of the helper described on the form (the format for assessing the perceived characteristics of each help-provider was similar to that used in Studies 1 and 2; analyses of responses to this questionnaire yielded total scores on several reliable multi-item factors). The participants were also asked several questions about their perceptions of each helper and his or her motive for helping. Three critical questions included on the questionnaire were as follows (again, the response format was similar to that used in Studies 1 and 2):

- How much do you like the reason that this helper gave for helping?
- Imagine yourself in a situation like the one described by the helper. How similar was his or her reason for helping to the reason that might motivate you to help in a situation like this?
- If you were the person described in this situation to whom the help was offered, and you knew *why* the helper was offering it to you, would you accept the help?

Analyses revealed that in these "everyday" helping situations, other-oriented helpers were rated as more likable, more honest, less devious, and as more effective helpers than were self-oriented helpers. In addition, participants: (1) indicated that they liked the other-oriented reasons for helping more than the self-oriented reasons, (2) rated the other-oriented reasons as more similar to the reason that might motivate them to help in a situation like this than the self-oriented reasons, and (3) indicated that they would be more willing to accept help from an other-oriented than a self-oriented helper. Although participants generally favored other-oriented helping over self-oriented helping, their judgments were found to be influenced by: (1) the closeness of the relationship between the helper and recipient, (2) the type of help provided, (3) the participants' gender, and (4) the gender of the helper-recipient dyad.

In general, an other-oriented helper was rated more favorably in a close than a distant relationship (additionally, participants indicated that they would be more willing to accept other-oriented help in a close relationship than in a distant one). Perhaps individuals rated other-oriented helpers in a distant relationship less favorably because they were more skeptical about the genuineness of a "concern for other" expressed by the helpers who had no prior relationship with the recipients.

Concerning the type of help provided, whereas participants indicated that they would be equally willing to accept other-oriented instrumental and other-oriented expressive help, they indicated that they would be more willing to accept self-oriented instrumental help than self-oriented expressive help. Providing action-oriented, instrumental help (e.g., assisting someone in painting his or her house) may be perceived as less personal and intimate than providing feelings-oriented, expressive help (e.g., comforting a sad or distressed individual). Therefore, providing expressive help for a selfish reason may seem more exploitative, and more of a violation of the (close or distant) relationship between the helper and recipient, than providing instrumental help for a selfish reason.

In general, other-oriented helpers in this preliminary study were rated more favorably by females than males, and self-oriented helpers were rated more favorably by males than females (additionally, female participants indicated they would be more willing to accept other-oriented help than did male participants; the opposite pattern was found for the willingness to accept self-oriented help). Similarly, participants favored other-oriented reasons for helping more in female dyads than in male dyads; in contrast, they favored self-oriented reasons more in male than female dyads. Another indication of the perceived gender-linked nature of self- and other-oriented helping emerged in this preliminary study: whereas other-oriented helpers were rated as more feminine than were self-oriented helpers, self-oriented helpers were rated as more masculine than were other-oriented helpers. Given our society's traditional sex-role socialization of females (emphasizing sensitivity and responsiveness to others) and males (emphasizing individualism and the value of endeavors stemming from self-interest; see Basow, 1992), perhaps it should not be surprising that in "everyday" helping situations, other-oriented helping was rated more favorably by (and for) females than males, and self-oriented helping was rated more favorably by (and for) males than females.

Summary and Concluding Comments

The major findings for Studies 1 and 2 were incongruent with the notion inferred from the helping literature (Batson, 1991, 1995; Eisenberg, 1982, 1986; Eisenberg et al., 1983, 1991; Hoffman, 1982, 1989; Krebs and Van Hesteren, 1994) that altruistically motivated helpers would be consistently evaluated more favorably than, and preferred over, egoistically motivated helpers. First, whereas the other-oriented help-providers in both studies (i.e., a lawyer in Study 1 and an orthopedic surgeon in Study 2) were rated as more likable, more honest, and less devious than the self-oriented help-providers, the self-oriented help-providers were rated as more ambitious, competent, and as earning more money than the other-oriented help-providers. Moreover, evidence from both studies suggests that the participants considered a help-provider's income to be associated with the characteristics perceived as more descriptive of a self-oriented than an other-oriented individual. Second, although the participants' "desire to hire" was found to be associated with (a) their perceptions of the help-provider's characteristics (Studies 1 and 2), (b) their own self-reported characteristics (Study 1), and (c) their anticipated affective state prior to seeking assistance (Studies 1 and 2), no clear relation was found in either study between the help-provider's orientation and the participants' desire to seek assistance from that help-provider.

In contrast to the ambivalence demonstrated in response to the altruistically and egoistically motivated professional help-providers presented in Studies 1 and 2, participants in a preliminary study of perceptions of "everyday" helpers demonstrated a clear preference for altruistically motivated assistance. Indeed, the other-oriented help-providers in the preliminary study were not only rated as more likable, more honest, and less devious than the self-oriented help-providers (as was true for the lawyers and physicians presented in Studies 1 and 2), but as more effective (i.e., competent) helpers too. Moreover, in contrast to the nonsignificant "desire to hire" results of Studies 1 and 2, participants in the preliminary study of "everyday" helping behavior indicated a greater willingness to accept aid from an individual whose assistance was motivated by a concern for others than an individual whose assistance was motivated by a concern for the self. Interestingly, participants' ratings of their willingness to accept assistance in the preliminary study were also found to be influenced by the closeness of the relationship between the helper and recipient, the type of help provided, and their gender. While it would be premature to draw any conclusions about the similarities and differences in individuals' perceptions of assistance provided in formal and informal settings, the pattern of results does suggest the broad range of situational and individual difference variables that may affect perceptions of, and reactions to, self-oriented and other-oriented help-providers.

Future experimental research will continue to systematically examine individuals' perceptions of altruistically and egoistically motivated helpers in professional and "everyday" helping situations (including instances of cross-gender, as well as same-gender, helping). Additionally, retrospective self-reports could be utilized to examine individuals' perceptions of help-providers' motives for offering assistance in more naturalistic settings. Such research could enable us to delineate more clearly the "situation" and "person" factors that influence individuals' responses to altruistically and egoistically motivated offers of assistance.

Notes

1. Following Bem's (1974) procedure, median splits on participants' masculinity and femininity scores on the BSRI were used to establish four sex-role groups (i.e., androgynous, masculine, feminine, and undifferentiated). An initial series of 2 x 2 x 2 x 4 (Gender of Participant x Gender of Lawyer x Lawyer Orientation x BSRI Group) ANOVAs revealed no consistent or interpretable findings involving BSRI Group. Therefore, this variable was not included in the ANOVAs reported in the text.
2. The correlations with "desire to hire" were also computed controlling for the effects of Gender of Participant and Gender of Lawyer. The pattern of partial correlations was found to be highly similar to the pattern of bivariate correlations reported in the text.
3. As in Study 1, median splits on participants' masculinity and femininity scores on the BSRI were used to establish four sex-role groups (i.e., androgynous, masculine, feminine, and undifferentiated). An initial series of 2 x 2 x 2 x 4 (Gender of Participant x Gender of Physician x Physician Orientation x BSRI Group) ANOVAs again revealed no consistent or interpretable findings involving BSRI Group. Therefore, as in Study 1, this variable was not included in the ANOVAs reported in the text.
4. The main effect for honesty was qualified by a significant interaction of Gender of Participant x Physician Orientation, $F(1,121) = 4.10$, $p < .05$. Simple effects *post hoc* tests revealed that although the male participants did not differ significantly in their ratings of the honesty of the other-oriented ($M = 6.29$) and self-oriented physician ($M = 6.14$), $F(1,121) = .13$, the female participants rated the other-oriented physician ($M = 7.00$) as more honest than the self-oriented physician ($M = 5.71$), $F(1,121) = 9.24, p < .01$.
5. The correlations with "desire to hire" were also computed controlling for the effects of Gender of Participant and Gender of Physician. As in Study 1, the pattern of partial correlations was found to be highly similar to the pattern of bivariate correlations reported in the text.
6. A central purpose of this study was to develop the stimuli and questionnaire for use in subsequent research on perceptions of "everyday" helping behavior. Toward this end, extensive manipulation checks were incorporated in the materials presented to the participants. In addition, only same-gender dyads (i.e., male helper-male recipient and female helper-female recipient) were included in the design of the study. As a result, this investigation is considered "preliminary," and the procedure and findings are presented here in an abbreviated manner.

References

Barnett, M. A. (1988). Reasons for not wanting help: Categories and developmental differences. *Journal of Genetic Psychology, 149*, 127–129.

Bart, P. (1994). Superstar, esq.: Legal eagles fly like stars. *Variety, 356* (October 3), 6, 26.

Basow, S. A. (1992). *Gender: Stereotypes and roles* (3rd Ed.). Pacific Grove, CA: Brooks/Cole.

Batson, C. D. (1990). How social an animal?: The human capacity for caring. *American Psychologist, 45*, 336–346.

Batson, C. D. (1991). *The altruism question: Toward a social-psychological answer.* Hillsdale, NJ: Erlbaum.

Batson, C. D. (1995). Prosocial motivation: Why do we help others? In A. Tesser (Ed.), *Advanced social psychology* (pp. 333–381). New York: McGraw-Hill.

Baumeister, R. F. (1995). Self and identity: An introduction. In A. Tesser (Ed.), *Advanced social psychology* (pp. 51–97). New York: McGraw-Hill.

Bem, S. L. (1974). The measurement of psychological androgyny. *Journal of Consulting and Clinical Psychology, 42*, 155–162.

Campbell, D. T. (1975). On the conflicts between biological and social evolution and between psychology and moral tradition. *American Psychologist, 30*, 1103–1126.

Caplan, L. (1995). Who ya gonna call? 1–800–sue me. *Newsweek, 125* (March 20), 36.

Carlo, G., Eisenberg, N., Troyer, D., Switzer, G., and Speer, A. L. (1991). The altruistic personality: In what contexts is it apparent? *Journal of Personality and Social Psychology, 61*, 450–458.

Clark, M. S. (1983). Some implications of close social bonds for help seeking. In B. M. DePaulo, A. Nadler, and J. D. Fisher (Eds.), *New directions in helping: Vol. 2. Help seeking* (pp. 205–233). New York: Academic Press.

Davis, M. H. (1983). Measuring individual differences in empathy: Evidence for a multidimensional approach. *Journal of Personality and Social Psychology, 44*, 113–126.

Eisenberg, N. (1982). The development of reasoning regarding prosocial behavior. In N. Eisenberg (Ed.), *The development of prosocial behavior* (pp. 219–250). New York: Academic Press.

Eisenberg, N. (1986). *Altruistic emotion, cognition, and behavior.* Hillsdale, NJ: Erlbaum.

Eisenberg, N., Lennon, R., and Roth, K. (1983). Prosocial development: A longitudinal study. *Developmental Psychology, 19*, 846–855.

Eisenberg, N., Miller, P. A., Shell, R., McNalley, S., and Shea, C. (1991). Prosocial development in adolescence: A longitudinal study. *Developmental Psychology, 27*, 849–857.

Fotheringham, A. (1994). The law according to the chequebook. *Maclean's, 107* (October 24), 60.

Gleick, E. (1996). Look who's talking. *Time, 147* (April 8), 41–42.

Hoffman, M. L. (1982). Development of prosocial motivation: Empathy and guilt. In N. Eisenberg (Ed.), *The development of prosocial behavior* (pp. 218–231). New York: Academic Press.

Hoffman, M. L. (1989). Empathy and prosocial activism. In N. Eisenberg, J. Reykowski, and E. Staub (Eds.), *Social and moral values* (pp. 65–86). Hillsdale, NJ: Erlbaum.

Hume, D. (1963). A treatise of human nature. In V. C. Chappell (Ed.), *The philosophy of David Hume* (pp. 11–312). New York: Modern Library (Original work published 1739).

Kaplan, D. A. (1994). Three for the defense. *Newsweek, 124* (July 11), 26–27.

Krebs, D. L., & Van Hesteren, F. (1994). The development of altruism: Toward an integrative model. *Developmental Review, 14,* 103–158.

Markus, H. R., and Kitayama, S. (1991). Culture and the self: Implications for cognition, emotion, and motivation. *Psychological Review, 98,* 224–253.

Nadler, A. (1991). Help-seeking behavior: Psychological costs and instrumental benefits. In M. S. Clark (Ed.), *Prosocial behavior* (pp. 290–311). Newbury Park, CA: Sage.

Phares, E. J., & Erskine, N. (1984). The measurement of selfism. *Educational and Psychological Measurement, 44,* 597–608.

Samuelson, R. J. (1992). I am a big lawyer basher. *Newsweek, 119* (April 27), 62.

Shaffer, D. (1994). *Social and personality development* (3rd Ed.). Pacific Grove, CA: Brooks/Cole.

Smith, A. (1966). *The theory of moral sentiments.* New York: A. M. Kelley (Original work published 1759).

Wallach, M. A., and Wallach, L. (1983). *Psychology's sanction for selfishness: The error of egoism in theory and therapy.* San Francisco, CA: W. H. Freeman.

7

The Linkage between Spurned Help and Burnout among Practicing Nurses

Wai Hing Cheuk, Bridget Swearse
Kwok Wai Wong, and
Sidney Rosen

In the study on helping and being helped, the area of how would-be helpers react when their offer of help is refused by a seemingly needy recipient received attention from researchers only recently. A model has been advanced to address this area of investigation (Cheuk and Rosen, 1992; Rosen, Mickler, and Spiers, 1986). Based on this model, the present study attempted to: (1) further establish the external validity of the model through assessing the spurning-burnout linkage in a sample of practicing nurses in Hong Kong, (2) explore whether social support from one's supervisor and one's colleague could buffer the adverse effects of spurning on burnout, and (3) examine the role of workload as a moderating factor.

According to the model, would-be helpers expect that their offer of help would be accepted. Subsequent rejection by the help recipient would be stressful to the helpers because the rejection violates their expectancy and carries negative implications on their self-image as being efficacious and caring to help others. Rejected helpers then cope through various modalities in order to restore their threatened self-image. The model further proposes that coping reactions to rejection are mediated by the extent to which the rejection violates helpers' prior expectations that the offer of help would be accepted by the recipient and the degree of importance the helper has attached to the acceptance of the offer, and moderated by situational factors such as the helper-recipient relationship and personal factors such as chronic self-perceptions of being efficacious to help others.

We first conducted laboratory experimental studies which allowed us to manipulate the outcome of an offer of help by a seemingly needy recipient, i.e., rejection or acceptance. The results showed that rejected helpers exhibited a variety of reactions that enabled them to maintain their self-image being threatened by the rejection. For instance, rejected helpers claimed that at the time they were considering whether to offer help, they actually had very little control over the decision as to whether to offer help. By making such a claim, rejected helpers could detach themselves from the decision which had led to an interpersonal failure—the rejection—and thereby maintain an illusion that they had not lost decision control. Rejected helpers also devalued the rejecter much more than the self, seemingly to diffuse the responsibility for the rejection from the self to the rejecter.

We also found support for the hypothesis that the impact of spurning on subsequent coping reactions would be mediated by violated expectancy of acceptance: When the extent of surprise at the outcome of the offer of help—as a measure of expectancy violation—was statistically controlled, the magnitude of the coping reactions was significantly reduced (Cheuk and Rosen, 1993). We also obtained support for the hypothesis of perceived importance to self or to the recipient serving also as the mediating variable: the reactions of the rejected helpers were the strongest when the acceptance was perceived as important to the self and important to the recipient (Cheuk and Rosen, 1996).

To assess whether the results we obtained with undergraduates experiencing an isolated rejection of help by a recipient can be generalized to reactions of professional caregivers who often face recurrent rejection of help by their clients, we examine if recurrent rejection of help would result in the long-term negative syndrome of burnout in different categories of professional helpers.

We found support for the spurning-burnout hypothesis in a sample of medical personnel (Mickler and Rosen, 1994), and in two samples of classroom teachers in Macau (Cheuk and Rosen, 1994; Cheuk, Wong, and Rosen, 1994). Cheuk and Swearse (unpublished) found evidence for the spurning-burnout hypothesis in another helping con-

text with a different group of professional caregivers—namely, nurses—
and a different category of help recipient—namely, patients—in Hong
Kong. The present study, as a related effort at establishing the external
validity for the spurned helpers' reactions, examined the spurning-
burnout hypothesis in yet another sample of practicing nurses in Hong
Kong. Our hypothesis was again that spurning would result in burnout.

Another objective of the present study was to explore the extent to
which social support could reduce the negative effects of being spurned.
A great deal of attention has been paid to social support in the past
twenty years and the literature so accumulated (e.g., Bishop, 1994;
Gottlieb, 1988; Shumaker and Brownell, 1984; Taylor, 1991) suggests
that social support can contribute directly to psychological well-being,
and can also buffer the adverse impact of stress on various indicators
of psychological health.

House (1981) differentiated social support into three different types:
informational, emotional, and material. In the context of nursing, informational social support refers to information from others that can
assist the spurned nurses to deal with the negative event of being
spurned. For instance, information from one's supervisor or colleague
may help the spurned nurses to realize that being spurned is not an
uncommon phenomenon and that patients reject help for a great number of reasons, which may not necessarily be related to the nurse's
task-oriented or interpersonal competence. Information from one's supervisor or colleague may assist the spurned nurses to relate to the
rejecting patients in ways that can overcome the resistance or to develop ways to relate to patients that would make their offers of help
more receptive.

Emotional social support refers to information from others that as-
sists the spurned nurses to deal with the emotional distress arising
from being spurned. For instance, words of concern and care from
one's supervisor or colleague would help soothe one's distress and be
beneficial in restoring one's threatened self-image.

There is some evidence that support from a particular source is
relatively more effective (e.g., Constable and Russell, 1986; Costanza,
Derlega, and Winstead, 1988; Rook, 1984; Russell, Altmaier, and Van
Velzen, 1987). For instance, Russell, Altmaier, and Van Velzen (1987)
surveyed teachers' stress in 47 job-related situations and found that
teachers who were more stressed were also more burned. Only support
from one's supervisor had a main effect and a buffering effect. These

researchers suggested that the uplifting of the teachers' self-esteem came more from supervisor support than from peer or family support. Constable and Russell (1986) investigated the impact of unpleasant working conditions, work pressure, and perceptions of control on burnout in practicing nurses. Unpleasant working conditions and work pressure were found to be associated with burnout. Only supervisor support was found to exert a main effect and a buffering effect.

Accordingly, in the present study, we explored whether or not supervisor support could reduce the adverse impact of spurning on burnout. To test the suggestion that the basis for the effectiveness of support from this source was an enhancement in the self-esteem of the stressed, we examined whether or not the support from the supervisor had been found to have bolstered one's self-esteem and whether or not the bolstering could reduce the impact of spurning on burnout. If it was the uplifting to one's self-esteem from the support that would buffer the spurned nurses from being burned, then spurned nurses who received support from their supervisor and found the support to have bolstered their self-esteem should experience less burnout than spurned nurses who received support from their supervisor but perceived that the support had not sufficiently uplifted their self-esteem. We thus predicted that spurned nurses who found the supervisor support to have bolstered their self-esteem would experience less burnout than would their counterparts who found the supervisor support to have bolstered their self-esteem to a lesser extent.

We suspect that supervisor support serves mainly as a form of emotional support, assisting the spurned nurses to deal more with their emotional distress and threatened self-perception than with the recurrent rejection by patients. It seems plausible that as fellow nurses are involved directly in interacting with patients than is the supervisor, information from fellow nurses would be more useful in assisting spurned nurses to overcome patient resistance than would information from the supervisor. We therefore examined whether or not spurned nurses received support from their colleagues and whether the support had helped them deal with the rejection. To the extent that the support from a colleague could help the spurned nurses to handle the rejection, the support should be able to reduce the adverse effects of spurning on burnout. We thus predicted that spurned nurses who received support from a colleague and found the support to have helped them cope with the rejection would experience less burnout than would their counterparts who received support from a colleague but had not perceived the support to have assisted them to cope with the rejection.

We were also interested in the extent to which the workload undertaken by the nurses would moderate the impact of spurning on burnout. A heavy workload, in addition to being a stressor in itself (e.g., Caplan et al., 1975), would also leave the nurses with little time to adequately cope with patient rejection, such as failing to develop ways to overcome the resistance. A heavy workload would therefore intensify the impact of spurning and burnout. We thus predicted that spurned nurses with a heavy workload would be more burned out than would their counterparts who had a less heavy workload.

Method

Respondents

Practicing nurses enrolled in a refresher program of study at the Open Learning Institute of Hong Kong (Hong Kong) were invited to participate in a study on their work experience. One-hundred seventy-two out of four-hundred nurses agreed to take part in the study. They were each given a questionnaire to be completed and returned in two weeks' time. The questionnaire, in Chinese, measured spurning, social support, workload, and burnout.

The sample was predominantly female (87 percent), the average age being 28.39 (SD = 6.34), and average years of working experience was nine (SD = 4.07).

Measures

Spurning. A twelve-item measure of perceived spurning in the nursing context, which was developed in a previous study (Cheuk et al., 1997), was used. Respondents rated the extent to which patients resist their offer of help, on scales each of which ranged from *applies very little to me* (1) to *applies very much to me* (11). An example is: "Patients feel more reluctant to approach me for help than to approach my fellow colleagues." Internal consistency among the 12 items (*alpha* = .717) was considered adequate. A composite was constructed through simple summation of the items. The sample showed an adequate distribution of scores (*M*= 50.28, SD = 11.14, with a range from 22 to 99).

Respondents were differentiated into those who were more spurned and those less spurned through dichotomizing the range of scores obtained.

Social support. Two dichotomized (feeling supported versus not feeling supported) items were used to measure support from one's supervisor and support from one's co-worker, respectively. Respondents were also asked to indicate, on an 11-point scale (1 = very little; 11 = very much), the extent to which the support from the supervisor had bolstered their self-esteem. Respondents were distinguished into those who found the support to have bolstered their self-esteem and those who found the support to have bolstered their self-esteem to a lesser extent by dichotomizing the scores obtained. Respondents were also asked to indicate, on an 11-point scale (1 = very little; 11 = very much), the extent to which the support from the colleague had bolstered their self-esteem. Respondents were distinguished into those who found the support to have bolstered their self-esteem and those who found the support to have bolstered their self-esteem to a lesser extent by dichotomizing the scores obtained.

Likewise, respondents were also asked to indicate, on an 11-point scale (1 = very little; 11 = very much) the extent to which the support from a colleague had helped them deal with the rejection. Respondents were categorized into those who found the support to have helped them deal with the rejection and those who found the support to have helped them deal with the rejection to a lesser extent by dichotomizing the scores obtained.

Burnout. We used a 16-item scale of burnout developed by Mickler and Rosen (1994), on scales ranging from *applies very little to me* (1) to *applies very much to me* (11). Five items were used to reflect emotional exhaustion (e.g., feel frustrated), six items were employed to indicate personal accomplishment (e.g., accomplish a lot at work), and five items assessed depersonalization (e.g., I don't care much what happens to my patients). The alpha of the items was .72, which was regarded as of acceptable magnitude. A composite of burnout was constructed by summing the items. The sample exhibited an adequate distribution ($M = 52.92$, SD = 13.60, with a range from 20 to 104).

Results

To examine the hypothesized effects of spurning on burnout, a two-way analysis of variance (more spurned versus less spurned; supervisor support versus no supervisor support) was conducted on the burnout measure. There was a significant main effect of spurning, $F(1,168) = 17.34$, $p < .0001$, indicating that nurses who were spurned expressed greater burnout ($M = 67.46$) than did nurses who were less spurned ($M = 57.11$).

In contrast to our expectation, the Spurning X Supervisor Support interaction effects did not reach significance, $F(1,169) = 2.16$, ns, showing that spurned nurses who received support from their supervisor experienced burnout ($M = 66.02$) to the same extent as did their counterparts who did not receive support from their supervisor ($M = 67.16$), $F(1,169) = 1.16$, ns.

To examine the hypothesized impact of supervisor support on self-esteem, a two-way analysis of variance (more spurned versus less spurned; bolstered self-esteem versus bolstered self-esteem less) was performed on the measure of burnout. The interaction effects revealed that spurned nurses who found the supervisor support to have bolstered their expressed self-esteem were burned to the same degree ($M = 63.19$) as were spurned nurses who found the supervisor support to have bolstered their esteem to a lesser extent ($M = 64.22$), $F(1,103) = 1.34$, ns. The results did not support our hypothesis of self-esteem bolstering as the basis of the effectiveness of supervisor support.

To assess the hypothesized effects of support from one's colleague, a two-way analysis of variance was conducted. The results indicated significant interaction effects: Spurned nurses who received support from their colleague expressed less burnout ($M = 52.31$) than did spurned nurses who did not receive support from their colleague ($M = 62.49$), $F(1,167) = 13.67$, $p < .0001$. Two other two-way analyses of variance were performed to examine whether or not bolstering to one's self-esteem and assisting in coping with the rejection served to moderate the impact of spurning on burnout. Interaction effects were found only in the latter case: Spurned nurses who found the support from a colleague to have helped them cope with the rejection expressed less burnout ($M = 56.89$) than did spurned nurses who found the support from a colleague to have helped them cope with the rejection to a lesser extent ($M = 68.59$), $F(1,121) = 12.32$, $p < .0001$.

A two-way analysis of variance (more spurned versus less spurned; heavy workload versus less heavy workload) was performed to assess the moderating impact of workload. As hypothesized, spurned nurses with a heavier workload suffered greater burnout ($M = 64.12$) than did their counterparts who had a less heavy workload ($M = 53.29$), $F(1,166)$ $= 9.47, p < .001$.

Correlational analyses were performed to assess the association between years of working experience and burnout, and between age and burnout. Our prediction was that both of the background variables would be negatively associated with burnout. The results showed a positive correlation between age and burnout, $r = .22, p < .05$, and nonsignificant association between years of working experience and burnout.

Discussion

The hypothesized main effect of spurning on burnout was obtained once again, thus replicating the results we found in a previous study with a different sample of practicing nurses in Hong Kong. So far we have acquired evidence that spurning was conducive to burnout in two categories of professional caregivers—classroom teachers in Macau and medical personnel in Hong Kong and the United States. These studies offered converging evidence that the model on rejected helpers' experience and reactions is applicable to an understanding of the reactions of professional caregivers facing recurrent rejections of their offers of help by their clients/patients. We will continue to examine the applicability of the model to other categories of helpers, such as social workers and counselors, to further establish its external validity.

The spurning-burnout linkage obtained in the present study and in a previous one (Cheuk et al., 1997) indicate that being spurned by patients is a potent stressor for nurses that would result in adverse consequences for the nurses themselves and for their perceptions of and relationships with patients. Initial nurse training programs should incorporate some type of inoculation on rejection of help by patients through guiding pre-service nurses to harbor realistic expectations of the occurrence of spurning, and teaching them how to prevent spurning and how to deal with it when it occurs.

The Spurning X Support from Supervisor interaction effects did not reach significance, indicating that spurned nurses who received support from their supervisor experienced burnout to the same extent as did their counterparts who did not receive support from this source. The results are not consistent with results of previous studies which documented the positive impact of supervisor support (e.g., Russell,

Altmaier, and Van Velzen, 1987). It was suggested that supervisor support is relatively more effective than peer support because of its greater ability to enhance the self-esteem of the stressed individuals. We obtained no evidence for this suggestion: Spurned nurses who found the supervisor support to have uplifted their self-esteem admitted burnout to the same extent as did their counterparts who found the supervisor support to have uplifted their self-esteem to a lesser extent. Perhaps our insignificant results were due mainly to a failure in our measure of supervisor support to pinpoint the basis for the usefulness of support from the supervisor. Future studies should explore such bases. Perhaps it has to do with the supervisors' power to monitor and reward/punish the performance of the nurses. It is also plausible that the support offered by the supervisor could assist the spurned nurses to deal effectively with the rejection and thereby restore their self-esteem.

The Spurning X Peer Support interaction effects showed that spurned nurses experienced less burnout when they received support from their peers than when they did not receive such support. The buffering impact of peer support has not been reported in previous studies on peer support (e.g., Constable and Russell, 1986). Perhaps the results have to do with the more generic, categorical nature of the support measure that we used in the present study. It could also be related to the more communal orientation of Chinese nurses under investigation. It could also be related to the type of tasks that nurses do, a failure at which would sometimes lead to fatal consequences for patients, thus calling for continued exchanges of resources and support among the nurses who happen to work together.

No Spurning X Bolstering Self-esteem interaction effects were obtained, indicating that having one's self-esteem bolstered from peer support did not contribute to coping with recurrent patient rejection. The results indicate, nevertheless, that spurned nurses' self-esteem can be affected by support from one colleague, but with its effects unrelated to burnout. On the other hand, the Spurning X Dealing with Rejection interaction effects reached significance, showing that spurned nurses who found the support from a peer to have helped them deal with the rejection expressed less burnout than did spurned nurses who found the peer support to have helped them deal with rejection to a lesser extent. Such results suggest that the basis for the beneficial buffering impact of peer support lies more in its enhancement of the ability of the spurned nurses to cope with recurrent patient rejection.

Granted that support from a colleague is effective in reducing the negative effects of spurning on burnout, what needs to be examined is how such support is communicated among nurses. For instance, is the exchange initiated by the spurned nurses or by the colleague offering the help? How do the partners feel about the supportive exchange? How is the exchange conducted? Future studies should examine these aspects of supportive interactions among nurses, paying attention also to the negative aspects of supportive interactions. In this connection, it has been said that a certain type of support from a particular source may not be perceived as appropriate to the relationship, which may trigger further stress, such as the need to respond to a seeming initiation of a relationship (e.g., Shinn, Lehman, and Wong, 1998). Even when the support is appropriate to the relationship, the receipt may induce other stress, such as a felt obligation to reciprocate in the future, which the recipient may feel unable to honor (e.g., Shumaker and Brownell, 1984) or as a sense of dependence (Fisher and Nadler, 1982).

The results indicated that a heavy workload exerted not only a debilitating (main) effects on burnout, but also hindered spurned nurses' ability to adequately cope with recurrent patient rejection. The results are consistent with what other studies have documented (e.g., Kahn and Byosiere, 1992). Hospital administrative personnel could thus make use of this information to properly arrange workload with a view to promoting the physical and psychological health of nurses, as well as their willingness to continue to stay in the nursing profession.

References

Bishop, G. D. (1994). *Health psychology: Integrating mind and body.* Boston, MA: Allyn & Bacon.

Caplan, R. D. Cobb, S., French, J. R. P., Harrison, R., and Pinneau, S. R. (1975). *Job demands and worker health.* National Institute of Safety and Health, U.S. Department of Health, Washington, D.C.: U.S. Government Printing Office.

Cheuk, W. H. and Rosen, S. (1994). Validating a "Spurning Scale" for teachers. *Current Psychology, 13,* 241–247.

Cheuk, W. H. and Rosen, S. (1992). Helpers' reactions: When help is rejected by friends or strangers. *Journal of Social Behavior and Personality, 7,* 445–458.

Cheuk, W. H. and Rosen, S. (1993). How efficacious, caring Samaritans cope with unexpected rejection. *Current Psychology, 12,* 99–112.

Cheuk, W. H. and Rosen, S. (1996). The moderating influence of perceived importance on rejected helpers' reactions. *Basic and Applied Social Psychology, 18*(2), 195–210.

Cheuk,. W. H., Wong, K. S., and Rosen, S. (1994). The effects of spurning and social support on teacher burnout. *Journal of Social Behavior and Personality, 9,* 657–664.

Cheuk, W. H. Wong, K.S., Swearse, B., and Rosen, S. (1997). Stress preparation, coping style, and nurses' experience of being spurned by patients. *Journal of Social Behavior and Personality, 12,* 1055–1064.

Constable, J. F. and Russell, D. W. (1986). The effects of social support and the work environment upon burnout among nurses. *Journal of Human Stress, 12,* 20–26.

Constanza, R. S., Derlega, V J., and Winstead, B. A. (1988). Positive and negative forms of social support: Effects of conversational topics on coping with stress among same-sex friends. *Journal of Experimental Social Psychology, 24,* 182–193.

Fisher, J. D., & Nadler, A. (1982). Determinants of recipient reactions to aid: Donor-recipient similarity and perceived dimension of problem. In T. A. Wills (Ed.), *Basic processes in helping relationships* (pp. 131–152). New York: Academic Press.

Gottlieb, B. H. (Ed.). (1988). *Marshaling social support: Formats, processes, and effects.* Newbury Park, CA: Sage.

House, J. S. (1981). *Work stress and social support.* Reading, MA: Addison-Wesley.

Kahn, R. L. and Byosiere, P. (1992). Stress in organizations. In M. D. Dunnette and L. Hough (Eds.), *Handbook of industrial and organizational psychology* (pp. 571–650). Palo Alto, CA: Consulting Psychologists Press.

Maslach, C. and Jackson, S. E. (1982). Burnout in health professionals: A social psychological analysis. In G. S. Sanders and J. Suls (Eds.), *Social psychology of health and illness* (pp. 227–250). Hillsdale, NJ: Lawrence Erlbaum.

Mickler, S. and Rosen, S. (1994). Burnout in spurned medical caregivers and the impact of expectancy training. *Journal of Applied Social Psychology, 24,* 2110–2131.

Rook, K. S. (1984). The negative side of social interaction: Impact on psychological well-being. *Journal of Personality and Social Psychology, 46,* 1097–1108.

Rosen, S., Mickler, S., and Collins, J. E. (1987). Reactions of would-be helpers whose offer of help is spurned. *Journal of Personality and Social Psychology, 53,* 288–297.

Rosen, S., Mickler, S., and Spiers, C. (1986). The spurned philanthropist. *Humboldt Journal of Social Relations, 13,* 145–158.

Russell, D. W., Altmaier, E., and Van Velzen, D. (1987). Job-related stress, social support, and burnout among classroom teachers. *Journal of Applied Psychology, 72(2),* 269–274.

Shinn, M., Lehman, S., and Wong, N. W. (1984). Social interactions and social support. *Journal of Social Issues, 40(4),* 55–76.

Shumaker, S. A. and Brownell, A. (1984). Towards a theory of social support: Closing conceptual gaps. *Journal of Social Issues, 40(4),* 11–36.

Taylor,. S. (1991). *Health psychology.* New York: McGraw-Hill.

8

Doctrinal Orthodoxy, Religious Orientation, and Anthropocentrism

C. Edward Snodgrass and Larry Gates

Chandler and Dreger (1993) define anthropocentrism as "a doctrine which posits humanity as the centerpiece of the universe and sees the well-being of mankind as the ultimate purpose of things" (p. 169). Their *Anthropocentrism Scale* (AS) was developed primarily as a means of validating the construct of anthropocentrism within a "nomological net" (Cronbach and Meehl, 1955) of adjacent constructs. As suggested by a survey of the relevant literature, basic anthropocentric attitudes were found, by Chandler and Dreger, to include, but not necessarily be limited to the following views: agreeableness to the exploitation of the environment, a perceived separateness of man and nature, views of humanity as superior to nature, and a perception of man's life on Earth as exceptional, which may also be transferred to one's beliefs about any afterlife. Consequently, AS items were formulated to reflect these basic anthropocentric attitudes.

After addressing basic psychometric issues regarding the AS, Chandler and Dreger (1993) conducted an assessment of its construct validity by evaluating Anthropocentrism Scale results against a backdrop of other measures. The interrelatedness of anthropocentrism to various constructs within its proposed nomological net was assessed by means of correlating Anthropocentrism Scale scores with scores from the following instruments: *Exner's Self-Focus Sentence Completion* (Exner,

1973); *The Xenophobia Scale* (Campbell and McCandless, 1951); *The Philosophies of Human Nature Scale* (Wrightsman, 1963); *Kameron's Scale* (Kameron, 1975, as cited in Chandler & Dreger, 1993). *Kameron's Scale* includes four subscales: *K1—Conservationist vs. Exploitationist, K2—Non man-under-nature vs. Man-under-nature and hostile toward animals, K3—Nonfear of outdoors vs. Fear of outdoors,* and *K4—Antitechnology vs. Protechnology. The Environmental Behavior List* (Chandler, 1981, as cited in Chandler & Dreger, 1993) and *Internal vs. External Control* (Rotter, 1966) were also included. The effects on AS scores of the categorical variables, parental socioeconomic status, sex, race, religion, political party, and political ideology were evaluated using separate ANOVAs for each.

Pearson rs indicated that high AS scores (anthropocentric) were correlated positively with ethnocentrism ($r = .36, p < .05$) and negatively with self-reported environmentally conscious behaviors ($r = -.47, p < .05$). AS scores were also correlated with exploitation of the environment (K1)($r = .60, p < .05$), with non-man-under-nature (K2)($r = .33, p < .05$), with fear of outdoors (K3)($r = .58, p < .05$), and with protechnology (K4)($r = .43, p < .05$). Though predicted, no significant correlations were found to exist between AS scores and egocentrism, perception of human nature, or locus of control. Furthermore, AS scores did not differ significantly as a function of sex, religion, political party, or political ideology.

The authors contend that the correlation between anthropocentrism and ethnocentrism are central to the understanding of anthropocentrism. This correlation, though not particularly high, does indicate that ethnocentric views can be extended to the nonhuman environment. In a companion study (Dreger & Chandler, 1993), a LISREL confirmatory factor analysis was also conducted with a sample of 74 participants. The predicted latent factors (Anthropocentrism & Ethnocentrism) were found to be positively correlated ($r = .585, p < .01$), with each showing separate relations to the other measured constructs.

The first of these two studies is introduced with an explanation of the historical foundations of anthropocentric attitudes. It is interesting that the negative role of religion is emphasized, with the Judeo-Christian heritage taking the brunt of the blame. At first glance, one experimental finding appears contradictory to this premise (i.e., there was no relationship between religion and anthropocentrism). However, possible group homogeneity, with regard to religion, was a likely cause of this, though not explicitly stated. Though the link between religion and anthropocentrism—generically speaking—is currently accepted (Schaeffer, 1970; Berry, 1988), it appears that one limitation regarding the validation of the AS is the lack of exploration of possible relationships between alternative religious variables and anthropocentrism.

Religion and Environmental Concern

As previously stated, Western religion (i.e., Judeo-Christian) has taken much of the blame for the environmental crisis. This notion was popularized within the academic community by White's (1967) "The Historical Roots of Our Ecological Crisis." He cites Genesis 1:26:

> And God said, let us make man in our image, after our likeness: and let them have dominion over the fish of the sea, and over the fowl of the air and over the cattle, and over all the earth, and over every creeping thing that creepeth upon the earth.

White's hypothesis, that Christianity is responsible for the anthropocentric worldview of the West, has been tested by many researchers of psychology, sociology, and religion. In 1984, Hand and Van Liere reported that among Judeo-Christian denominations, independent of social background variables, there were significant differences regarding environmental attitudes. It was found that the more conservative denominations (e.g., Mormons and Baptists) were generally less concerned about environmental issues and had a stronger "mastery over nature" belief set than the more liberal denominations (e.g., Episcopal, Presbyterian, and Methodist; [p. 561]). Similarly, Shaiko (1987) found that even among "environmentalists" differences are demonstrated between Judeo-Christian and non-Judeo-Christian groups and among various Judeo-Christian denominations, in measures of mastery over nature and environmental concern. Furthermore, Eckberg and Blocker (1989) hypothesized that the "sacredness of the Bible" would serve as a predictor of environmental attitudes (p. 510). Subjects were categorized based on their religion and denomination. Along with a measure of environmental concern, a measure of biblical literalism was also administered. It was a measure of biblical literalism, that above all other measures, correlated *consistently* with lowered environmental concern, thus providing "firm" support to White's thesis (p. 516).

This research has been criticized to some degree by Greeley (1993) who contends that political ideology and "religious image" should be taken into account and that direct relations between religion and environmental concern are "spurious" (p. 27). Religious image is characterized by one's "more gracious narrative image of God as Mother, Spouse, Lover, Friend, as opposed to Father, Master, Judge, and King" (p. 22). This image was stated to be intertwined within the framework of a denomination embracing the concept of biblical literalism, (i.e., *Fundamentalism*); however this narrative image of God proved to have predictive power, beyond that of denomination. Consequently it was determined that "Christians who reject the various levels of rigidity, are as likely as anyone else to support environmental spending" (pp. 27–28). Though the findings of this research do support the importance of the above variables, they are limited by the fact that environmental concern was measured by a single survey item related to governmental spending.

A 1993 study by Guth, Kellstedt, Smidt, and Green was conducted in a similar manner to that of Eckberg and Blocker (1989), however political correlates and more demographic variables were taken into account. Even above and beyond these political and demographic variables, similar results were found. Fundamentalism again predicted a lack of environmental concern in comparison to other "religious identities" that even exceeded political ideology—which was predicted by Greeley (1993) to be an underlying variable influencing environmental concern (p. 376). It is clear that various aspects of religion, in many ways, may influence beliefs regarding the importance of environmental issues. Certainly, fundamentalism/literal biblical interpretation seems central to this theme.

Fundamentalism

Marsden (1980) and Wilcox, Linzey, and Jelen (1991) describe the fundamentalist approach to religion as incorporating biblical literalism, high supernaturalism, belief in the second coming and the end of times, and furthermore an unconcerned view regarding the reform of this *world*. At a glance, it seems quite logical that these views would possibly be correlated with an absence or lack of environmental concern. Indeed, based on the research that has addressed these hypotheses, the correlations, are in fact, stated to exist.

Similar to its correlation with a lack of environmental concern (hypothetically stemming from anthropocentrism) discussed earlier, fundamentalism has also been found to correlate moderately with many other discriminatory attitudes regarding race, gender, sexual orientation, and political ideology (McFarland, 1989). However, the research on prejudice and religion is not traditionally explained only by correlates of fundamentalism, but rather, very often by measures of *religious orientation*. This variable, so far, has been ignored by researchers as a possible religious correlate of environmental concern.

Religious Orientation

Extrinsic and Intrinsic Religious Orientation. Though the measurement and scientific study of religious behaviors (e.g., church attendance, prayer, etc.) provide useful information, many social scientists contend that a more accurate understanding of piousness must extend well beyond these measures. It has been found that within the population lie a variety of attitudes toward religion based on the *motives* that influence personal religious beliefs and behaviors. Through the measurement of these underlying motives, a more useful, however complex, understanding of religiousness is gained (Wulff, 1991). One very popular mode of viewing religiosity at a theoretical level is in terms of Allport's (1959) Extrinsic (E) and Intrinsic (I) religious orientations. Individuals characterized by the E orientation

> are disposed to use religion for their own ends. . . . Extrinsic values are always instrumental and utilitarian. Persons with this orientation may find religion useful in a variety of ways—to provide security and solace, sociability and distraction, status and self-justification. The embraced creed is lightly held or else selectively shaped to fit more primary needs. In theological terms the extrinsic type turns to God, but without turning away from self.

On the other hand, individuals having an intrinsic religious orientation

> find their master motive in religion. Other needs, strong as they may be, are regarded as of less ultimate significance, and they are, so far as possible, brought into harmony with the religious beliefs and prescriptions. Having embraced a creed the individual endeavors to internalize it and follow it fully. It is in this sense that he *lives* his religion. (Allport & Ross, 1967, p. 434)

The rationale for this distinction can be seen in Allport's earlier writing. In *The Individual and His Religion* (1950), Allport states that,

A faith centered in self-advantage is bound to break up. To endure at all it must envisage a universe that extends beyond personal whims and is anchored in values that transcend the immediate interest of the individual as interpreted by himself. (p. 120)

The history of conceptualizing degrees of Allport's I and E orientations as *measurable* began with Wilson (1960), in his analysis of extrinsic religiousness and anti-Semitism, followed by Feagin (1964), who added the intrinsic dimension to his measurement. These instruments were later expanded upon by Allport and Ross (1967), who, in their seminal study on prejudice and churchgoers, improved upon the reliability of Feagin's scale, renaming it the Religious Orientation Scale (ROS). During the following decades the ROS has been utilized extensively in the scientific study of religion. Consequently, in his 1985 review and meta-analysis, Donahue (1985) states that "no approach to religiousness has had greater impact on the empirical psychology of religion" (p. 400). Gorsuch concurred, referring to the I and E typologies as "the most empirically useful definitions of religion" (1988, p. 210).

Such acceptance does not come without debate, however. There has been criticism concerning the utility of the ROS, dating as early as 1971 (Dittes; Hunt & King); and even some twenty years later (Kirkpatrick & Hood, 1990) the debate continues. Some of the conflict over the ROS stems from the findings of factor-analytic research by Genia (1993), Gorsuch and Macpherson (1989), and Kirkpatrick (1989). It was found, in each of these studies, that with further investigation of the factor structure of the ROS, three dimensions actually appear, replacing the original two-factor structure. These findings have convinced some (e.g., Kirkpatrick, 1989; Kirkpatrick & Hood, 1990, 1991) to propose the discontinued study of I/E religiosity, calling for more elaborate multidimensional measures.

Others, however (e.g., Gorsuch, 1988; Gorsuch & McPherson, 1989; Masters, 1991), see these findings as a positive sign for continued study of the I/E paradigm. The results of Gorsuch and McPherson's (1989) study were in agreement with the other factor analytic studies in that the Intrinsic dimension remained intact, while the Extrinsic dimension was found to consist of two separate and distinct elements, labeled *Ep* and *Es*. In their discussion of the resulting I/E-Revised Scale, Gorsuch and McPherson describe Ep as "personally oriented" while Es was described as "socially oriented" (1989, p. 348).

Religion as Quest

In the search for *alternative* explanations of religiousness, Batson (1976) and Batson and Ventis (1982) developed a unique typology, extending beyond the I/E framework, however also based, ironically, on the same early writings of Allport. Allport states that, "the final attribute is its essentially heuristic character. An heuristic belief is one that is held tentatively until it can be confirmed or until it helps us discover a more valid belief" (1950, p. 81). In agreement with Allport's statement that, "the mature religious sentiment is ordinarily fashioned in the workshop of doubt" (1950, p. 83), Batson and Ventis named their third dimension of religious orientation "Religion as Quest." Quest has been later described as

> involving honestly facing existential questions in their complexity, while at the same time resisting clear-cut pat answers. An individual who approaches religion in this way recognizes that he or she does not know, and probably never will know, the final truth about such matters. Still, the questions are deemed important, and, however tentative and subject to change, the answers are sought. (Batson & Schoenrade, 1991a, p. 417)

In an attempt to quantify the extent to which this mode of religiousness exists, the nine-item Interactional scale (popularly designated as the Quest scale) was devised (Batson, 1976). Later, a six-item Quest scale was introduced and recommended (Batson & Ventis, 1982). In 1991, a final revision was made after issues of reliability were examined (Batson & Schoenrade, 1991b). It should be noted that the Quest orientation has been one of controversy since its inception. Donahue (1985) and Wulff (1991, p. 238) argue that the "enduring" tentativeness and doubt, exemplified by the Quest orientation, are not representative of the "mature" sentiment Allport envisioned. To date, the quest orientation remains quite controversial, and as Wulff states, "Clarifying and assessing the quest orientation is surely one of the psychology of religion's most urgent tasks" (1991, p. 242).

Correlates of Religious Orientation

Donahue (1985) found fairly consistent results overall in his meta-analysis of over 70 published studies regarding I, E, and Quest. The I orientation was found to have no consistent predictive abilities regarding prejudice, or many other variables not directly linked to religiousness; however I did predict many traditional religious variables (church attendance, etc.), while, not surprisingly, E was found to be significantly correlated with prejudice and noncorrelated with traditional measures of religiousness. E was also found to be correlated with measures of dogmatism, fear of death, and belittlement of an innocent victim.

Though the I and E orientations are given adequate support for their validity, Donahue remains skeptical of the utility of the Quest orientation, contending that it is possibly a measure of agnosticism, or immature religious doubt. Batson and Schoenrade (see 1991a) disagree, citing a preponderance of studies that advocate the validity of the quest scale. Regarding the correlates of Quest, it has been found that Quest is negatively correlated with racial and gender-related prejudice (McFarland, 1989), positively correlated with complexity of religious thought (Batson & Raynor-Price, 1983), and positively associated with helping behavior in response to a victim's needs (Batson, 1976).

Present Study

The purpose of this study was to examine the relationships of Christian doctrinal orthodoxy and religious orientation (including Quest) to anthropocentric beliefs as measured by the AS, thereby adding to the research on religio-psychological variables of environmental concern. By doing so, some contribution to the construct validity of the AS was expected to be made by the expansion of its nomological net.

Given the correlation between anthropocentrism and ethnocentrism, it was hypothesized that individuals scoring high in doctrinal orthodoxy (approaching fundamentalism), would tend to be more anthropocentric, as they tend to be more ethnocentric. The same hypothesis was made for those found to be extrinsically religious. It is the instrumentality of the Extrinsic orientation on which this second hypothesis was based. For the purposes of this study, the distinction between Ep and Es was considered possibly extraneous. Whether the correlation would extend down to Ep and Es as two independently unique relationships was not hypothesized, though this possibility was explored. It was hypothesized that high Quest scores would be negatively correlated with anthropocentrism, just as they are associated with lowered ethnocentrism. Finally, no specific hypotheses were made with regard to individuals who are intrinsically religious; however this relationship was also explored.

Method

Subjects

Participants included in this study were 144 undergraduates enrolled in various psychology courses at a medium-sized southern university. Of the 100 women in the sample, 31 were African American, 68 were Caucasian, and 1 was Asian American. Of the 44 men in the sample, 9 were African American and 35 were Caucasian. Participants' ages ranged from 19 to 49, with a mean of 26.6 and a standard deviation of 7.69. Participants were given extra course credit for their participation in the study.

Instruments

Anthropocentrism Scale. The AS is a 30-item, 7-point Likert scaled instrument, consisting of items designed to gauge varying degrees of anthropocentric attitudes. Chandler and Dreger (1993) report a possible range of scores from 30 to 210, with a reported mean, for their sample, of 119.3 and standard deviation of 23.77. Additional psychometric properties of the AS were explored in two phases. First, after examining item-test reliability coefficients, five items were dropped from the original 35-item AS (Chandler, 1978, 1981, as cited in Chandler & Dreger, 1993), leaving 30 items, ranging from alphas of .23 to .66. Test-retest reliability (2-week interval) for a 32-item version of the AS was reported to be .91.

Doctrinal Orthodoxy Scale

The Doctrinal Orthodoxy Scale (DOS) was developed by Batson (1976, p. 32), in his "development of a three dimensional model of religious orientation." The DOS is a 12-item scale, constructed as a measure of doctrinal orthodoxy, specifically within the Christian tradition. Five of the items specifically mention Jesus Christ in their syntax (see Batson, 1976). As for the psychometric properties of the DOS, limited information was found in the literature. It was reported that with the exception of one item ("I believe in a transcendent realm"), all items were significantly correlated with each other in the positive direction ($p < .05$). The median correlation coefficient was reported as $r > .50$ (Batson, 1976, p. 33). From a rational-intuitive standpoint, the items included on the DOS seem to adequately tap the construct of fundamentalism as described by Marsden (1980) and Wilcox, Linzey, and Jelen (1991). Furthermore, McFarland (1989) equates Christian orthodoxy to fundamentalism; it was on this premise that the DOS was included.

I/E-Revised Scale

After revising the ROS based on the findings of previous factor analytic research, a 14-item I/E-Revised Scale (I/E-R) was proposed by Gorsuch and McPherson (1988). The I/E-R included three Ep (extrinsic-personal) items, three Es (extrinsic-social) items, and eight I (intrinsic) items. The I/E-R appeared to be confirmed as a more psychometrically sound instrument than its 20-item predecessor with regard to the new two-factor structure of the extrinsic scale, and though the revised extrinsic scales (Ep and Es) each have regrettably low reliabilities (alpha = .57 and .58, respectively), the combined Ep/Es reliability (.65) was considered no worse than that of the original Extrinsic scale (.66). Therefore, Gorsuch and McPherson recommended the use of the I/E-R in future research examining religiosity in the context of the I/E framework.

Revised Quest Scale

Similar to the criticisms of the ROS, questions regarding the construct validity (Donahue, 1985; Hood & Morris, 1985) and the reliability (McFarland, 1989; Ponton and Gorsuch, 1988) of the Quest scale have been brought to attention. Validity concerns were addressed by Batson and Schoenrade (1991a) convincingly, with a thorough presentation of prior research findings related to the specific questions raised. Reliability concerns, however, were not so easily dismissed. In a companion report, Batson and Schoenrade (1991b) reported that though test-retest reliability (.63) was acceptable (Batson and Schoenrade, 1985 as cited in Batson & Schoenrade, 1991b), internal reliability data for the six-item scale was quite unstable, with the average Cronbach's alpha estimated to be near .50. Recognizing that this was probably due to the low number of items included on the scale, six additional items were added. The resulting 12-item Revised Quest scale was reported as having adequate internal consistency, with alpha coefficients now ranging from .75 to .82. The 12-item scale was also reported as being highly positively correlated (ES ranging from .85 to .90) with the six-item scale.

Procedure

The AS, DOS, I/E-R, and Quest scales were combined back to back on separate pages, but numbered consecutively throughout. To maintain consistency, all item responses were based on a 7-point Likert scale, scored 0–6, with 1-point increments. Separate electronic scoring sheets were included in the instrument handout. Participants were read a statement regarding the purpose of the study, along with instructions. It was explained that their participation was strictly voluntary, and they could, at any time, withdraw from the study. Care was made to limit potential examiner bias by offering no explanations regarding the rationale of the study or for the types of items included in the handout. Prior to testing, it was stated that anyone having questions could contact the examiner after completion of the study.

Results

Psychometric Properties

Prior to correlational analyses, the psychometric properties of the instruments being utilized were investigated. The data are summarized in Table 8.1.

Adequate inter item reliability coefficients (Cronbach's alpha) were found for all instruments, within the sample. Relatively normal distributions of all scales, excluding doctrinal orthodoxy, were found. Among the sample, DOS scores maintained a highly negative skew, indicating the collective acceptance of Christian doctrinal orthodoxy.

Correlations

To examine the independent effects of the specified measures of

TABLE 8.1
Means, Standard Deviations, Range, and Reliabilities for Scores
on the AS, I, E, Es, Ep, Quest, and DOS Scales

	Mean	St. dev.	Actual range	Possible range	Reliability[a]
Anthropocentrism Scale	95.22	24.87	36-153	0-180	.87
Intrinsic Orientation	33.88	9.04	1-48	0-48	.82
Extrinsic Orientation	16.67	6.07	0-35	0-36	.69
Ext./Personal	11.84	4.09	0-18	0-18	.74
Ext./Social	4.83	3.72	0-17	0-18	.73
Quest	33.63	11.56	4-63	0-72	.77
Doctrinal Orthodoxy	63.40	13.64	5-72	0-72	.95

[a]Cronbach's coefficient alpha

religious orientation on the dependent variable (AS scores), a zero-order intercorrelation matrix was computed (see Table 8.2). With an alpha level set at .05, significant positive correlations were found to exist between AS scores and E, Ep, DOS, and I. Quest scores were significantly negatively correlated with AS scores.

Regression Analyses

To examine the total amount of variance in AS scores accounted for by the religious variables, two standard multiple regression analyses were performed. The first analysis included DOS, I, E, and Quest as independent variables. E was broken down into its subscales for use in the second regression analysis; resulting in five independent variables: DOS, I, Ep, Es, and Quest. Otherwise, the second analysis was conducted just as the first. The results are summarized in Tables 8.3 and 8.4.

In the first analysis, with an alpha level set at .05, the independent variables, together as a block, were found to predict a significant amount of variance in AS scores ($R = .516$, $p < .001$). However, of the variables in the equation, only intrinsic religious orientation accounted for a significant amount of unique variance ($sr^2 = .261$, $p < .001$). Within the second analysis, the inclusion of Ep and Es, in lieu of E, had negligible effects on the outcome of the regression.

TABLE 8.2
Intercorrelations between Variables of Interest

Variable	1	2	3	4	5	6	7
1. Anthropocentrism	--	.49	.17	.27	-.03	-.24	.41
		(.000)	(.046)	(.001)	(.738)	(.003)	(.000)
2. Intrinsic		--	.23	.40	-.07	-.32	.65
			(.005)	(.000)	(.427)	(.000)	(.000)
3. Extrinsic			--	.80	.75	.22	.29
				(.000)	(.000)	(.007)	(.000)
4. Ext./Personal				--	.21	.07	.55
					(.013)	(.382)	(.000)
5. Ext./Social					--	.28	.13
						(.001)	(.108)
6. Quest						--	-.24
							(.004)
7. Doctrinal Orthodoxy							--

[Coefficient / (2-tailed Significance)] N=144

Discussion

Summary of Findings

In this study it was found that significant relationships exist between anthropocentrism as measured by the AS, and the religious variables of interest: religious orientation (I, E, and Quest) and doctrinal orthodoxy. The strength of the correlations found between anthropocentrism and the independent variables, Quest ($r = -.24, p < .01$) and DOS ($r = .41, p < .001$), appear to be analogous to past research reported by MacFarland (1989) in his study of religious correlates of prejudice. Though Quest has not been utilized in studies of anthropocentrism or environmental concern, the correlation between fundamentalism and lack of environmental concern has been firmly established in past research (e.g., Hand & Van Liere, 1989; Guth, Kellstedt, Smidt & Green, 1993) and is congruent with the correlation found between doctrinal orthodoxy and anthropocentrism.

Somewhat surprising within the present sample were the differences in effect size of the relationships of E and I to Anthropocentrism. The E orientation has typically been associated with stronger correlations to attitudes typically viewed in a negative light, specifically those

TABLE 8.3
Summary of First Standard Multiple Regression of Religious Variables on
the Anthropocentrism Scales (N=144)

Variables	B	SE B	β	p	sr² (unique)
Intrinsic	.981	.273	.356	.000	.261
Extrinsic	.302	.331	.074	.363	
Quest	−.248	.176	−.115	.160	
Doctrinal Orthodoxy	.229	.178	.126	.201	

$R^2 = .267$, Adjusted $R^2 = .245$, $R = .516$, (F [4,139] = 12.63, $p = <.001$)

related to prejudice (Donahue, 1985). The I orientation, conversely, has been associated with smaller, or a lack of, similar correlations. For the present sample the effect was reversed, with the I orientation having the strongest correlation with anthropocentrism ($r = .49$, $p < .001$) of all variables.

In their study of racial prejudice and religious orientation, Allport and Ross (1967) observed a similar role reversal of I and E for two of their subsamples: Pennsylvania Presbyterians ($n = 53$), and Tennessee Methodists ($n = 35$). For each of these subsamples, the I orientation was more strongly correlated with measures of racial prejudice than the E orientation. Allport and Ross attribute this, without elaboration, to "salient racial issues in the local community" (p. 439). This explanation may be short-sighted, however. Certainly, one would be justified to assume that most "local racial issues" would affect the intrinsic and extrinsic, alike, thus negating differential effects regarding religious orientation. It is quite possible that the correlations observed were due to the specific underlying religious doctrine of the participants, a doctrine which may have been *more* fully accepted by the intrinsically religious.

To better understand the results of the present study, the correlation between the I orientation and anthropocentrism must be viewed in the context of the high level of doctrinally orthodox Christian beliefs of the sample. Given the fact that the I orientation is one in which the religious creed is fully embraced (Allport, 1959), the correlation with anthropocentrism can be understood due to the fact that doctrinal orthodoxy is also correlated with anthropocentrism. It is as if the I orientation serves to intensify the embraced religious doctrine. It is possible that the participants scoring high in the intrinsic orientation more accurately understand the tenets of the doctrine to which they purport to

TABLE 8.4
Summary of Second Standard Multiple Regression of Religious Variables on
the Anthropocentrism Scales ($N=144$)

Variables	B	SE B	β	p	sr^2 (unique)
Intrinsic	.978	.274	.355	.000	.260
Ext/Personal	.422	.578	.069	.467	
Ext/Social	.196	.534	.029	.714	
Quest	−.249	.534	−.115	.161	
Doctrinal Orthodoxy	.207	.200	.113	.303	

$R^2 = .267$, Adjusted $R^2 = .240$, $R = .517$, ($F [4,138] = 10.47$, $p = <.001$)

subscribe. It is from this perspective that the observed correlation between I and AS scores becomes much less surprising.

Limitations

Due to the nature of the instruments used (i.e., paper and pencil), a mono-method bias (Cook and Campbell, 1979) is likely present; thus the constructs of interest may be only partially represented. A more accurate understanding of the variables could be gained by the use of alternate measures of these constructs (e.g., behavioral measures). There is also a substantial threat to the external validity of this study due to the overrepresentation of doctrinal orthodoxy. More than half of the participants scored the maximum possible score on the DOS. This overrepresentation is possibly due to the geographical location of the sample (i.e., "the South"). It must be understood that these results may not be, and likely are not, representative of other geographical regions in the United States. Furthermore, with regard to gender and race, Caucasian women were somewhat overrepresented ($n = 68$), while African American men were underrepresented ($n = 9$). Finally, participants in this study were all enrolled in college courses; therefore results may not generalize to the population not enrolled in college, specifically those who never attended college.

Conclusions

Regarding the construct validity of the AS, the results of the analyses indeed place religion, specifically the measures of doctrinal orthodoxy and religious orientation, within the nomological net of adjacent constructs. In addition, further support was provided for Lynn White's (1967) thesis, relating "the roots of our ecological crisis" to Christianity. It must be understood that White's *causal* relationship cannot be proven, because of reliance on correlational methods. However, there certainly appears to be convincing evidence that the relationship itself does consistently surface in research examining relationships between religion, especially the more conservative, fundamentalistic religion, and environmental concern (Hand and Van Liere, 1984; Eckberg and Blocker, 1989; Guth et al., 1993).

If White *is* correct in his statement that "Since the roots of our trouble are so largely religious, the remedy must also be essentially religious" (1967, p. 1207), then one might surmise that society, at least in part, is approaching this remedy. For example, the establishment of the Deep Ecology movement is influencing many, by placing a magnitude of spiritual value on the natural environment and humanity's relationship to the environment (Deval and Sessions, 1985). One also finds a similar tone among religious authors such as Thomas Merton and Father Thomas Berry. It is yet to be seen, however, whether we are indeed, as Berry states, "returning to our native place after a long absence, meeting once again with our kin in the earth community" (1988, p. l).

References

Allport, G. W. (1950). *The individual and his religion.* New York: Macmillan.

Allport, G. W. (1959). Religion and prejudice. *Crane Review, 2,* 1–10.

Allport, G. W., & Ross, M. W. (1967). Personal religious orientation and prejudice. *Journal of Personality and Social Psychology, 5,* 432–443.

Batson, C. D, (1976). Religion as prosocial: Agent or double agent? *Journal for the Scientific Study of Religion, 15,* 29–45.

Batson, C. D., & Raynor-Price, L. (1986). Religious orientation and complexity of thought about existential concerns. *Journal for the Scientific Study of Religion, 22,* 38–50.

Batson, C. D., & Schoenrade, P. A. (1991a). Measuring religion as quest: 1) Validity concerns. *Journal for the Scientific Study of Religion, 30,* 416–429.

Batson, C. D., & Schoenrade, P. A. (1991b). Measuring religion as quest: 2) Reliability concerns. *Journal for the Scientific Study of Religion, 30,* 430–447.

Batson, C. D., & Ventis, W. L. (1982). *The religious experience: A social-psychological perspective.* New York: Oxford University Press.

Berry, T. (1988). *The dream of the earth.* San Francisco: Sierra Club Books.

Campbell, D.T., & McCandless, B.R. (1951). Ethnocentrism, xenophobia and personality. *Human Relations, 4,* 185–192.

Campbell, E. K. (1983). Beyond anthropocentrism. *Journal of the History of the Behavioral Sciences, 19,* 54–67.

Chandler, E. W., & Dreger, R. M. (1993). Anthropocentrism: Construct validity and measurement. *Journal of Social Behavior and Personality, 8,* 169– 188.

Cook, T.D, & Campbell, D.T. (1979). *Quasi-Experimentation: Design & analysis issues for field settings.* Boston: Houghton Mifflin.

Cronbach, L. J., & Meehl, P. E. (1955). Construct validity in psychological tests. *Psychological Bulletin, 52,* 281–302.

Deval, B., & Sessions, G. (1985). *Deep ecology: Living as if nature mattered.* Layton, UT: Gibbs Smith.

Dittes, J. E. (1971). Typing the typologies: Some parallels in the career of church-sect and extrinsic-intrinsic. *Journal for the Scientific Study of Religion, 10,* 375–383.

Donahue, M. J. (1985). Intrinsic and extrinsic religiousness: Review and meta-analysis. *Journal of Personality and Social Psychology, 48,* 400–419.

Dreger, R. M., & Chandler, E. W. (1993). Confirmation of the construct validity and factor structure of the measure of anthropocentrism. *Journal of Social Behavior and Personality, 8,* 189–202.

Eckberg, D. L., & Blocker, T. J. (1989). Varieties of religious involvement and environmental concerns: Testing the Lynn White thesis. *Journal for the Scientific Study of Religion,* 509–517.

Exner, J. E., Jr. (1973). The self focus sentence completion: A study of egocentricity. *Journal of Personality Assessment, 37,* 437–455.

Feagin, J. R. (1964). Prejudice and religious types: A focused study of southern fundamentalists. *Journal for the Scientific Study of Religion, 4,* 3–13.

Genia, V. (1993). A psychometric evaluation of the Allport-Ross I/E scales in a religiously heterogeneous sample. *Journal for the Scientific Study of Religion, 32,* 284–290.

Gorsuch, R. L. (1988). Psychology of religion. In M. R. Rosenzweig, & L. W. Porter (Eds.), *Annual review of psychology: Vol. 39* (pp. 201–221). Palo Alto, CA: Annual Reviews.

Gorsuch, R.L., & McPherson, S. E. (19893. Intrinsic/Extrinsic measurement: I/E-Revised and single-item scales. *Journal for the Scientific Study of Religion, 28,* 348–354.

Greeley, A. (1993). Religion and attitudes toward the environment. *Journal for the Scientific Study of Religion, 32,* 19–28.

Guth, J. L., Kellstedt, L. A., Smidt, C. E., & Green, J. C. (1993). Theological perspectives and environmentalism among religious activists. *Journal for the Scientific Study of Religion, 32,* 373–382.

Hand, C.M., & Van Liere, K. D. (1984). Religion, mastery-over-nature, and environmental concern. *Social Forces, 63,* 555–570.

Hood, R. W., & Morris, R. J. (1985). Conceptualization of quest: A critical rejoinder to Batson. *Review of Religious Research, 26,* 391–397.

Hunt, R. A., & King, M. B. (1971). The intrinsic-extrinsic concept: A review and evaluation. *Journal for the Scientific Study of Religion, 10,* 339–356.

Kirkpatrick, L. A. (1989). A psychometric analysis of the Allport-Ross and Feagin measures of intrinsic-extrinsic religious orientation. In Lynn, M., & Moberg, D. (Eds.), *Research in the Social Scientific Study of Religion* (pp. 1–30). Greenwich, CT: JAI Press.

Kirkpatrick, L. A., & Hood, R. W. (1990). Intrinsic-extrinsic religious orientation: The boon or bane of contemporary psychology of religion? *Journal for the Scientific Study of Religion, 29,* 442–462.

Kirkpatrick, L. A., & Hood, R. W. (1991). Rub-a-dub-dub: Who's in the tub? Reply to Masters. *Journal for the Scientific Study of Religion, 30,* 318–321.

Marsden, G. (1980). *Fundamentalism and American culture*. New York: Norton.

Masters, K. S. (1991). Of boons, banes, babies, and bath water: A reply to the Kirkpatrick and Hood discussion of intrinsic-extrinsic religious orientation. *Journal for the Scientific Study of Religion, 30,* 312–317.

McFarland, S. G. (1989). Religious orientations and the targets of discrimination. *Journal for the Scientific Study of Religion, 28,* 324–336.

Ponton, M. O., & Gorsuch, R. L. (1988). Prejudice and religion revisited: A cross-cultural investigation with a Venezuelan sample. *Journal for the Scientific Study of Religion, 27,* 260–271.

Rotter, J. B. (1966). Generalized expectancies for internal versus external control of reinforcement. *Psychological Monographs, 80* (Whole No. 609), 1–28.

Schaeffer, F. A. (1970). *Pollution and the death of man: The Christian view of ecology*. Wheaton, IL: Tyndale.

Shaiko, R.G.(1987). Religion, politics, and environmental concern: A powerful mix of passions. *Social Science Quarterly, 68,* 244–262.

White, L. (1967). The historical roots of our ecological crisis. *Science, 155,* 1203–1207.

Wilcox, C, Linzey, S. & Jelen, T. (1991). Reluctant warriors: Premillennialism and politics in the Moral Majority. *Journal for the Scientific Study of Religion, 30,* 245–258.

Wilson, W. C. (1960). Extrinsic religious values and prejudice. *Journal of Abnormal and Social Psychology, 60,* 286–288.

Wrightsman, L. S. (1964). Measurement of philosophies of human nature. *Psychological Reports, 14,* 743–751.

Wulff, D. M. (1991). *Psychology of religion: Classic and contemporary views*. New York: Wiley.

9

Intrinsic Religious Motivation and Attitudes toward Death among the Elderly

Richard Clements

Several researchers have examined the possibility of a connection between "religion" (variously defined) and attitudes toward death and dying, typically hypothesizing a negative relationship between religiosity and death anxiety (i.e., the more "religious" an individual is, the less anxiety that person will feel regarding death). However, the studies conducted in this area have yielded conflicting results. Some studies have found that anxiety regarding death and dying is lower among religious people than it is among nonreligious people (Alvarado, Templer, Bresler, & Thomas-Dobson, 1995; Feifel & Nagel, 1981; Jeffers, Nichols, & Eisdorfer, 1961; Martin & Wrightsman, 1965; Templer, 1972); some have found that death anxiety is higher among religious people than it is among nonreligious people (Feifel & Branscomb, 1973); some have found no relationship between death anxiety and religiosity (Kurlychek, 1978; Templer & Dotson, 1970); and others have found that death anxiety is lower among people who adhere most closely to traditional religious beliefs and those who reject such traditional beliefs completely than it is among people who are undecided in their attitude toward traditional beliefs or only moderately committed to those beliefs (Aday, 1984; McMordie, 1981).

Several potential explanations can be offered for the discrepancies in these research results, but three of the most plausible explanations are the use of simplistic measures of "religion," widely varying (often unidimensional) measures of death anxiety, and differing samples. Regarding the first point, many of the past studies in this area have used rather superficial measures of religion, such as denominational affiliation, frequency of church attendance, etc. However, in order to assess the impact of religion on a person's attitudes, such as a person's attitudes toward death and dying, one must attempt to measure internal aspects of the person's religion (i.e., aspects such as the person's motivation for religious belief and the nature and complexity of their religious ideas, beliefs, and conceptions), instead of looking only at external religious behavior and affiliation. Regarding the second point, Hoelter and Epley (1979) have argued that the use of a wide array of unidimensional measures of death anxiety in past research may have led to the masking or distorting of relationships between religiosity and death anxiety because a variety of positive and negative relationships may exist between various types of religiosity and the various dimensions of death anxiety, leading to offsetting effects between these relationships when unidimensional measures of death anxiety and unsophisticated measures of religiosity are used. Finally, the impact of differing samples is perhaps best illustrated by comparing the results of two studies, both of which used a multidimensional measure of death anxiety and a relatively sophisticated measure of religion, the Intrinsic Religious Motivation Scale (Hoge, 1972, based on Allport & Ross, 1967). Thorson and Powell (1989) used a sample of older males (mean age = 70.8 years) and found no significant relationship between intrinsic religious motivation and subjects' total scores on the death anxiety scale, but did report that two individual items on the death anxiety scale were significantly correlated with scores on the IRM scale. In contrast, Powell and Thorson (1991) used a younger sample of both males and females (mean age = 50.1 years) and found a significant negative relationship between intrinsic religious motivation and subjects' total scores on the death anxiety scale ($r = -.362$, $p < .001$), i.e., subjects with high levels of intrinsic religious motivation reported lower levels of death anxiety than did subjects with low levels of intrinsic religious motivation.

The present study sought to address some of the shortcomings of previous research in this area by utilizing two different multidimensional measures of death anxiety (the Collett-Lester Fear of Death Scale-Revised [Lester, 1990] and the Multidimensional Fear of Death Scale [Hoelter, 1979]), two different measures of religion, both of which are more sophisticated than the measures that have been used in many of the past studies in this area (the Intrinsic Religious Motivation Scale [Hoge, 1972]; and the shortened format of the faith development interview [Swensen, 1989a, based on Fowler, 1981]), and a sample confined to a specific age range (65 and over).

Two hypotheses were examined in this study. The first hypothesis was that subjects with high scores on the Intrinsic Religious Motivation Scale (i.e., persons with "extrinsic" religious motivation) would report significantly higher levels of death anxiety than subjects with relatively low scores on the IRM scale (i.e., persons with "intrinsic" religious motivation). The second hypothesis was that subjects with low scores on the faith development interview (i.e., those at lower, less complex stages of religious faith) would report significantly higher levels of death anxiety than would subjects with relatively high scores on the faith development interview. Both of these hypotheses, like many of the hypotheses formulated by previous researchers positing a negative relationship between measures of "religiosity" and death anxiety, are based on the following rationale. One of the functions of religion is to provide individuals with some explanations and/or insights regarding a variety of existential issues, including the nature and meaning of death and the possibility of continued existence after physical death. A person who finds these explanations plausible and comforting and who has internalized these viewpoints would seem to be less likely to regard various aspects of death as anxiety-provoking than would other individuals.

Method

Subjects

Two criteria were used to select people for participation in this research project: the subject had to be 65 years old or older, and the subject had to be non-institutionalized (i.e., living independently rather than in a nursing home or similar institution). Forty-five people (30 females and 15 males, all Caucasians) participated in the study. Subjects ranged in age from 65 to 87 ($M = 72.1$; $SD = 6.1$). Table 9.1

TABLE 9.1
Frequency Distribution for Marital Status, Education,
and Religious Affiliation of the Sample

	Males	Females	% of sample
Marital Status			
Single (never married)	0	2	4.4%
Married	13	9	48.9%
Widowed	1	18	42.2%
Divorced	*1*	*1*	*4.4%*
Total	15	30	100%
Education (highest level completed)			
Eighth Grade	0	1	2.2%
High School	1	11	26.7%
Vocational or Technical School	0	3	6.7%
Some college (no degree)	3	6	20.0%
Bachelor's Degree	3	4	15.5%
Master's Degree	2	5	15.5%
Ph.D., M.D., J.D., etc.	*6*	*0*	*13.3%*
Total	15	30	100%
Religious Affiliation			
Protestant	8	23	68.9%
Methodist	5	12	37.8%
Presbyterian	2	2	8.9%
Church of Christ	1	1	4.4%
Lutheran	0	2	4.4%
Assembly of God	0	1	2.2%
Baptist	0	1	2.2%
Christian Reformed	0	1	2.2%
Episcopalian	0	1	2.2%
United Brethren in Christ	0	1	2.2%
Independent	0	1	2.2%
Roman Catholic	0	4	8.9%
Jewish	3	1	8.9%
Unitarian Universalist	0	1	2.2%
No religious affiliation	*4*	*1*	*11.1%*
Total	15	30	100%

shows the frequency distribution for the variables of marital status, education, and religious affiliation.

Measures

Personal Data Questionnaire. This questionnaire consisted of questions regarding the subject's sex, age, race, marital status, education, income level, religious affiliation, religious activities, and the number of deaths of persons close to the subject (family, friends, etc.) which had occurred in the past year.

Multidimensional Fear of Death Scale (MFODS). Hoelter (1979), aware of the increasing amount of evidence indicating that death anxiety is a multidimensional, rather than unidimensional, phenomenon, and of the need for a measuring instrument that could accurately assess these dimensions, developed the Multidimensional Fear of Death Scale (MFODS) by factor-analyzing the results of an administration (to 375 undergraduates) of a questionnaire containing items from the Fear of Death Scale (Boyar, 1964), the Death Anxiety Scale (Templer, 1970), and several items developed by Hoelter in two pretests. Hoelter operated on the basis of the following definition of death anxiety: "[Death anxiety is] an emotional reaction involving subjective feelings of unpleasantness and concern based on contemplation or anticipation of any of the several facets [dimensions] related to death" (Hoelter, 1979, p. 996). Factor analysis of the forty-two items on the MFODS yielded eight factors: fear of the dying process, fear of the dead, fear of being destroyed, fear for significant others, fear of the unknown, fear of conscious death, fear for the body after death, and fear of premature death. These eight dimensions were duplicated in a second factor-analytic study done on the MFODS by Walkey (1982) with a New Zealand sample that included both students and non-students. The subscale reliabilities reported by Walkey were high and very similar to those reported by Hoelter, lending support to Hoelter's claim of eight independent subscales with high reliabilities.

Collett-Lester Fear of Death Scale (Revised). This instrument, like the MFODS, was designed to be a multidimensional measure of death anxiety. The original scale has been the most widely used multidimensional measure of death anxiety in past research (Niemeyer, Bagley, & Moore, 1986). The revised version retained the four subscales of the original questionnaire (fear of death of self, fear of dying of self, fear of death of others, and fear of dying of others), but contained an equal number of items for each subscale (eight items per subscale) and utilized a more logical scoring system. Lester (1990) reported the following Cronbach's alpha coefficients for the four subscales, respectively: .91, .89, .72, and .88.

Intrinsic Religious Motivation Scale. The Intrinsic Religious Motivation Scale (Hoge, 1972) is based on the distinction drawn by Allport and Ross (1967) between "extrinsic" and "intrinsic" religious motivation. "Extrinsics" are individuals who are religious because of benefits that accrue to them from being religious, such as security and solace, sociability, and status in the community, whereas "intrinsics" are typically described as individuals who seek to internalize their religious beliefs, make those beliefs a central aspect of their lives, and live out those beliefs in their lives. Hoge's scale has greater reliability and greater predictive validity than each of the three scores yielded by Allport and Ross's Intrinsic-Extrinsic scales. The Intrinsic Religious Motivation Scale is a ten-item scale containing statements relating to the motivations for one's religious faith. Subjects indicate their degree of agreement/disagreement with each item on a 4-point Likert scale and these responses are then added together to yield a total score; the lower the subjects' score, the more they tend toward an intrinsic, rather than extrinsic, orientation toward religion, and conversely, the higher their score on this scale, the more they tend toward an extrinsic religious orientation.

Faith Development Interview. Fowler (1981) developed an interview format for assessing a person's faith development consisting of nineteen open-ended questions. He developed this format empirically by interviewing 359 people and articulating six stages of faith based on their responses. "Faith," as Fowler conceives it, is not confined to people who are formal members of one religious denomination or another. His interview is based on a conception of faith that transcends traditional denominational and doctrinal boundaries and can therefore be applied to all people regardless of their formal religious affiliation (i.e., regardless of whether a person is a member of an organized religion, an agnostic, or an atheist).

Swensen (1989a) has shortened Fowler's interview format to five open-ended questions, including such questions as "What is the purpose of human life?" and "Can you describe the beliefs and values or attitudes that are most important in guiding your life?" Swensen has also developed a rating manual for scoring each of these five interview questions. On each question, the subject is given a score from 2 to 5, representing his or her "stage of faith development" on that item; thus, a person's score on the interview can range between 10 and 25. Swensen (1989b) used the shortened version of the faith development interview in a study of cancer patients and their spouses and reported interrater reliability figures of .86, .87, and .88 for the three judges who scored the 92 protocols using Swensen's rating manual.

Results

Hypothesis 1: Death Anxiety and Religious Motivation

The results of the multivariate regression equation using the eight subscales of the MFODS as dependent variables and the Intrinsic Religious Motivation Scale (IRM) as the independent variable were statistically significant (F (8, 25) = 3.186, p < .05); subjects whose motivation for religious faith tended toward the "intrinsic" side of the spectrum of religious motivation reported less death anxiety than did subjects who exhibited "extrinsic" religious motivation (see Table 9.2). Within this multivariate equation, the regression coefficient for only one of the eight fear of death subscales was significant in the hypothesized direction: the coefficient for fear of the unknown (F (1, 32) = 23.662, p < .01). One of the individual regression equations for the MFODS subscales was statistically significant, the equation for fear of the unknown (F (1, 42) = 8.697, p < .01), with the equation for one other subscale (fear of dying) approaching significance (F (1, 41) = 4.045, p = .051).

The results of the multivariate regression equation using the four subscales of the Collett-Lester Fear of Death Scale (Revised) as dependent variables and the IRM Scale score as the independent variable approached, but did not reach, statistical significance (F (4,40) = 2.533, p = .055). Within this multivariate equation, three of the four regression coefficients for the fear of death subscales were significant (the coefficients for fear of death of self, fear of dying of self, and fear of dying of others; see Table 9.3).

Hypothesis 2: Death Anxiety and Stage of Faith Development

The results of the multivariate regression equation using the eight subscales of the MFODS as dependent variables and the subject's score on the stage of faith interview as the independent variable were not statistically significant (F (8, 25) = .623, p = .751). The results of the multivariate regression equation using the four subscales of the Collett-Lester Fear of Death Scale-Revised as dependent variables and score on the stage of faith interview as the independent variable were also not statistically significant (F (4, 40) = .706, p = .592).

TABLE 9.2
Regression Analyses—Multidimensional Fear of Death Subscales and the
Intrinsic Religious Motivation Scale

Multivatirate regression equation						
Dependent variable(s)	Multivariate F	p	Univeriate F	p	Adjusted R^2	
All 8 MFODS subscales	2.186	.012*	—	—		
Fear of dying			3.540	.069	.071	
Fear of the dead			.252	.619	.000	
Fear of being destroyed			.601	.444	.000	
Fear for significant others			.000	.998	.000	
Fear of the unknown			23.662	.000*	.407	
Fear of conscious death			.055	.817	.000	
Fear for body after death			2.117	.155	.033	
Fear of premature death			.392	.536	.000	

*$p<.05$ **$p<.01$.

Regression equations for each of the MFODS subscales				
Dependent variable	F	p	r (with IRM score)	r^2
Fear of dying	4.045	.051	.30	.090
Fear of the dead	1.472	.232	.18	.033
Fear of being destroyed	2.169	.149	−.23	.051
Fear for significant others	.151	.700	.06	.004
Fear of the unknown	14.678	.000**	.51**	.259
Fear of conscious death	2.484	.123	−.24	.057
Fear for body after death	.250	.620	.08	.006
Fear of premature death	.466	.499	.11	.011

**$p<.01$.

Discussion

The data from the present study provided some support for the hypothesis that people whose religious motivation tends to be primarily intrinsic fear certain aspects of death less than do people who tend to be more extrinsic in their religious orientation. Specifically, subjects with intrinsic religious motivation showed significantly less fear of the unknown ($r = .51$, $p < .01$), less fear of the death of self ($r = .30$, $p < .05$), less fear of the dying of self ($r = 39$, $p < .01$), and less fear of the dying of others ($r = .30$, $p < .05$) than did subjects with extrinsic religious motivation. These results differ somewhat from those obtained by Thorson and Powell (1989), who reported significant correlations between religious motivation and two individual items on their

TABLE 9.3
Multivariate Regression Analyses—Collett-Lester Fear of Death Scale (Revised)
Subscales and the
Intrinsic Religious Motivation Scale

Multivatirate regression equation					
Dependent variable(s)	Multivariate F	p	Univeriate F	p	Adjusted R^2
All four CL-R subscales	2.533	.055	—	—	
Fear of death of self			4.099	.049*	.066
Fear of dying of self			7.479	.009*	.128
Fear for death of others			.059	.810	.000
Fear of dying of others			4.130	.048*	.066

Regression equations for each of the MFODS subscales				
Dependent variable	F	p	r (with IRM score)	r^2
Fear of death of self	4.099	.049*	.30*	.087
Fear of dying of self	7.479	.009*	.39**	.148
Fear for death of others	.059	.810	.04	.001
Fear of dying of others	4.130	.048*	.30*	.088

$p<.05$ **$p<.01$.

death anxiety scale but no general relationships between religious motivation and death anxiety in a sample of older males. Two potential explanations for the differences between the results of their study and the results of the present study would be the different measures of death anxiety that were used in these two studies and the possibility that the two samples differed from each other in some systematic way (other than gender composition; in the present study, males and females scored at similar levels on the IRM scale and on ten of the twelve death anxiety subscales, which would seem to eliminate gender as an explanation for the differing results of the two studies).

The finding that religious motivation was significantly related to various types of death anxiety in the present sample may have implications for the counseling of older individuals facing terminal illness or death. Specifically, individuals with extrinsic religious motivation may have more fears about death and thus be in greater need of counseling regarding this issue than individuals with intrinsic religious motivation. These results also suggest that the Intrinsic Religious Motivation Scale would be worth including in future studies of attitudes toward death.

The data from the present study failed to support the hypothesis of a negative relationship between death anxiety and stage of faith development. This may mean that such a relationship does not exist, but it could also be that such a relationship was not found because of the restricted range of scores on the interview in the present sample. This interview still offers promise as a measure of "religion" in psychological research, particularly if future studies use the full-length version of the interview as originally developed by Fowler (1981) instead of using the shortened version employed in the present study. The usefulness of this interview might also be enhanced by describing transitional steps between the various stages of faith, which would allow for finer gradations of subjects' responses to interview items.

References

Aday, R. H. (1984). Belief in afterlife and death anxiety: Correlates and comparisons. *Omega, 15*, 67–75.

Allport, G. W., & Ross, J. M. (1967). Personal religious orientation and prejudice. *Journal of Personality and Social Psychology, 5*, 432–443.

Alvarado, K. A., Templer, D. I., Bresler, C., & Thomas-Dobson, S. (1995). The relationship of religious variables to death depression and death anxiety. *Journal of Clinical Psychology, 51*, 202–204.

Boyar, J. I. (1964). The construction and partial validation of a scale for the measurement of fear of death. Doctoral dissertation, University of Rochester.

Feifel, H., & Branscomb, A. B. (1973). Who's afraid of death? *Journal of Abnormal Psychology, 81*, 282–288.

Feifel, H., & Nagel, V. G. (1981). Another look at fear of death. *Journal of Consulting and Clinical Psychology, 49*, 278–286.

Fowler, J. (1981). *Stages of faith.* San Francisco: Harper & Row.

Hoelter, J. W. (1979). Multidimensional treatment of fear of death. *Journal of Consulting and Clinical Psychology, 47*, 996–999.

Hoelter, J. W., & Epley, R. J. (1979). Religious correlates of fear of death. *Journal for the Scientific Study of Religion, 18*, 401–411.

Hoge, D. R. (1972). A validated Intrinsic Religious Motivation Scale. *Journal for the Scientific Study of Religion, 11*, 369–376.

Jeffers, F. C., Nichols, C. R., & Eisdorfer, C. (1961). Attitudes of older persons to death. *Journal of Gerontology, 16*, 53–56.

Kurlychek, R. T. (1978). Assessment of attitudes toward death and dying: A critical review of some available methods. *Omega, 9*, 37–47.

Lester, D. (1990). The Collett-Lester Fear of Death Scale: The original version and a revision. *Death Studies. 14*, 451–468.

Martin, D., & Wrightsman, L. S. (1965). The relationship between religious behavior and concern about death. *The Journal of Social Psychology, 65*, 317–323.

McMordie, W. R. (1981). Religiosity and fear of death: Strength of belief system. *Psychological Reports, 49*, 921–922.

Neimeyer, R. A., Bagley, K. J., & Moore, M. K. (1986). Cognitive structure and death anxiety. *Death Studies, 10,* 273–288.

Powell, F. C., & Thorson, J. A. (1991). Constructions of death among those high in intrinsic religious motivation: A factor-analytic study. *Death Studies, 15,* 131–138.

Swensen, C. H. (1989a). Rating scale for shortened format of Fowler's faith development interview. Unpublished document, Purdue University, West Lafayette, IN.

Swensen, C. H. (1989b, August). *Stage of religious faith and reactions to cancer.* Paper presented at the annual convention of the American Psychological Association, New Orleans, LA.

Templer, D. (1972). Death anxiety in religiously very involved persons. *Psychological Reports, 31,* 361–362.

Templer, D. I., & Dotson, E. (1970). Religious correlates of death anxiety. *Psychological Reports, 26,* 895–897.

Thorson, J. A., & Powell, F. C. (1989). Death anxiety and religion in an older male sample. *Psychological Reports, 64,* 985–986.

Walkey, F. H. (1982). The multidimensional fear of death scale: An independent analysis. *Journal of Consulting and Clinical Psychology, 50,* 466–467.

10

Counterfeit Courage: Toward a Process Psychology Paradigm for the "Heroic Rescue Fantasy"

Nathaniel J. Pallone
James J. Hennessy

As devotees of the fiction of James Thurber well remember, the heroic rescue fantasy has long served as a mainstay in droll humor. Thurber's Walter Mitty spent inordinate amounts of time daydreaming about how heroically he might, could, or would behave were a fire to erupt in an elevator shaft or a masked gunman to invade the dull precincts of the insurance company where he worked—and about the degree of affectionate gratitude that would inevitably be showered upon him by those comely lasses who were his co-workers following this display of manly virtue and who, in the absence of that display, seemed barely to notice him. So long as they remain entirely within the realm of fantasy, we universally regard such dreamy aspirations for future glory won by virtue of dauntlessly heroic behavior as innocuous enough. But Thurber's character never colluded with a masked gunman to invade an office, nor set a fire which he himself expected to extinguish, nor secreted a bomb in a place in which he, and only he, could conveniently discover and disarm the device.

In earlier work (Pallone and Hennessy, 1992; 1993; 1996), we have been concerned with the engines that drive both prosocial and antisocial risk-taking behavior. We have opined that, among both genuine heroes (e.g., police, fire, and public safety officers decorated for bravery) and those who commit unrelentingly antisocial and often gratuitously violent criminal acts, there can be discerned impairment in the capacity to assess the costs, risks, and benefits associated with particular ways of behaving toward particular behavioral objects. With less evidence (whether clinical or empirical) we proposed that similar impairment is likely in "adventurous" risk-takers (e.g., those who might select hang-gliding as pastime for an afternoon) whose behavior is neither distinctly prosocial nor antisocial. Rather more speculatively, we also conjectured that, when such impairment is seen to operate relatively more globally than specifically (i.e., in relation to a wide variety of behavioral objects rather than in relation to a circumscribed set toward which the behaver has become particularly sensitized) there obtains persuasive—albeit admittedly not yet quite compelling—reason to attribute such impairment to neuropsychological anomaly or dysfunction.

Because our view that heroism and violent criminality may share remarkably similar biological roots had received some media attention and because some members of the press understood that we hoped to address as well the matter of the "heroic rescue fantasy" in the general biopsychosocial model for risk-taking behavior under development, we were asked for public comment after an incendiary device exploded in Centennial Park in Atlanta during the 1996 Summer Olympics, with a security guard almost immediately identified as the prime suspect. Prudence should have dictated that comment be declined until we had finalized what was then only a fragmentary conceptual model and submitted it to the scrutiny of our professional colleagues through publication in a scholarly journal. In the event, prudence did not prevail; and thus it was that our conjecture that the security guard under intense suspicion was unlikely to be found liable (a view seconded only many months later by Federal law enforcement officials) became known to listeners to public radio stations in the New York-Philadelphia megalopolitan corridor some five days after the Atlanta explosion.

In some measure, addressing ourselves to our colleagues in this article represents an attempt to atone for that lack of prudence. For reasons that become evident, our data are largely drawn from (generally rather lengthy) interviews (and results of psychometric instruments completed by some interviewees) with nonrandom takers of risks of varying character that are too small to permit valid statistical inference and are thus discussed in clinical terms. Hence, we present in this article a model for the heroic rescue fantasy in relation to other manifestations of risk-taking behavior predicated on the principles of process psychology that, we hasten to add, we still regard as a work in progress.

Farley's Taxonomy and Its Variants

Although most researchers and commentators would distinguish at the conceptual level between *risk-taking* as a behavior and *thrill-seeking* (or, less often, "thrill-experiencing") as its phenomenological representation, even the most robust of the several relevant taxonomies blurs the distinction by assuming that risky behavior invariably reveals thrill-seeking as one of its propellants. We will later observe, however, that at least among the prosocial risk-takers we have interviewed clinically—and particularly when the risky behavior has been emitted in a "togetherness" or cohesive social group situation (e.g., police officers during a hostage situation)—we have often not been able to discern an inclination to seek thrills as anything remotely resembling an enduring trait of personality.

Be that as it may, no taxonomy is more comprehensive than Farley's (1986), which pivots on three axes: 1) the extent to which the actor actively seeks thrills through risky behavior; 2) whether the behavior thus elicited is inflected toward positive or negative social goals; and 3) whether the behavior thus elicited requires mental or physical "exertion." Distinguishing between "risk-takers and adventurers [who] seek excitement and stimulation wherever they can find or create it" from those who "cling to certainty and predictability, avoiding risks and the unfamiliar," Farley labels the former *T* types (i.e., *capital T* types) and the latter *t* types (i.e., *lower-case t* types). Among T types, "thrill-seeking can lead . . . to outstanding creativity . . . but it can [also] lead to extremely destructive, even criminal, behavior." In summarizing research on the capital T types using a variety of measures (some patterned after scales from the Eysenck Personality Inventory), Farley has identified four subtypes among habitual thrill-seekers in a schematic that differentiates what he calls the "criminal mastermind" from the creative artist:

- Constructive T (T +)/Mental, a group that encompasses "people who seek stimulation mainly in the mental domain, such as artists, scientists, entertainers."
- Constructive T (T +)/Physical, a group that includes "people who seek stimulation mainly in the physical domain, such as adventurers and physical risk-takers."
- Destructive T (T –)/Mental, a group that encompasses "people who seek stimulation mainly in the mental domain, such as criminal masterminds, schemers, and con artists."
- Destructive T (T –)/Physical, a group that includes "people who seek stimulation mainly in the physical domain, such as violent delinquents and criminals."

Farley's (1986, 45–46) model is somewhat less elegant in respect of etiology. Farley posits that the genesis of thrill-seeking or thrill-avoidance is likely neurophysiological; and, in an analogue to a process psychology paradigm, he holds that thrill-seeking behavior is both mediated by, and mediates, social and or stimulus factors:

[W]e all seek unconsciously to maintain an optimal level of "arousal" or activity in the central nervous system. . . . If arousal is too high or too low, we try to adjust it to some middle ground, often by choosing environments and experiences that are either soothing or stimulating. Some of our research and that of others implicates such physiological arousability as the basis for stimulation-seeking, while other research suggests a role for biochemistry (such as monoamine oxidase . . .). These interpretations may not be incompatible, but the precise biological bases are not certain at present. Experiences around the time of birth or perhaps early nutrition may also play a role.

In a relatively complementary study, Alexander et al. (1995) investigated developmental psychosocial (but not neurobiological) antecedents among subjects who would likely be classified as T+/Physical in the Farley schema (firefighters) and those who who would likely be classified as T–/Physical (incarcerated felons). Prosocial risk-takers self-reported significantly fewer episodes of victimization in aggression over the life span than did antisocial risk-takers, a finding that may help explain the *direction* or intended goal of thrill-seeking behavior.

Whatever its source, according to Farley (1986), thrill-seeking appears to fluctuate inversely with age:

[Thrill-seeking] is most often found among those in the 16 to 24 age range. From then it drops off gradually, as my colleagues and I found in two large studies of people from approximately 10 to 75 years old . . . . [m]ost people reach their strongest expression of [thrill-seeking behavior] in their late teens to early 20s, with a decline into old age.

Farley's observations about the age-intensity link in thrill-seeking and risk-taking are highly congruent both with the findings of Colligan and his associates (1989) on age-related decline in scores on the mania and psychopathic deviation scales of the MMPI in the Mayo Clinical restandardization study and those of Hare and his colleagues (1988) on the age-related decline in criminal behavior among offenders categorized as psychopaths. That link is further confirmed by White, Labouvie, and Bates (1985) and Bates, White, and Labouvie (1994), who found, in longitudinal studies of a large sample of adolescents and young adults, that sensation seeking as measured psychometrically correctly predicts alcohol and substance abuse over time. For these subjects, involvement in the drug world may have been a major source in satisfying their thrill-seeking urges; and such involvement (especially with CNS stimulants as the drugs of choice) may further reinforce thrill-seeking as a behavioral pattern.

In contrast to the multifaceted Farley paradigm, Levenson (1990) employed only one axis in a study which compared and contrasted antisocial (habitual drug offenders), prosocial (police and fire officers decorated for bravery in the line of duty), and adventurous (skilled mountain climbers) risk-takers on such variables as emotional arousability, conformity, moral reasoning, psychopathy, and proclivity to use or abuse of mood-altering substances. Though we might well expect "heroes" to differ from "villains," if not each group also to differ from adventurers on each of these variables, Levenson found no differences between the three groups in moral development, empathy, or independence versus conformity. But significant differences were found on substance abuse proclivity, emotionality, depression, psychopathy, disinhibition, and susceptibility to boredom. Hence, Levenson concluded (pp. 1073, 1079) that the three groups

appear to represent both different psychological types and different forms of risk taking. . . . [D]ifferent types of risk taking have very different antecedents and consequences . . . . [Pro-social risk takers] literally risk their lives in the performance of their duties [but] the reasons for pro-social risk taking may be very different from those for . . . sensation-seeking. It is important to distinguish doing harm to others for personal gratification (antisocial behavior) from the antistructural violation of social norms in the service of positive social change.

Four Faces of Risk-Taking Behavior

In the figure that accompanies this paper, we present a schematic representation for four faces of risk-taking behavior consistent with the principles of process psychology articulated by Cattell (1980) and extended by Smith (1988) and in our own earlier work. In brief, those principles hold that behavior is generated by means of interaction among biopsychosocial variables; that, as a result of the knowledge explosion in the neurosciences of the past three decades, particular attention should be paid to neurologic and neuropsychological influences in accounting the contribution made by biological variables; and that, among the stimulus determinants of behavior (social and environmental influences), particular attention should be paid to sensitization to variant interpersonal environments and to the creation of opportunity for behavior. That schematic can be addressed most parsimoniously by considering pathways and divergences cross-sectionally.

Neuropsychological Substratum

Risk-taking of whatever sort involves systematic minimization of costs and risks and magnification of anticipated benefits. The proposition that consistently unrealistic assessment of behavioral objects and of ways of behaving is anchored in compromised neurologic and neuropsychological processes has enough support in recent research in the neurosciences (Klinteberg et al., 1987; Schälling et al., 1988; Brown and Linnoila, 1990; Linnoila and Virkkunen, 1992; Higley et al., 1992; Mehlman et al., 1995; Pandey et al., 1995; Blanco et al., 1996; Coccaro et al., 1996) that we feel comfortable in positing it as a persuasive (though admittedly not yet compelling) proposition. Not surprisingly, the general tenor of that research tends to implicate naturally occurring or induced anomalies in the production of monoamine oxidase and/or serotonin, or anatomical damage to (or merely naturally occurring variations in) brain structures where these substances customarily are metabolized. Mehlman, Higley, and their colleagues (1995), for example, observe that persistent anomalies in the production and or metabolism of brain serotonin represent precursors to "trait-like impulsivity, while, conversely . . . higher than average . . . activity [is related] to greater rigidity and inhibition of many forms of behavior." Some investigators might well categorically "reduce" what personality

FIGURE 10.1
Four Paths to Risk-Taking: Commonalities and Divergences

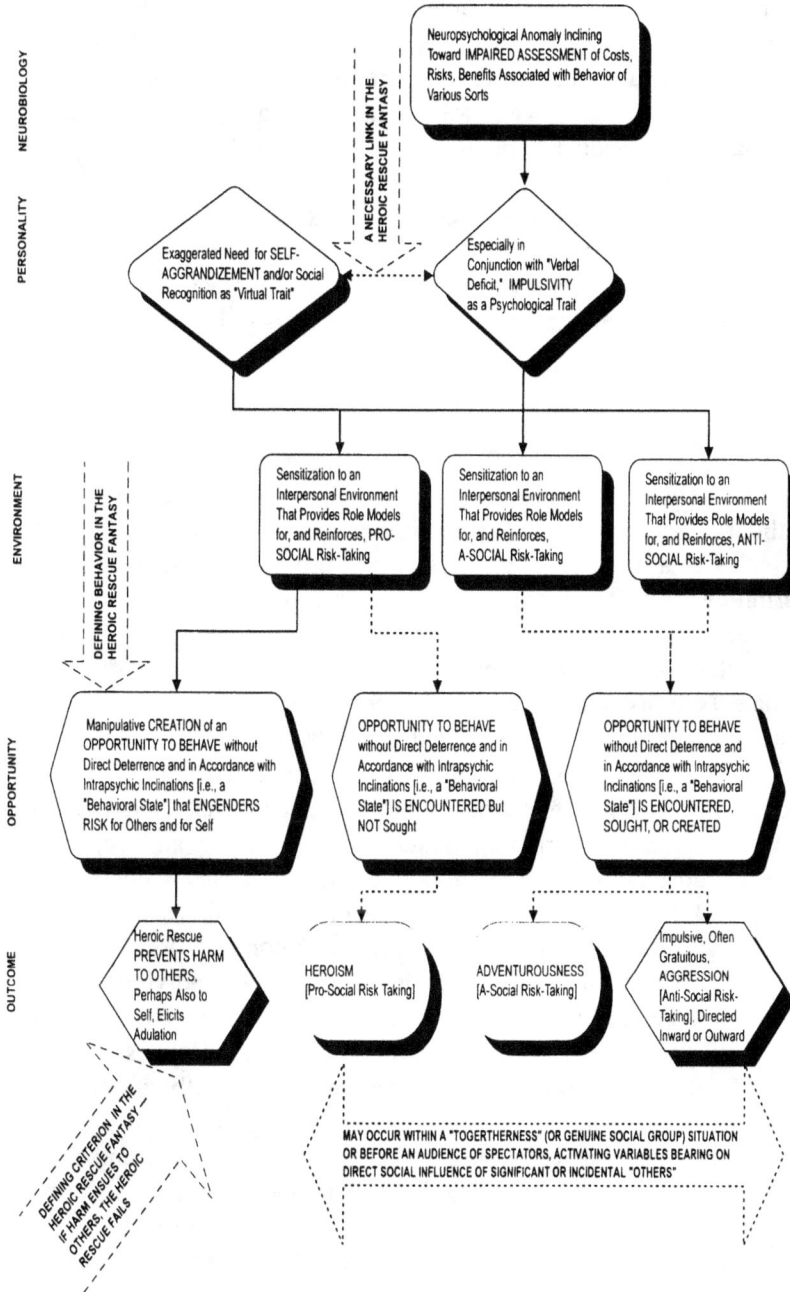

psychologists term impulsivity to anomalies in the serotonergic system.

But, in some contrast to contemporary advocates of the position that neurobiology alone constitutes destiny, we do not hold that such anomalies in and of themselves inexorably dictate risk-taking (or any other) behavior; rather what we might term an *inclination* remains *dormant* until activated through interaction with other (psychological, social, environmental) variables. Indeed, following Cattell, one might well conclude that the proper focus in process psychology in an era of neuroscience information revolution is to model conceptually how such dormant, neurogenic inclinations are activated, interact with other engines of behavior, and transmute into actual units of behavior.

Personality Traits

Eysenck and Eysenck (1978) have defined *impulsivity* as "action without thought;" and they might be willing to accept the emendation "without *adequate* thought." There is every reason to believe that what originates as a neurogenic anomaly may, through systematic (or even intermittent) reinforcement, "mature" into a relatively enduring psychological trait (understood as a habitual way of behaving toward a certain class of behavioral objects). A neurogenic inclination to overestimate benefits and underestimate costs and risks associated with behavior may thus well perpetuate through "action without thought."

Yet impulsivity is but one of perhaps an untolled number of personal characteristics; interaction with other personal characteristics may produce ever more intriguing patterns of perceiving and behaving. There is substantial research support for the Wechsler's observation (1958, 160–177) concerning the character of cognitive functioning that "a significant Verbal minus Performance constellation (V-P) [is] frequently met with in subjects labeled as acting-out individuals." We have elsewhere reviewed the considerable body of evidence that what we termed the "verbal deficit pattern" (Pallone and Hennessy, 1996, 210–215), in which the subject demonstrates substantially greater nonverbal than verbal intelligence (equivalent at least to a full standard deviation), is systematically observed among both juveniles and adults who persistently engage in antisocial (and, to a lesser extent, adventurous) risk-taking and have also drawn parallels between the verbal deficit pattern and the quasi-psychopathological condition termed *alexithymia*

(Keltikangas-Jarvinen, 1982; Taylor, Bagby, and Parker, 1992; Reif, Jeuser, and Fichter, 1996). We have suggested that people who are *both* neurogenically impulsive *and* at verbal deficit are at high risk to become excessively stimulus bound (Pallone and Hennessy, 1996, 242–243):

> Especially when the difference between verbal and non-verbal intelligence is relative large (and most particularly when both are subnormal), we may expect that the relative incapacity to mediate the data of experience verbally will result in impairment or constriction in the capacity to differentiate, construe, fantasize, and or imagine, since these cognitive operations are largely mediated verbally.... The person who is limited in the capacity to construe may become, on that account, more *stimulus-bound* than one who is able to construe imaginatively a variety of possible meanings for, or responses to, stimuli or able to construe alternate meanings for the behavior of others.

We have encountered the verbal deficit pattern less frequently among the police officers decorated for bravery whom we have examined clinically; and (not unexpectedly, given relatively formal procedures for preservice selection even in very small departments) in no case have we found a significant V-P difference with both readings at subnormal levels. Because our subject sample remains too small to permit valid statistical inferences, we can only offer the impression that it appears to be the case that nonverbal intelligence typically exceeds verbal intelligence but only at a level that approximates ten IQ points or so (about 0.67 a standard deviation), a difference that clearly could be attributed to chance even if our sample were large enough to warrant formal statistical analysis. Clinically, however, the decorated officers we have interviewed display an unmistakable impatience with words, strong disdain for lengthy explanation (even of relatively complex phenomena), and a clear preference for action over thought. Whether, with a larger sample, such a clinical impression will reveal an empirically demonstrable preference for "action without thought" among *bona fide* heroes remains a matter of conjecture.

We believe impulsivity (especially when expressed in the underestimation of costs and risks associated with behavior) is implicated in all four forms of risk-taking behavior here discussed. We posit as essential in the teleologic emergence of the heroic rescue fantasy an interaction between impulsivity and so pervasive and persistent a need for self-aggrandizement and/or social recognition (Jackson, 1984) that it approximates the level of a "virtual trait" and is discernible in what in the Freudian canon might be called the continual search for narcissistic supplies. Such a conjunction might contribute to heroism in some peculiar way; we have not yet encountered such a case.

Although there is considerable agreement among neuroscientists concerning the probable neurogenesis of trait impulsivity and some reason to believe that the verbal deficit pattern in intellectual functioning has its roots in brain dysfunction (recent twin studies concerning the "heritability" of complex psychological traits aside), no consensus obtains concerning the possible/probable neurogenesis of an inordinate need for self-aggrandizement. Some zealots hold the position that an inflated sense of self-importance can be inferentially attributed to dysfunction in the limbic system, but the reasoning that precedes this conclusion seems convoluted, shuffling between hard science and anthropomorphically poetic analogy: among humans, a sense of self-importance (perhaps the root for grandiosity, though not necessarily for self-aggrandizement) is often the linchpin for paranoia, the principal symptom in which is pervasive, intractable fear; paranoia (or at least refractory and objectively unwarranted fear) can be generated through an overproduction of dopamine in the limbic system; ergo . . . ? Thus far, the evidence seems to reveal an unreconstructed commitment to the neurology = destiny formulation. The explanations of the psychoanalysts and the developmentalists, pivoting on notions of maternal indulgence or deprivation, seem to us to have at least as much to offer. Whatever its source, the conjunction between persistent self-aggrandizing and the concomitant hypervigilance for opportunities to display superiority on the one hand and impulsivity, with or without verbal deficiency, on the other clearly represents a volatile mixture.

Variant Psychosocial Environments

There is every reason to believe that each of us *self-selects* those psychosocial environments that we find most congenial and comfortable, largely because they are peopled by folks like us. Moreover, as we search for congenial environments, we become sensitized to cues that reveal preferences and tolerances for behaviors of various sorts. The bookworm, the computer "nerd," and the legendary Joe Six-Pack usually immerse themselves in quite variant interpersonal networks.

Role models likely provide the most readily accessible index to those behaviors (not to say also, costume) which are normative and/or tolerable within variant psychosocial environments. Some interpersonal networks provide no role models for risk-taking behavior (but instead perhaps, for "rigidity and inhibition"); they are unlikely to attract people in whom impulsivity has become an embedded trait. Yet others provide role models for prosocial, antisocial, or asocial risk-taking. There may be some element of chance operating to determine to which psychosocial environment the impulsive person is exposed initially and systematically, or such exposure may result from a more-or-less conscious search, in which a variety of other personality traits (and values) are also implicated. Exposure progresses to sensitization by means both of direct social reinforcement and vicarious conditioning.

Generally accepted civic ideals in advanced societies and the precepts of many (though not all) formal religions fairly explicitly urge prosocial (although not necessarily risky) behavior in order to protect the safety of another, even a previously unknown other. The willingness to risk one's own safety to protect that of another under threat ratchets toward heroism. But organized programs of socialization to the values that underlie heroic behavior are encountered infrequently—perhaps only in the training of public safety officers (police and other law enforcement officers, firefighters, corrections officers, prison guards, armed probation and parole officers, and some branches of the military). There are many interesting issues that deserve exploration in the relationship between psychosocial developmental experiences involving early exposure to prosocial models of risk-taking behavior and the decision to pursue a public safety career; society values heroism, but rarely studies its dynamics and antecedents.

The Opportunity to Behave

Very nearly paralleling the emergence of sharp focus on neurologic bases for behavior, renewed emphasis has been placed in sociology (and criminology) over the past three decades on opportunity as an important stimulus determinant of behavior (Sells, 1963). In its new dispensation, opportunity is interpreted to account both a relevant behavioral object and lack of direct deterrence. According to Clarke (1984), the principal architect of opportunity-based criminogenesis, "Opportunity . . . is a rather more complex concept than implied by simple counts of targets. . . . Opportunities . . . are not merely presented and perceived [but also] can be sought and created by those with the necessary motivation." Clearly, sensitization to a particular interpersonal environment with tolerance (admiration?) for this or that sort of behavior interpenetrates behavioral opportunity.

But, within the context of risk-taking behavior, the matter of whether opportunity is "encountered" or "created" is key. Our data thus far incline us to believe that it is rare that an act of genuine heroism results from an effort, whether conscious or not, to *create* an opportunity for prosocial risk-taking. Instead, both among the public safety officers and the tiny handful of heroic private citizens we have interviewed, heroic behavior has been stimulated by external events and or (especially in the case of private citizens) by randomly encountered appeals for help; in no case have we intuited a posture that, in retrospect, might suggest an act of heroism searching for an opportunity to happen. Especially among police officers, the (admittedly post-event) attitude we have encountered most frequently has been minimization, expressed in phrases such as "No big thing; part of the job." Among the relative handful of private citizens who have behaved heroically we have interviewed, an air of diffidence has frequently been communicated (virtually, of the "Aw, shucks" genre). Not quite incidentally, we have been deeply impressed by the fact that the heroic private citizens to a person had issued a summons for "official" assistance (generally from police, fire, or emergency medical sources) before themselves leaping into the fray and, in essence, regarded their own behavior essentially as a stop-gap measure until such assistance arrived. (If only to underscore that a small sample may be extremely biased, we might also mention the "one that got away." This was a private citizen who had heroically rescued a "victim" previously unknown to him from suicide by drowning. Although he had tentatively agreed to a clinical interview, after the tale of the rescue had been reported in a "supermarket" tabloid we learned from his newly-appointed attorney that such interview was to be contingent upon a substantial fee that rivaled those already proffered for "story rights" by scriptwriters for made-for-TV films.)

Among the asocial risk-takers (rock climbers, bungee-jumpers, hang-gliders, stock car racers) we have examined, it is very nearly invariably the case that opportunity has been consciously sought. Among the antisocial risk-takers in our data base (aggressive criminal offenders, rapists, pedophiles), there appears to be considerable spread;

among repetitive offenders, it is often the case that the first opportunity to behave antisocially was more-or-less encountered, while subsequent opportunities were deliberately created.

Creation of an opportunity that in fact engenders risk *both* for others and for the actor himself/herself constitutes the defining behavior in the heroic rescue fantasy. To satisfy the need for self-aggrandizement, the level of risk must be clearly perceived and serious enough to engender fear in others, else the heroic rescue could not be enacted. As an example: In one of the earliest cases in our data base, during a weekday matinee a 21-year-old head usher in an upscale motion picture theater, who perceived himself as under-employed and under-appreciated, set a fire in the waste can in a smoking lounge adjacent to the ladies' room. Once sufficient smoke had emerged into the theater and caused concern (that failed to rise to the level of panic, however), he entered the lounge and extinguished the fire calmly and heroically. He had correctly calculated that few men would be present in the theater during a weekday matinee (and thus that a "carelessly dropped cigarette" in the men's smoking lounge would not constitute a credible account) and that the majority of members of the audience (whom he reasoned would likely be women not otherwise employed during normal working hours and thus not likely "liberated," independent, or assertive) would not be likely to undertake to attempt to extinguish the fire themselves. Alternately, of course, had our usher known the research that suggests that a V-P difference in the case of women generally tilts in the direction of verbal intelligence, he might have reasoned that the members of the audience were more likely on that account to summon responsible help than to attempt an heroic rescue. In this case, the rescuer subjected both others and himself to perceptible and palpable danger; and that is quite in contrast to Walter Mitty, whose heroic rescue scenarios always remained in fantasy and, consequently, jeopardized no one and violated no law.

Behavioral Outcome

Our schema proposes that the heroic rescue fantasy emerges from the interplay between:

(a) neurologic anomaly affecting realistic assessment of costs, risks, and benefits;

(b) perpetuating as impulsivity expressing itself in the underestimation of costs and risks and overestimation of benefits and perhaps supported by alexithymia; interacting with

(c) a persistent need for self aggrandizement likely born of psychosocial developmental experiences; leading to

(d) sensitization to interpersonal environments that provide role models for and positively reinforce prosocial risk-taking behavior; yielding to

(e) the manipulative creation of an opportunity to behave in such fashion as to engender risk to others and to the self; and eventuating

(f) in the enactment of a heroic rescue that prevents harm to others and thus elicits praise, admiration, adulation, and possibly formal reward.

That behavioral outcome is the defining criterion in the heroic rescue fantasy; the heroic rescue has failed if harm comes to others. Optimally, of course, no (or little) harm ensues to the rescuer himself/ herself. Adulation may, of course, prove short-lived. Although our usher received high praise from management, patrons, and even fire safety officers, adjusters and investigators for the property insurance company called upon to reimburse the costs of restoration of the damaged area were not satisfied that the fire could be attributed to a lighted cigarette disposed of carelessly. Convincing evidence that the fire and ensuing damage were the product of "voluntary misbehavior" on the part of a member of the theater staff would have the effect of negating the insurance company's obligations under the policy in force. Armed with only the flimsiest of circumstantial evidence and no physical evidence at all, insurance investigators nonetheless gave our man to understand that they were prepared to ask the public prosecutor to lodge against him the charge of attempted sexual assault, with aggravation—because the fire had been set in a lounge adjacent to the ladies' room. The sentence for such a charge might range to a maximum of thirty years, while the sentence for arson was limited to seven years. In the event, the rescuer was induced to plead guilty to the reduced charge of "reckless endangerment," to which a three-year sentence attaches. Sentence was suspended in favor of probation, one condition of which was restitution in the form of monetary damages. Within a space of ten weeks, adulation had given way to disgrace.

Our schematic also explicitly proposes that, while neurobiology and those prior developmental and learning experiences that give rise to such personality traits and near or virtual traits as impulsivity and need for self-aggrandizement may account for "inclination" or "propensity," a critical contribution to the character of the behaviors here considered is made by the character of the interpersonal environment in which the developing person matures and the norms of which he/she internalizes. Hence, we suggest that heroism emerges from a mix that includes neurogenic impulsivity (but not self-aggrandizement), sensitization to prosocial interpersonal environments, and a (more-or-less chance) encounter with an opportunity to behave impulsively in prosocial ways. By *heroism,* we mean a prosocial act, perhaps implicating the self in danger, the purpose of which is to right a wrong which is being done (or which is threatened) to another person (e.g., thwarting an effort to rob, maim, or murder another; rescuing a vulnerable person from impending harm) or, on occasion, to an object of significance (e.g., an effort to deface a patriotic or religious symbol).

Alternately, when neurogenic impulsivity melds with socialization in an interpersonal environment that rewards antisocial risk-taking, and most particularly when need for self-aggrandizement enters the mix, impulsive antisocial aggression follows. In cases in which gratuitous violence has been employed (i.e., aggressive behavior beyond that required to gain compliance with a perpetrator's demands, as when the liquor store clerk indeed empties the cash drawer but is rewarded for compliance with a pistol whipping nonetheless), we have the impression from our data that both a high level of need for self-aggrandizement and quite major verbal deficits have been implicated.

By its very nature, planning and enacting the heroic rescue fantasy imply secrecy and, in turn, solitary activity. But acts of heroism, adventurousness, or antisocial aggression often occur within "togetherness" situations or even within the context of genuine social groups, whether a criminal gang, a personal interest group of parachutists or rock climbers, or working groups of public safety officers. As a general principle, we believe that variables bearing on the direct social influence of significant (or perhaps only incidental) "others" then enter the mix in such fashion as to cue the behaver toward the pattern of social reinforcement customary within the interpersonal environment to which he/she has become sensitized.

Among public safety officers, we have observed that the presence of others has often contributed to massive minimization by the heroic actor, even months and sometimes years following the event. In some cases, the heroic actor has even claimed not to recall his/her heroic behavior, despite official records. In those cases, we suspect, minimization and/or the "forgetting" of the heroic experience may function as an attempt to narrow the social distance between oneself and one's colleagues that is engendered by virtue of the heroic act itself.

In yet another case, heroic intent clothed itself in deliberate deception. We interviewed at length several members of a special weapons and tactics (SWAT) team of municipal police officers who had been engaged in an eight-hour stand-off during a hostage situation involving a single gunman (later confirmed as heavily under the influence of central nervous system stimulants) and two elderly residents in a suburban community. As dusk yielded to night, one officer broke ranks, acting contrary to the standing orders of his superordinate, stealthily entered the house, and disarmed the hostage taker. His confreres reported to the press that, as he broke ranks, he said, "Enough of this [expletive deleted]; I got a hot date waiting." In our subsequent meetings with this officer, who was virtually simultaneously reprimanded and decorated for bravery, it became evident that the "hot date waiting" statement lacked even a remote resemblance to reality. Rather, that verbalization had been consciously couched in terms that could be understood and accepted by colleagues who cultivated a "macho" image. After many hours of discussion, this well-educated, highly sensitive officer admitted that it was easier to clothe himself in macho statements than to declaim that a wrong called to be righted, or that he believed (contrary to the opinion of his superordinate) that the probability for harm to the hostages increased as the stand-off dragged on beyond nightfall. We are not at all certain that his colleagues, though personally perhaps rougher around the edges and though they had remained obedient to their superior officer's instructions, might not have employed similar locutions to mask similar values.

Reprise

On the basis largely of data from interviews and examinations of takers of risks of varying sorts, this paper has essayed to sketch a process psychology paradigm for the heroic rescue fantasy and to contrast a prototypical sequence therefor with corresponding sequences in antisocial, asocial, and prosocial risk-taking. It has been proposed that the heroic rescue fantasy emerges from the interplay between (a) neurologic anomaly affecting realistic assessment of costs, risks, and benefits, associated with behavior of various sorts, (b) perpetuating as impulsivity expressed as persistent underestimation of costs and risks and perhaps supported by a condition of alexithymia or verbal deficit in cognitive functioning, interacting with (c) a persistent need for self-aggrandizement (or social recognition or narcissistic supplies) likely born of psychosocial developmental experiences, leading to (d) sensitization to interpersonal environments that provide role models for and positively reinforce prosocial risk-taking behavior, yielding to (e) the manipulative creation of an opportunity to behave in such fashion as to engender risk to others and to the self, and eventuating (f) in the enactment of a heroic rescue that prevents harm to others and thus elicits praise, admiration, adulation, and possibly formal reward. The conjunction between impulsivity expressing itself in the underestimation of costs and risks (neurogenic or not) and need for self-aggrandizement is proposed as necessary in the heroic rescue fantasy; the manipulative creation of an opportunity to behave that engenders risk to others and to the self is proposed as the defining behavior; and a rescue that prevents harm to others is proposed as the defining criterion.

References

Alexander, E.C., H.N. Wolfson, D.J. Scrams, and B.M. Rienzi. (1995). Provocation, hostility, aggression, and victimization: Firefighters and incarcerated felons. *Journal of Offender Rehabilitation*, 22 (1/2), 47–58.

Bates, M.E., H.R. White, and E. Labouvie. (1994). Changes in sensation-seeking needs and drug use. In P. Venturelli (Ed.), *Drug Use in America: Social, Cultural, and Political Perspectives*. Boston: Jones & Bartlett, 67–75.

Blanco, C., L. Orensanz-Muñoz, C. Blanco-Jerez, and J. Saiz-Ruiz. (1996). Pathological gambling and platelet MAO activity: A psychobiological study. *American Journal of Psychiatry*, *153*, 119–127.

Brown, G.L. and M.I. Linnoila. (1990). CSF serotonin metabolite (5-HIAA) studies in depression, impulsivity, and violence. *Journal of Clinical Psychiatry*, *51*, 31–41.

Cattell, R.B. (1980). *Personality and Learning Theory: The Structure of Personality in Its Environment*. New York: Springer.

Clarke, R.V. (1984). Opportunity-based crime rates: The difficulties of further refinement. *British Journal of Criminology*, *75*, 77–85.

Coccaro, E.F., R.J. Kavoussi, Y.I. Sheline, J.D. Lish, and J.G. Csernansky. (1996). Impulsive aggression in personality disorder correlates with tritiated paroxetine binding in the platelet. *Archives of General Psychiatry*, *53*, 531–536.

Colligan, R.C., D. Osborne, W.M. Swenson, and K.P. Offord. (1989). *The MMPI: A Contemporary Normative Study*, (2nd ed.). Odessa, FL: Psychological Assessment Resources.

Eysenck, S.B.G. and H.J. Eysenck. (1978). Impulsiveness and venturesomeness: Their position in a dimensional system of personality description. *Psychological Reports, 43*, 1247–1255.

Farley, F. (1986). The big T in personality. *Psychology Today*, May, 44–52.

Hare, R.D., L. McPhereson, and A.E. Forth. (1988). Male psychopaths and their criminal careers. *Journal of Consulting & Clinical Psychology, 56*, 710–714.

Higley, J.D., P.T. Mehlman, D.M. Taub, S.B. Higley, J.H. Vickers, S.J. Suomi & M. Linnoila. (1992). Cerebrospinal fluid monoamine and adrenal correlates of aggression in free-ranging rhesus monkeys. *Archives of General Psychiatry, 49*, 436–441.

Jackson, D.N. (1984). *Personality Research Form Manual*, (3rd ed.). Port Huron, MI: Research Psychologists Press.

Keltikangas-Jarvinen, L. (1982). Alexithymia in violent offenders. *Journal of Personality Assessment, 46*, 462–467.

Klinteberg, B., D. Schälling, G. Edman, L. Oreland, and M. Asberg. (1987). Personality correlates of platelet monoamine oxidase (MAO) activity in female and male subjects. *Neuropsychobiology, 18*, 89–96.

Levenson, M.R. (1990). Risk taking and personality. *Journal of Personality & Social Psychology, 58*, 1073–1080.

Linnoila, M.I. and M. Virkkunen. (1992). Aggression, suicidality, and serotonin. *Journal of Clinical Psychiatry, 53*, 46–51.

Mehlman, P.T., J.D. Higley, I. Faucher, A.A. Lilly, D.M. Taub, J. Vickers, S.J. Suomi, and M. Linnoila. (1995). Correlation of CSF 5-HIAA concentration with sociality and the timing of emigration in free-ranging primates. *American Journal of Psychiatry, 152*, 907–913.

Pallone, N.J. and J.J. Hennessy. (1992). *Criminal Behavior: A Process Psychology Analysis*. New Brunswick, NJ: Transaction Publishers.

Pallone, N.J. and J.J. Hennessy. (1993). Tinderbox criminal violence: Neurogenic impulsivity, risk-taking, and the phenomenology of rational choice. In R.V. Clarke and M. Felson (Eds.), *Routine Activity and Rational Choice: Advances in Criminological Theory*. New Brunswick, NJ: Transaction Publishers, 127–158.

Pallone, N.J. and J.J. Hennessy. (1996). *Tinder-Box Criminal Aggression: Neuropsychology, Demography, Phenomenology*. New Brunswick, NJ: Transaction Publishers.

Pandey, G.N., S.C. Pandey, Y. Dwivedi, P.G. Janicak, and J.M. Davis. (1995). Platelet serotonin-2A receptors: A potential biological marker for suicidal behavior. *American Journal of Psychiatry, 152*, 850–855.

Reif, W., J. Heuser, and M.M. Fechter. (1996). What does the Toronto alexithymia TAS-R measure? *Journal of Clinical Psychology, 52*, 423–429.

Schälling, D., G. Edman, M. Asberg, et al. (1988). Platelet MAO activity associated with impulsivity and aggressivity. *Personality and Individual Differences, 9*, 597–605.

Sells, S.B. (1963). Dimensions of stimulus situations which account for behavior variance. In S.B. Sells (Ed.), *Stimulus Determinants of Behavior*. New York: Ronald, 3–15.

Smith, B. (1988). Personality: Multivariate systems theory. In J. Nesseleroade and R.B. Cattell (Eds.), *Handbook of Multivariate Experimental Psychology* (2nd ed.). New York: Plenum, 687–736.

Taylor, G.J., R.M. Bagby, and J.D.A. Parker. (1992). The revised Toronto alexithymia scale: Some reliability, validity, and normative data. *Psychotherapy & Psychoso-matics, 57,* 34–41.

Wechsler, D. (1958). *The Measurement and Appraisal of Adult Intelligence* (4th ed.). Baltimore: Williams & Wilkins.

White, H.R., E.W. Labouvie, and M.E. Bates. (1985). The relationship between sensa-tion seeking and delinquency: A longitudinal analysis. *Journal of Research in Crime & Delinquency, 22,* 198–211.

11

Pathological Narcissism and Serial Homicide: Review and Case Study

Louis B. Schlesinger

> *But even where it emerges without any sexual purpose, in the blindest fury of destructiveness, we cannot fail to recognize that the satisfaction of the instinct is accompanied by an extraordinarily high degree of narcissistic enjoyment, owing to its presenting the ego with a fulfillment of the latter's old wishes for omnipotence.*
>
> —Sigmund Freud, *Civilization and Its Discontents*

Homicide, the ultimate form of human aggression, is not a unitary event, but a complex behavior with different clinical pictures, different dynamics, and different prognoses. Serial homicide is a relatively rare phenomenon (Drukteinis, 1992) at the extreme end of the aggressive spectrum. Here, the offender kills not because of a logical motive, or as an outgrowth of a psychotic disorder, but because of an internal pressure to commit the act (Revitch and Schlesinger, 1989). If, as Fromm (1973) and others suggest, aggression should be viewed as an aspect (or outgrowth) of personality functioning, the motivation to commit serial murders would thus stem in large part from an individual's underlying personality makeup. That is, in such cases aggression has been integrated within the personality (Kernberg, 1992).

The psychopathology of narcissism has been increasingly studied ever since the condition "narcissistic personality disorder" was included in the third revision of the *Diagnostic and Statistical Manual* (1980). Specifically, the relationship between narcissism and aggression, murder, and serial murder is being explored. Liebert (1985), for example, believes that most cases of serial murder occur among the borderline/narcissistic personality disorders. In Liebert's view, even the older cases reported in the literature (e.g., Revitch, 1965) would probably be classified, according to current nosological standards, as borderline or narcissistic.

The purpose of this article is to explore the relationship between serial homicide and pathological narcissism through a review of the literature and an illustrative case report.

Psychopathology of Serial Homicide

Revitch and Schlesinger (1978, 1981, 1989) developed the concept of a motivational spectrum in classifying homicide. At one end of the spectrum are homicides committed as a result of external (sociogenic or environmental) factors; at the other end are homicides committed as a result of internal (endogenous or psychogenic) pressures that drive (compel) the offender to act. Compulsive homicides are frequently repetitive (serial) and ritualistic. Fantasies may precede the murder by many years (Schlesinger and Kutash, 1981). Once started, the homicide may be repeated frequently, or there may be intervals with years in between.

In many cases reported in the literature, an offender who has committed a bizarre (usually sexual) murder and has served a lengthy prison term will repeat a similar crime when paroled. The case of William Heirens, famous for his saying "Catch me before I kill more, I can't help myself," is illustrative (Kennedy, Hoffman, and Haines, 1947). Prior to his spree of gynocide, Heirens broke into homes and also was a panty fetishist. He described severe anxiety, perspiration, and headaches when he tried to resist the urge to kill again.

Such cases of compulsive serial offenders have been described in the literature as far back as 1886 (Krafft-Ebing, 1934). In one case reported by Krafft-Ebing, a twenty-three-year-old man made at least four sexual attacks on women and killed several other women. After killing one of his victims, a fourteen-year-old girl, he mutilated her body, tore out her intestines and genitals, bit off a piece of flesh, and sucked blood from the wound. He also strangled a twenty-eight-year-old woman and ripped out her intestines and then tried to choke his nineteen-year-old cousin. All of these activities were accompanied by erection and ejaculation. Jack the Ripper, the compulsive serial offender who terrorized England, sadistically murdered five prostitutes, and possibly two other women whose mutilated bodies were found in a river; he earned his name through a tantalizing letter he wrote to the press, where he threatened to continue his murders: "I am down on whores and shan't quit ripping them."

Another serial killer, Peter Kurten, terrified Dusseldorf, Germany, in the late 1920s. In his childhood he was fascinated by the torture of dogs; and from the age of thirteen through his later adolescence, he had sexual relations with pigs, goats, and sheep, finding particular excitement in stabbing sheep while having sex with them. He committed his first murder at the age of nine and spent the rest of his life in and out of prison for murdering or attempting to murder various women. Once released from prison, he began a reign of terror, during which his compulsion to kill was so strong that he attacked not only women but men and children, choking them and cutting their throats. On one occasion, he killed a five-year-old and a fourteen-year-old girl on the same day. Other cases in the literature, reviewed by Schlesinger and Revitch (1997), have involved cannibalism, vampirism, necrophilia, and similar acts.

The incidence of serial murder is difficult to determine, since accurate statistics are not kept. Stote and Standing (1995) believe that serial homicide rates have increased, but only as much as have overall homicide rates in general. Holmes and DeBurger (1988) classify serial murder into four subtypes based on phenomenology of the act and motivation: (1) visionary—serial murder as a result of psychotic commands; (2) mission oriented—the goal to kill certain types of people, such as prostitutes; (3) hedonistic—murder as a result of thrill seeking; and (4) power control—gratification from complete control of the victim.

Revitch and Schlesinger (1981, 1989) believe that the vast majority of compulsive serial murderers have an underlying basis of sexual conflict. In such cases, there is a combination of hostility to women, preoccupation with maternal sexual conduct, overt or covert incestuous preoccupation, guilt over sex and rejection of sex as impure, and feelings of sexual inferiority. Some unhealthy emotional involvement with the mother has been found in many of these cases. The mother may be rejecting and punitive or, to the contrary, seductive, at times openly so. In some cases, the child may have experienced or witnessed the mother's promiscuity. In adult serial murderers, hostility to women is the outstanding characteristic. Adolescent and preadolescent offenders are chiefly preoccupied with maternal sexual conduct and sexual morality (Revitch, 1965); some of these individuals even develop a fantasy of the mother's purity. One fourteen-year-old boy who choked a ten-year-old girl and cut her neck expressed dislike for all girls but entertained a fantasy of his mother's purity and insisted that his parents abstained from sexual relations.

The role of fantasy in serial homicide has been noted by Prentky et al. (1989) and by Myers et al. (1993). According to these authors, fantasy eventually leads to action; and then the action is strongly driven by the fantasy, which takes on more and more power. Hale (1994) has emphasized the role of humiliation and embarrassment as motivation for serial murder. In Hale's view, the victim revives memories of someone who embarrassed and humiliated the offender earlier in life. The murderer then transfers feelings of humiliation into rage, in an attempt to remove the initial memory; but the memory is not expelled and the killings continue. Drukteinis (1992) explores the conversion of a childhood trauma into mastery by murder; in such cases, the perpetrator attempts to gain complete mastery and dominance by torturing and humiliating the victim.

According to Money (1990), serial sexual killing is not a result of psychogenesis, but a consequence of a neurobiological abnormality: "[t]he brain becomes pathologically activated to transmit messages of attack simultaneously with messages of sexual arousal and mating behavior" (p. 28). Many years earlier, MacLean (1962) spoke of the interconnection and proximity of the limbic structures connected with feeding and aggression (amygdala) and the structures connected with sexual functions (septum and hippocampus). MacLean also pointed to the display of genitals in male squirrel monkeys during a fight, highlighting the interconnection between sex and aggression.

Narcissism and Serial Homicide

Kohut (1966, 1968) described rage and aggression in narcissistic psychopathology and its relationship to low self-esteem: "The most violent forms of narcissistic rage arise in those individuals for whom a sense of absolute control over an archaic environment is indispensable because the maintenance of self-esteem—and indeed of the self—depends on the unconditional availability of the approving mirroring function of an admiring self object or on the ever present opportunity for a merger with an idealized one" (Kohut, 1972, p. 386). Many other writers (Fox, 1974; Noshpitz, 1984; Hurlbert and Apt, 1991; Rosen, 1991; Schulte, Hall, and Crosby, 1994; Hockenberry, 1995) also have noted the relationship between severe forms of narcissism and severe aggression, but not necessarily murder.

The relationship between narcissism and murder in both the adult and the adolescent has been observed by several investigators. Miller and Looney (1974) postulate that an adolescent offenders recidivism can be predicted by the degree to which that offender has dehumanized the victim; the description of dehumanization, as evidenced in case studies, is replete with narcissistic psychopathology. Thus, the most pathologically narcissistic offender, with total and permanent dehumanization, is at highest risk for repetition. McCarthy (1978), in his comprehensive study of ten adolescent murderers, cites narcissism and narcissistic injury and insults as major ingredients fueling homicidal behavior: "Both sadistic fantasies and homicidal acts or explosively violent assaults can be understood as attempts at redress of a common narcissistic vulnerability" (p. 25). Marohn (1987), in his psychobiography of the notorious western folk hero John Wesley Hardin, also concludes that narcissism was a major factor in the multiple murders committed during Hardin's adolescence. Revitch and Schlesinger (1978) report a case of a sixteen-year-old serial murderer's description (obtained while under the influence of intravenously injected sodium amytal) of his sadistic fantasies, his feelings of power and control when the victims begged him not to hurt them; after describing these fantasies he yelled out "Super David, the ruler," indicating how he wished people would view him.

Stone (1989) surveyed celebrated murder cases, including serial murders, and concluded that "many of the perpetrators can, with a fair degree of certainty, be considered examples of malignant narcissism" (p. 643), and that those murderers who do not admit their crimes are on the most extreme end of malignant narcissism, far beyond the scope of treatment. In many of the cases that he studied, Stone found humiliation and narcissistic injury predating and directly contributing to the murder; many of these offenders had also been brutalized as children.

Focusing solely on serial murder, Ansevics and Doweiko (1991) reviewed reports on eleven cases in a search for common themes, characteristics, and developmental patterns in the compulsive, repetitive murderer. They concluded that "the serial murderer reflects a variation of the borderline personality disorder and should be treated as such rather than as an antisocial personality disorder" (p. 115). A common variation of borderline psychopathology is narcissism, as manifested in self-glorifying fantasies motivated by a need to compensate for sexual inadequacies. Ten of the eleven murderers studied by Ansevics and Doweiko had experienced what amounts to severe narcissistic injury following rejection of a female in adulthood, to the extent that the subjects decompensated and developed rage directed against women.

Liebert (1985) uses narcissistic and borderline personality disorders in profiling serial murder cases to assist in investigation and apprehension. He believes that the narcissistic individual has "incorporated too much of the bad from the maternal relationship and can split this introjected badness from his own personality and perceive it as originating from the outside. . . . The individual no longer possesses the badness—it is the other person, the female victim, who has it. . . . He may either project his introjected dissociative badness onto his victim and justify his own violence or displace his violence toward his bad mother onto the victim and destroy the mother's badness" (p. 192). Sexual and aggressive impulses become easily fused as a result of the underlying structural weakness of the narcissistic and borderline personality, and the murder thus becomes "a substitute for normal erotic pleasure" (p. 197). Regarding the fusion of sex and aggression, Freud (1905) noted that the sexual instinct is composed of different components, "some of which detach themselves to form perversions. Our clinical observation thus calls our attention to fusions, which have lost their expression in the uniform normal behavior" (p. 572). Thus, in serial homicide a fusion of sex and aggression is made easier by the weakened personality structure found in borderline and narcissistic cases.

In analyzing a spree serial murder, Pollack (1995) agrees with Abrahamsen (1973) that violence is used in such cases as a defense in the service of narcissism. The offender in this case manifested characteristics of "pathological grandiosity in response to rejection and humiliation" (p. 265), as well as the need for power and control described by Holmes and DeBurger (1988). Pollack concludes that the psychopathology of malignant narcissism—specifically, the erection of narcissistic defenses as a response to very destabilizing interpersonal relationships and life events—is a major consideration in understanding the serial murderer. Meloy (1988) believes that in particularly severe and malignant cases narcissism, sadism, and aggression are combined.

Hickey (1991) developed a trauma control model of serial murder and found that highly developed narcissistic features are present in cases of repetitive murder. Similarly, Lowenstein (1992) emphasizes pathological omnipotence as a central feature in the serial murderer. Finally, Gacono (1992) made a detailed Rorschach analysis of a sexual murderer and found borderline personality, sadism, and significant pathological narcissism as factors relevant to the homicide.

All the above-noted characteristics (see Table 11.1 for a summary) and theories are helpful in the phenomenological/psychodynamic search for understanding behavior as complex and multidetermined as serial murder. Different examiners stress different aspects of the same case— that is, various facets of behavior and various levels of consciousness—depending on their own perspective and orientation (Perr, 1975).

In the following case, the element of pathological narcissism is so striking that it clearly plays a major role in understanding this particular offender and the disorder of serial murder in general.

Case Report

A thirty-year-old male (John) was convicted of the murder of a twenty-five-year-old woman and the subsequent murder of a twenty-six-year-old woman and her two young children, ages six and eight. Although not charged, he was also suspected of two later murders and apparently confessed (off the record) to his attorney, but refused to do so officially. At the time of the evaluation, the defendant was raising either a diminished capacity or an insanity defense.

John became a suspect in the initial murders because he was ac-

TABLE 11.1
Narcissistic Characteristics in the Serial Murderer

Author	Characteristics
Liebert (1985)	easy fusion of sexual and aggressive impulses due to structural weakness of narcissistic personality disorder
Stone (1989)	coexistence of narcissistic and antisocial traits
Hickey (1991)	narcissistic features used to control trauma
Ansevics and Doweiko (1991)	self-glorifying fantasies to compensate for sexual inadequacies; experiences of narcissistic injury and rejection from female
Lowenstein (1992)	pathological omnipotence and antisocial behavior
Pollock (1995)	pathological grandiosity in response to rejection and humiliation; narcissistic defenses in response to destabilizing life events

quainted with both of the adult victims. He had had a sexual relationship with the first victim and knew the second victim because she was dating a friend of his. When initially questioned by the police, he denied guilt; but when he was interviewed a second time, he gave a full confession, which he later recanted in part. He told the police that he had shaved all his body hair and entered the home of both women without any clothing on, except for sneakers that he covered with socks. His motive here was not to leave any hair or fiber evidence that could be traced to him. He was also careful not to leave any fingerprints (using latex gloves). The defendant told the police that he had read books on criminology and criminal law in an attempt to become an expert on how to commit a murder without detection. Additionally, following the murder of the second victim, he poured alcohol into her vagina, in order to remove any traces of DNA, since he had had sex with her. He indicated that he came upon this idea after viewing the movie *Presumed Innocent*, where a similar method was presented.

It is extremely difficult to understand all the psychodynamics involved in these homicides, since John gave many different versions to many different individuals. With regard to the first victim, Laura, he stated that he visited her "just to have sex." Following sexual relations, Laura tried to convince him to stay with her all night, whereas he wanted to go home. She then threatened to tell his girlfriend about their sexual relationship and Laura tried to cut him with a knife. He retaliated by starting to choke her: "I took her upstairs; I don't know why. I was still choking her. I asked her why she wanted to do this to me and expose everything. I left her on the bed and I left and I went home." This is not exactly what the physical evidence showed: there was medical evidence of forcible sex, the victim had been hog-tied, and her head was smashed.

Six months after this homicide, the defendant killed the girlfriend of one of his friends. He gave a similar story, stating that he went over to visit her, had sex with her, and then got into an argument during which she too threatened to tell his girlfriend about their sexual encounter. Again, according to John, a fight ensued; he choked the victim, tied her up, and killed her. He then killed her two young children, who apparently saw John and knew him because he had been to their home on a number of occasions to visit their mother and her boyfriend, John's friend. After killing these three individuals, the defendant went to a restaurant, ate dinner, bought beer, returned home, and slept well.

The DNA analysis came back; and since alcohol preserves—rather than destroys—semen, a perfect DNA match was made. The defendant then changed his story, stating that he knew alcohol preserves semen and actually wanted to get caught.

When asked why he had killed these people, John was unable to give a clear answer except to say that he was angry and felt that the women would expose their sexual relationship with him to others. When asked whether he got any type of powerful or sexually arousing feeling from the killings, he stated, "No, I am powerful in any way I need to be powerful. I get respect from everyone. I can conquer whatever I have to conquer; it is something I was born with. I do whatever it takes to overcome whoever it may be. When I tell you to do something, it's not intimidation or fear; either you do it or deal with me." When asked whether any feelings of inadequacy might underlie some of his behavior, he stated: "I have no fears or worries. People try to overcompensate when they fear something. I have no fear, none whatsoever."

Psychological testing showed an individual of average intelligence with no significant organicity. Diagnostically, he falls within the spectrum of the severe personality disorders with strong narcissistic and less pronounced antisocial traits. There were several primitive and regressive Rorschach perceptions, such as "blood blotted and smudged on a piece of paper, running down a piece of paper"; "Drops of blood"; and "Two boar hogs; their heads have been cut off, just their heads. Their heads have been severed. They are posted on a wall like a trophy." These responses are consistent with severe characterological disturbance falling within the borderline spectrum, also typical of individuals with malignant narcissism, and there is a tremendous aggressive component as well.

Most of John's explanations of his perceptions on the Rorschach were logical, and his perceptions bore a reasonably adequate relationship to the stimulus material on which they were based. The Rorschach also revealed a marked lack of empathic capacity, as evidenced by his providing only one human (movement) perception—a trait consistent with both narcissistic and antisocial features. His perception of "ovaries of a woman," given to the traditionally considered male card, suggested conflict with his male self-image. His response on the MMPI showed a strong need to appear without any socially undesirable characteristics, to the extent that he might even lie to achieve this impression.

TAT stories were replete with themes of narcissism and control: "He wants to be great at it; he wants to become a world-renowned violinist." Several stories also suggested severe conflict and anger toward women and a generalized negative view of females: "His wife had an affair; it's her nature. She's been doing it all along. It makes him angry. He dies of syphilis; she gets it from having so many affairs; she is a whore; she was born that way." "He killed his wife because she was unfaithful; he strangled her. She had an affair and flaunted it, and he couldn't take it anymore. She made him into an animal because of her actions. Once a woman finds out that you love her, she changes and starts doing what she wants to do because she figures no matter what, you will be there; you will follow her; she figures she's got you; you are not going anywhere, so why not have an affair."

The defendant was unemployed during the time period when the six murders occurred. He was previously in the Army but was expelled for attempting to steal and manipulate money out of subordinates. His early life is difficult to assess. He tried to present himself as coming from a typical middle-class background with indulgent parents and siblings; and he had, in fact, achieved some success as a high school athlete and was apparently well regarded in his adolescent years as a result. But his statements could not be confirmed or invalidated by interviews with family members, since they has severed all ties with him after learning the details of the various homicides.

Discussion

Pathological narcissism clearly played a major role in this case. John supplied a motive for his homicides by trying to give the impression that the women he murdered wanted him sexually and would expose their sexual relationship to his girlfriend. He displayed no emotion at all following the murders; in fact, after murdering the second victim and her two children, he went to a restaurant, had dinner, slept well, and showed no discernible remorse or anxiety. Narcissism poured out of John in various test findings, particularly TAT stories with themes of omnipotence and control. He also described himself as being powerful in all ways and having no fear at all.

John probably felt some degree of humiliation and embarrassment after being expelled from the military, where he had served as a drill sergeant who exerted excessive control over his men, often resorting to acts of sadism and manipulation. He had been unemployed for a considerable period of time when the murders began—another possible source of humiliation. Hale (1994) has noted that a sense of humiliation can serve as a trigger for serial murder. Drukteinis (1992) also stresses the role of humiliation and the serial murderer's need to gain complete dominance over his victims. In addition, John had enormous hostility toward women—a characteristic noted by Revitch and Schlesinger (1989) as a major factor in adult sex murderers. Holmes and DeBurger's (1988) power-control type of serial murder is evident in this case, and is probably the closest of these authors' subtypes associated with narcissism. Fantasy also must have been involved in this case, since John planned the various homicides with extraordinary detail, even shaving his body and entering the homes without clothes on. Whether he had an unhealthy emotional relationship with his mother is impossible to determine, but the fact that he described his family in such a rosy way suggests the opposite.

No matter what theoretical orientation one adopts, the role of narcissism seems to be fundamental in understanding the personality makeup of this serial murderer, with his overwhelming need to present himself as strong, powerful, and always in control. Liebert (1985) has noted the poor level of personality integration found in narcissistic cases, predisposing such offenders to an intrusion into consciousness of primitive sexual/aggressive impulses. A better-integrated personality with similar traits and dynamics might have stronger controls and thus would display no acting-out behavior. Further clinical study is needed in order to understand why individuals with characteristics and experiences similar to those of the serial murderer do not commit serial murder. Such studies could contribute substantially to our understanding of serial murderers and their clinical treatment.

References

Abrahamsen, D. (1973). *The murdering mind*. New York: Harper & Row.

Ansevics, N. L. and Doweiko, H. E. (1991). Serial murderers: Early proposed developmental model and typology. *Psychotherapy and Private Practice, 9*, 107–122.

Drukteinis, A. M. (1992). Serial murder—the heart of darkness. *Psychiatric Annals, 22*, 532–538.

Fox, R. P. (1974). Narcissistic rage and the problem of combat aggression. *Archives of General Psychiatry, 31*, 807–811.

Freud, S. (1905). Three contributions to a theory of sex (the sexual aberrations). In *Basic writings of Sigmund Freud*, trans. A. A. Brill. New York: Random House.

Fromm, E. (1973). *The anatomy of human destructiveness*. New York: Holt, Rinehart & Winston.

Gacono, C. D. (1992). Sexual homicide and the Rorschach: A Rorschach case study of sexual homicide. *British Journal of Projective Psychology, 37*, 1–21.

Hale, R. (1994). The role of humiliation and embarrassment in serial murder. *Psychology: A Journal of Human Behavior, 31*, 17–23.

Hickey, E. (1991). *Serial murderers and their victims*. Monterey, CA: Brooks/Cole.

Hockenberry, S. L. (1995). Dyadic violence, shame, and narcissism. *Contemporary Psychoanalysis, 31*, 301–325.

Holmes, R. M. and DeBurger, J. E. (1988). *Serial murder*. Beverly Hills, CA: Sage Publications.

Hurlbert, D. F., and Apt, C. (1991). Sexual narcissism and the abusive male. *Journal of Sex and Marital Therapy, 17*, 279–292.

Kennedy, F., Hoffman, H., and Haines, W. (1947). A study of William Heirens. *American Journal of Psychiatry, 104*, 113–121.

Kernberg, O. (1992). *Severe personality disorders*. New Haven: Yale University Press.

Kohut, H. (1966). Forms and transformations of narcissism. *Journal of the American Psychoanalytic Association, 14*, 243–272.

Kohut, H. (1968). The psychoanalytic treatment of narcissistic personality disorders. *Psychoanalytic Study of the Child, 23*, 86–113.

Kohut, H. (1972). Thoughts on narcissism and narcissistic rage. *Psychoanalytic Study of the Child, 27*, 360–399.

Krafft-Ebing, R. von (1934). *Psychopathia sexualis,* F. J. Rebman, trans. Brooklyn, NY: Physicians and Surgeons Book Company (Originally published in 1886).

Liebert, J. (198S). Contributions to psychiatric consultation in the investigation of serial murder. *International Journal of Offender Therapy and Comparative Criminology, 28*, 187–200.

Lowenstein, L. F. (1992). The psychology of the obsessed compulsive killer. *The Criminologist, 16*, 26–38.

MacLean, P. D. (1962). New findings relevant to the evolution of psychosexual functions of the brain. *Journal of Nervous and Mental Disease, 135*, 289–301.

Marohn, R. C. (1987). John Wesley Hardin, adolescent killer: The emergence of a narcissistic behavior disorder. *Adolescent Psychiatry, 14*, 271–296.

McCarthy, J. B. (1978). Narcissism and the self in homicidal adolescents. *American Journal of Psychoanalysis, 38*, 19–29.

Meloy, J. R. (1988). *The psychopathic mind: Origins, dynamics, and treatment.* Northvale, NJ: Jason Aronson.

Miller, O. and Looney, J. (1974). The prediction of adolescent homicide: Episodic dyscontrol and dehumanization. *American Journal of Psychoanalysis, 34*, 187–198.

Money. J. (1990). Forensic sexology: Paraphiliac serial rape (biastophilia) and lust murder. *American Journal of Psychotherapy, 44*, 26–36.

Myers, W. C., Reccoppa, L., Burton, K., and McElroy, R. (1993). Malignant sex and aggression: An overview of serial sexual homicide. *Bulletin of the American Academy of Psychiatry and Law, 21*, 435–451.

Noshpitz, J. D. (1984). Narcissism and aggression. *American Journal of Psychotherapy, 38,* 17–34.

Perr, I. N. (1975). Psychiatric testimony and the *Rashomon* phenomenon. *Bulletin of the American Academy of Psychiatry and Law, 3*, 83–98.

Pollock, P. H. (1995). A case of spree serial murder with suggested diagnostic opinions. *International Journal of Offender Therapy and Comparative Criminology, 39*, 258–268.

Prentky, R. A., Burgess, A. W., Rokous, F., Lee, A., Hartman, C., Ressler, R., and Douglas, J. (1989). The presumptive role of fantasy in serial sexual homicide. *American Journal of Psychiatry, 146*, 887–891.

Revitch, E. (1965). Sex murder and the potential sex murderer. *Diseases of the Nervous System, 26*, 640–648.

Revitch, E. and Schlesinger, L. B. (1978). Murder: Evaluation, classification, and prediction. In I. L. Kutash, S. B. Kutash, and L. B. Schlesinger (Eds.), *Violence: Perspectives on murder and aggression* (pp. 138–164). San Francisco: Jossey-Bass.

Revitch, E., and Schlesinger, L. B. (1981). *Psychopathology of Homicide.* Springfield, IL: Charles C. Thomas.

Revitch, E., and Schlesinger, L. B. (1989). *Sex murder and sex aggression: Phenomenology, psychopathology, psychodynamics, and prediction.* Springfield, IL: Charles C. Thomas.

Rosen, I. (1991). Self esteem as a factor in social and domestic violence. *British Journal of Psychiatry, 158*, 18–23.

Schlesinger, L. B. and Kutash, I. (1981). The criminal fantasy technique: A comparison of sex offenders and substance abusers. *Journal of Clinical Psychology, 37*, 210–218.

Schlesinger, L. B. and Revitch, E. (1997). *Sexual dynamics of antisocial behavior* (2nd ed.). Springfield, IL: Charles C. Thomas.

Schulte, H. M., Hall, M. J., and Crosby, R. (1994). Violence in patients with narcissistic personality pathology: Observations of a clinical series. *American Journal of Psychotherapy, 48,* 610–623.

Stone, M. (1989). Murder. *Psychiatric Clinics of North America, 12,* 643–651.

Stote, R. and Standing, L. (1995). Serial and multiple homicide: Is there an epidemic? *Social Behavior and Personality, 23,* 313–317.

Contributors

SHELDON ALEXANDER is professor of psychology at Wayne State University, Detroit, Michigan. His principal interests are in the psychology of justice and fairness at both organizational and interpersonal level of social behavior, with particular attention to the antecedents and consequences of procedural injustice. He is best known for his lanmark paper in *Social Justice Research* on procedural and distributive justice in the behavior of organizations and for his chapter on organizational justice in the 1995 American Psychological Association volume *Changing Employment Relations.*

MARK A. BARNETT is professor of psychology at Kansas State University, Manhattan, Kansas. His principal research interests concern an individual's social and emotional responses to others. His studies have examined factors that influence the development and expression of prosocial emotions and behaviors (e.g., empathy, helping) and how observers react to the plight of others in extreme circumstances (e.g., homelessness, victimization in rape). Recent publications include studies of moral development in *Basic and Applied Social Psychology* and crossover longitudinal studies of perceptions of homelessness in the *Journal of Social Distress.*

JEFFREY S. BARTEL is pursuing graduate study in psychology at Kansas State University, Manhattan, Kansas. He is interested in the development and expression of prosocial behavior and has completed research on personality differences between spontaneous helpers and long-term volunteers.

KIRK R. BLANKSTEIN is associate professor of psychology at the University of Toronto at Mississauga and an editor in the Plenum series on advances in studies of communication and affect. His principal research interests are in perfectionism, the causes and consequences of test anxiety, and the personality correlates of coping and problem-solving ability. Recent publications include studies on the frequency of perfectionistic thinking in the *Journal of Personality and Social Psychology* and on problem-solving in *Cognitive Therapy and Research*.

WAI H. CHEUK is associate professor at the Open University of Hong Kong. A doctoral alumnus of the University of Georgia, his research interests are in social support, close friendships, and rejection stress. He has previously contributed to *Current Psychology*.

RICHARD CLEMENTS is assistant professor of psychology at Indiana University Northwest, Gary. Substance use disorders, geropsychology, the relationships between religion and psychology, and clinical applications are among his principal interests. He has contributed to the *Journal of Psychology and Theology* and to *Alcoholism: Clinical and Experimental Research* and has authored a chapter on goal-setting in Hecker and Deacon's volume *The Therapist's Notebook* (1998).

GORDON L. FLETT is professor of psychology at York University, Toronto. His principal research interests are in perfectionism in relation to psychological adjustment and in the links between depression and personality traits. Recent publications include a landmark paper in *Psychological Bulletin* on the continuity of depression and a review of conceptual on methodological issues in research on personality and depression in the *European Journal of Personality*. His book on perfectionism (co-edited, with Paul L. Hewitt) is shortly to be published by the American Psychological Association Press.

LARRY GATES is professor of psychology at the University of Southern Mississippi, Hattiesburg. His research interest include Jungian personality theory and patterns of human development. He has contributed to *Psychological Perspectives, Journal of Religion and Health,* and *Journal of Evolutionary Psychology.*

KIMBERLY K.G. HARPER, an alumna of the department of psychology, Kansas State University, Manhattan, Kansas, is a market analyst at Experian Corporation, Lincoln, Nebraska. Her research interests include perceptions of helping behaviors within and across races.

JAMES J. HENNESSY is professor and lately chairperson, Division of Psychological and Educational Services, Graduate School of Education, Fordham University, Lincoln Center, New York City. Best known for studies of the interaction between race, social class, and differentiated cognitive functioning, his current research interests center on the psychobiology of risk-taking and the "crime personalities" of American cities. Among many other works, his books published by Transaction include *Tinder-Box Criminal Aggression: Neuropsychology, Demography, Phenomenology* (1996), *Fraud and Fallible Judgment: Varieties of Deception in the Social and Behavioral Sciences* (1995), and *Criminal Behavior: A Process Psychology Analysis* (1992, 1994), each with Nathaniel J. Pallone.

PAUL L. HEWITT is associate professor, clinical psychology, at the University of British Columbia, Vancouver. His research focuses on multidimensional perspectives on perfectionism, with particular emphasis on interpersonal dimensions. His papers on perfectionism, stress, and depression have appeared in the *Journal of Abnormal Psychology.* His book on perfectionism (co-edited, with Gordon L. Flett) is shortly to be published by the American Psychological Association Press.

ROBERT W. HILL is associate professor of psychology at Appalachian State University, Boone, North Carolina. He is currently studying the assessment of perfectionistic and narcissistic personality characteristics. His studies on perfectionism have recently appeared in the *Journal of Social Behavior and Personality* and the *Journal of Personality Assessment.*

HELEN E. LINKEY is associate professor of psychology at Marshall University, Huntington, West Virginia. Her principal research interests are in the psychology of justice and fairness, the effects of divorce on children, the psychology of religion, and male influence behaviors. Notable publications include her study on dominance in dyads expressed through nonverbal behaviors, which appeared in the *Journal of Research in Personality.*

NATHANIEL J. PALLONE is University distinguished professor (psychology) at Rutgers – The State University of New Jersey, where he previously served as dean and as academic vice president. His research interests focus on the psychobiology of risk-taking, both pro- and antisocial. Among many other works, his books published by Transaction include *Tinder-Box Criminal Aggression: Neuropsychology, Demography, Phenomenology* (1996), *Fraud and Fallible Judgment: Varieties of Deception in the Social and Behavioral Sciences* (1995), and *Criminal Behavior: A Process Psychology Analysis* (1992, 1994), each with James J. Hennessy, and *On the Social Utility of Psychopathology: A Deviant Majority and Its Keepers?* (1986) and *Rehabilitating Criminal Sexual Psychopaths: Legislative Mandates, Clinical Quandaries* (1990).

DONNA PICKERING is a doctoral candidate in psychology at York University, Toronto. His work on adaptation and coping has appeared in *Personality and Individual Differences.*

SIDNEY ROSEN is professor emeritus of psychology at the University of Georgia, Athens. After completing his graduate study at the University of Michigan, he directed the Ph.D. program in social psychology at Georgia from its inception in 1969 until his retirement in 1987. Dr. Rosen's earlier research focused on interpersonal processes and communication patterns. In more recent years, he has concentrated on prosocial behavior, in particular on the distinct and often contrasting perspectives and reactions of help givers and help receivers.

LOUIS B. SCHLESINGER is clinical associate professor in the department of psychiatry at the New Jersey Medical School of the University of Medicine and Dentistry of New Jersey, Newark, and a member of the adjunct faculty in the department of psychology at John Jay College of Criminal Justice, City University of New York. He is author or editor of six books, of which the most recent are *Sexual Dynamics in Antisocial Behavior* (1997) and *Explorations in Criminal Psychopathology: Clinical Syndromes with Forensic Implications* (1996).

C. EDWARD SNODGRASS is a doctoral candidate at the University of Southern Mississippi, Hattiesburg, where he is conducting research on the wellsprings of ecological world views. His research interests center on how social institutions influence the way in which an individual perceives his/her relationship with the natural environment.

LEE ANN STEADMAN, an alumna of the department of psychology at Kansas State University, Manhattan, Kansas, is currently a field sales associate for Sprint North, Atlanta, Georgia. Her research interests are in industrial and organizational psychology.

BRIDGET SWEARSE is associate professor at the Open University of Hong Kong, where she coordinates the program in nursing studies. He research interests focus on sources of job-related stress among practicing nurses and on in-service education in the nursing profession.

BIRGIT S. VALDEZ is currently enrolled in the doctoral program in clinical psychology at the University of Kansas. She has completed research on variables associated with decisions to engage in particular sexual behaviors. She will serve as a psychologist in the U.S. Army after completing her studies.

GUY D. VITAGLIONE is a doctoral candidate in psychology at Kansas State University, Manhattan, Kansas. His research interests concern empathy and helping behavior and he is presently studying how "empathic anger" may activate prosocial behaviors on behalf of a victim. His work has appeared in the *Journal of Applied Social Psychology.*

GRAHAM WAGSTAFF, who earned the Ph.D. at the University of Newcastle-upon-Tyne, is reader in psychology at the University of Liverpool, UK. His research has ranged across several topics in the psychology of justice and law, including equity theory, punishment, and eyewitness accuracy. His publications include a series of articles developing and revising the principle of equity in justice, published in *Current Psychology* and in the *British* and *European Journals of Social Psychology.* He is also a founding member of the British Society of Experimental and Clinical Hypnosis and has published widely on the cognitive psychology of hypnosis and suggestibility and on hypnosis and law. His *Hypnosis, Compliance, and Belief* is a substantive text on the social psychology of hypnosis.

SHANNON WHEATMAN is completing doctoral research in the Department of Psychology at the University of Georgia. Her research interests include self-esteem, group processes, and the psychology of the law. She holds a graduate degree from the School of Law at the University of Nebraska.

KWOK S. WONG, a specialist in educational administration, is a lecturer at the Hong Kong Institute of Education. Her research interests include job-related stress among kindergarten principals.

GREGORY P. YOUSEY is a staff psychologist at r/h/a Health Services, Rockwell, North Carolina, where he works with severely impaired adult patients. His current research interests include Down's Syndrome and interventions for self-injurious behavior.

Index of Topics and Names*

---

* Names of each contributor to the chapters which comprise this book are included, along with those of the first author of works cited.

Jackson, D., 171
Jack the Ripper, 185
James, W., 33
Janoff-Bulman, R., 68
Jeffers, F., 151
Joiner, T., 59
Judeo-Christian religious heritage, 134, 135
"just desert," ix, 8, 19
justice, ix, 1–31, 81–85, ; distributive, 14
John Paul II, Pope, vii

Kahn, A., 73
Kahn, R., 130
Kanfer, F., 68
Kansas State University, 99, 108
Kant, E., 24
Kaplan, D., 94
Karniol, R., 4
Katz, M., 16
Kelley, H., 57
Keltikangas-Jarvinen, L., 171
Kennedy, F., 184
Kernberg, O., 184
Kernis, M., 38, 52
Kluegel, J., 16
Kirkpatrick, L., 138
Klinteberg, B., 168
Kohlberg, L., 4, 24
Kohut, H., 186
Krafft-Ebbing, R., 184, 185
Krebs, D., 97, 107, 115
Kurlychek, R., 151

Lamm, H., 14, 73
Lane, I., 73
lawyer, motivation of, 99–117
laziness, voluntary, 10, 12
Lefcourt, H., 58, 60
"left-wing" politics, 15
Lemaine, G., 35, 39
Lenin, N., 24
Leppin, A., 66
Lerner, M., 2, 3, 4, 10, 13, 14
Lester, D., 153

Leventhal, G., 2, 5, 13, 14, 73, 83
Levenson, M., 167
Lewinshohn, P., 60
librarians, 87–95
Liebert, J., 184, 188, 190, 194
Linnoila, M., 168
Linkey, H., ix, 73–86, 199
Lowenstein, L., 189, 190

MacIntyre, A., 6
MacLean, P., 186
Markus, H., 98
Marohn, R., 187
Marsden, G., 136, 142
Martin, D., 151
Martin, T., 67
Marx, K., 24
Masters, K., 138
McCarthy, J., 187
McClintock, C., 19, 74
McFarland, S., 137, 140, 142
McGrath, J., 74
McMordie, W., 151
Meehl, P., 133
Mehlman, P., 168
Meloy, R., 189
Merton, R., 34, 35, 36, 49, 52
Merton, T., 148
Metalsky, G., 57
Meyer, J., 11, 14
Meyers, I., 94
Mickler, S., 122, 126
Mikula, G., 2, 5
Mikulincer, M., 67
Miller, D., 2, 3
ministers, religious, 87–95
Mitty, W., 163, 175
Molander, P., 20
monoamine oxidase, 168
Money, J., 186
Montada, L., 4
morality, 4, 15–16
Morgan, W., 73
Morris, S., 48
Mosher, S., 69